LUMBER KINGS AND SHANTYMEN

LOGGING AND LUMBERING IN THE OTTAWA VALLEY

DAVID LEE

JAMES LORIMER & COMPANY LTD., PUBLISHERS

TORONTO

James Lorimer & Company Ltd. acknowledges the support of the Ontario Arts Council.
We acknowledge the support of the Government of Canada through the Book
Publishing Industry Development Program (BPIDP) for our publishing activities. We
acknowledge the support of the Canada Council for the Arts for our publishing
program. We acknowledge the support of the Government of Ontario through the
Ontario Media Development Corporation's Ontario Book Initiative.

Cover design: Meghan Collins

Library and Archives Canada Cataloguing in Publication

Lee, David
    Lumber kings and shantymen : logging and lumbering in the Ottawa Valley /
by David Lee.

Includes bibliographical references and index.
ISBN 10: 1-55028-922-5   ISBN 13: 978-1-55028-922-0

    1. Logging—Ottawa River Valley (Quèbec and Ont.)—History—18th century.
2. Logging—Ottawa River Valley (Quèbec and Ont.)—History—19th century.
3. Lumber trade—Ottawa River Valley (Quèbec and Ont.)—History—18th century.
4. Lumber trade—Ottawa River Valley (Quèbec and Ont.)—
History—19th century. 5. Lumbermen—Ottawa River Valley (Quèbec and Ont.)—
Biography. 6. Ottawa River Valley (Quèbec and Ont.)—History.
I. Title.

SD538.3.C2L398 2006   634.9'8'09713809034   C2006-900035-2

James Lorimer & Company Ltd., Publishers
317 Adelaide St. West
Suite 1002
Toronto, Ontario
M5V 1P9
www.lorimer.ca

Printed and bound in Canada.

CONTENTS

1. The Ottawa Valley — A Distinct Society?   7

2. The River, the Valley, the Forests, the People   13

3. Governments and the Ottawa Valley   31

4. Square Timber   59

5. Lumber   89

6. Pulp and Paper   145

7. Shantymen   157

8. Timber Barons and Lumber Kings   197

9. Was It Worthwhile Cutting
   Down All Those Trees?   225

10. Endings and Remainders   239

Notes   245

Index   275

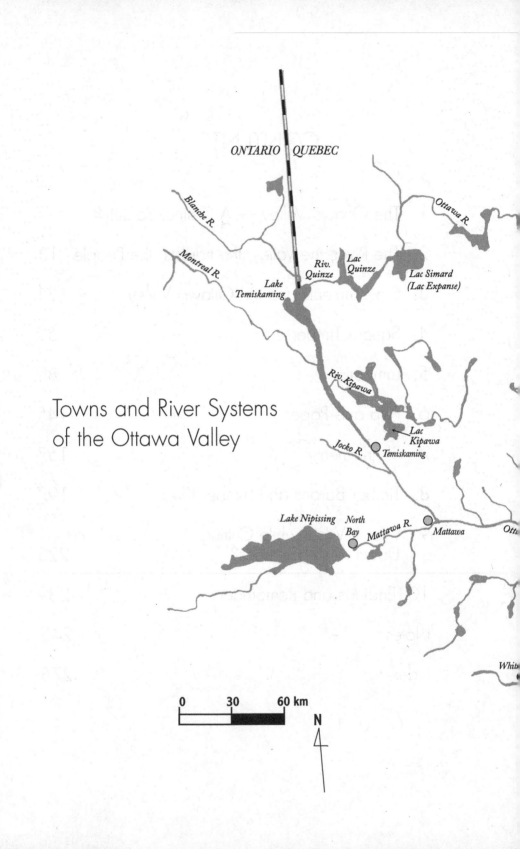

Towns and River Systems
of the Ottawa Valley

ONTARIO | QUEBEC

Blanche R.

Ottawa R.

Montreal R.

Riv.
Quinze

Lac
Quinze

Lac Simard
(Lac Expanse)

Lake
Temiskaming

Riv. Kipawa

Lac
Kipawa

Jocko R.

Temiskaming

Lake Nipissing

North
Bay

Mattawa R.

Mattawa

Ott

Whit

0   30   60 km

N

Grand
Lac Victoria

Ottawa R.

Lac
Capimitchigama

Lac Baskatong

Riv. Noire (Black R.)

Riv. Coulonge

Riv. Gatineau

Riv. Rouge

Riv. Petite-Nation

Maniwaki

Riv. Lièvre

Petawawa R.

Allumette Is.

Davidson

Calumet Is.

Buckingham

Ottawa R.

To
Montreal

Papineauville

Pembroke

Hawkesbury

onnechere R.

Renfrew

Chelsea

Hull

Rockland

Sand Pt./Braeside

Arnprior

Ottawa R.

Ottawa

Madawaska R.

Carleton Place

Nation R.

Missippippi R.

Smiths
Falls

Perth

Rideau R.

To Joanne, who has stood by me all these years

1

THE OTTAWA VALLEY — A DISTINCT SOCIETY?

When Canadians think of the old days of logging, timbering, and lumbering a number of mythic images come to mind. The rugged shantyman who endured long winters toiling in the frigid bush, isolated from the world. The swashbuckling "feller" who brought down the lofty pines. The skilled and haughty axeman who could hew timbers square with the precision and art of a sculptor. The brave (or foolhardy) river driver who risked death as he crept into the heart of a log-jam to dislodge the "key-log." The *macho*, devil-may-care river driver who could dance across rolling logs as they hurtled down cascading rivers. The colourfully attired raftsman who caroused his way down the Ottawa and the St. Lawrence rivers all the way to Quebec City on timber rafts. The rugged, unpolished timber barons and lumber kings who made huge fortunes in the Valley's pine forests and ruled vast empires. These romantic figures, these mighty men, could be found in New Brunswick and in other parts of Quebec and Ontario, but it was in the Ottawa Valley that they were made into myth and legend. It was here, for example, that Joe Mufferaw/Montferrand, larger-than-life, but real, performed deeds that were carried across North America in story and song. The Ottawa Valley was the epitome of the swaggering logging and lumbering life in Canada.

There was a time when people across Canada, as well as in England, Scotland, and the United States, talked of the Valley of the Ottawa and its abundances. Many in these places may not have been able to locate the Valley on a map, but they knew it as a seemingly inexhaustible source of square timber and lumber, the very materials they needed to build their cities. For much of the nineteenth century, the Ottawa Valley was the leading Canadian supplier of these coveted commodities.[1] The Valley was blessed with one of the world's richest endowments of coniferous trees — spruce and hemlock, but most importantly, red and white pine. Soon after European settlement began in 1800, a large and dedicated workforce set about harvesting this endowment. Vast stands of conifers were cut down and the square-timber, lumber, and pulp-and-paper industries came to dominate the economy. The Valley quickly became known for its mighty pines and the mighty men who harvested them. Only a few men managed to make a fortune from the pines, but many succeeded in making a living.

Inevitably, the all-dominating forest industries shaped society in the Valley. Charlotte Whitton, loyal daughter of the Valley and eventual mayor of Ottawa, wrote that its men "were said to have pine sap in their blood."[2] Another writer has noted that "while places like Newfoundland are identified with the men who went 'out to sea,' the Ottawa Valley is identified with the men who went 'into the bush.'"[3] Few residents of the Valley lived lives untouched by the pursuit of pine. Even those who never ventured into the bush — merchants, tradesmen, professionals — were affected. Indeed, it could be said that the population's dedication to felling, hauling, processing, and getting all this wood to market created a unique personality in the society. And just as this society flowered with the growth of timber, lumber, and pulp and paper in the nineteenth century, it began to wilt when those industries went into decline in the twentieth. Nevertheless, traces of this social distinctiveness can still be found today in parts of the Valley.

One social trait that was linked to logging and timbering (but has now died out) was an inclination to fighting; the Ottawa Valley gained a fine reputation for brawling and general rowdiness in the early years of the nineteenth century, and much of it was perpetrated by shantymen. Sometimes the fighting was sparked by ethnic differences. At other times shantymen were incited into fighting other shantymen by employers seeking to defend their timber limits against rivals or wanting to assert their right to be the first to drive logs downriver in the spring. Sometimes violence erupted simply because of an excess of whisky. And sometimes there was no obvious reason to prompt a fight beyond the competitive spirit of men who spent long monastic periods far from the refinements of polite society. In any case, one feature of life in the Valley was a passion for fighting, whether it was large-scale free-for-alls or one-on-one fisticuffs. The Valley writer Joan Finnigan has recounted many tales of manly mayhem carried out by legendary English, French, Scottish, and Irish pugilists. As she has noted, "along with church-going, 'recreational violence' was the most popular form of entertainment" in the Valley.[4] In reality, however, the unruliness did not last a long time; indeed, things had quieted down considerably by the middle of the nineteenth century. Nor is it likely that the violence was more vigorous here than in other frontier areas of North America. Still, the Valley's reputation as a place populated by pugnacious shantymen, fellers, axemen, river drivers, and raftsmen lingered a long time.[5]

An inclination to fighting, of course, was not enough to make life in the Valley different from other parts of the country, but other unique cultural practices are easy to pick out — the particular type of fiddling and step-dancing, for example. Studies have shown that the ethnic diversity of the population worked to produce unique forms of these arts in the Valley. Old-timers have pointed out that these forms emerged when men of diverse origins were thrown together in remote logging shanties for a whole winter. Shantymen of Irish, French, Scottish, and English backgrounds fiddled and danced in their traditional styles through long winter nights and came up with distinctive, new variants of their art. Ottawa Valley fiddlers would play a melody in a variety of styles and then blend them all into an exciting, hybrid rendition. Similarly, Ottawa Valley step-dancing is unique in its complexity; it has been described as "a cornucopia of diversified foot actions," all adapted from the various traditions that "mixed among one another in the lumber camps."[6] These music and dance forms continue to have an ardent following in some parts of the Valley today. In addition, studies by linguists have revealed remarkably distinctive speech patterns in the English-speaking population of the Ottawa Valley. Mainly of Irish origin, these patterns include not only pronunciation (the Ottawa Valley "brogue" or "twang") but also special words and expressions. This unique English dialect can still be heard in rural areas on both sides of the Ottawa River, especially where the forest industries were so powerful in the past.[7]

The land this distinct society occupied — the Ottawa Valley — was a geographic and cultural unit, even though it has never been a political unit. A political boundary has bisected the Valley through most of its settled history: for more than 200 years (except for the period from 1841 to 1867) the people on one side of the Ottawa River have lived in a different jurisdiction from those on the other. Political division, however, did not cause social division. The boundary never gave Valley people a split personality. After all, whether they lived in Upper Canada/Ontario or Lower Canada/Quebec, the inhabitants shared a common experience. First of all, they shared the Ottawa River. It was this broad stream that made settlement of the Valley possible. For most of the nineteenth century, people depended on the Ottawa River to get them into and out of their settlements, to carry the goods they needed to build their lives, to bring them news from the outside world, and, most important, to get the forest products they lived by to market. The river could be used in both summer and winter, and before roads and railways were built, it allowed people from both sides of the border to visit and socialize. Many families had members living in two provinces, but a line on a map had little effect on their lives. In some ways, political division actually deepened feelings of affinity in the Valley as residents of both sides of the river long felt neglected by government officials in far-off Toronto and Quebec City. Much of Pontiac County in the province of Quebec, for example, was (and still is) accessible only by means of Ontario roads. As well, institutions such as the Roman Catholic church paid no heed to the border: for over a century (until 1963), all Valley parishes belonged to one diocese headed by the bishop of Ottawa.[8] Most of all, however, it was their shared experiences in the forest industry that united the people of the Valley. The timber barons and lumber kings who dominated the industry harvested forests on both sides of the river, and the thousands of men who worked for them would often cut trees in Ontario one year and in Quebec the next. The result was a distinct society living in an easily defined geographic unit.

In this study the Ottawa Valley will be understood to embrace all the land drained by the Ottawa River above the old Long Sault rapids (now submerged by the Carillon hydroelectric dam). In Ontario, the Valley covers Renfrew, Lanark, Carleton, and Russell counties, most of Nipissing and Prescott, and the northern townships of Grenville, Frontenac, and Hastings. In Quebec, it includes Pontiac, Gatineau, Papineau, and Labelle counties, some of Témiskamingue, as well as the Rouge River Valley in Argenteuil. With its many tributaries, the Ottawa watershed encompasses about 60,000 square miles, an area as large as England and Wales combined. On the north, the Valley is bounded by the height of land from which rivers flow towards James Bay. On the west, south, and east, it is bounded by heights of land from which water drains towards the Great Lakes and the St. Lawrence River.

This book will examine the three forest-based industries — square timber, lumber, and pulp and paper — that dominated the Ottawa Valley economy over its first century and a quarter (roughly 1800 to 1925) and left such a powerful imprint on its people. It will tell of the Valley's mighty pines and the mighty men who harvested them. It will tell of how life in the Valley differed from life elsewhere.

2

THE RIVER, THE VALLEY, THE FORESTS, THE PEOPLE

Although it is called a tributary of the St. Lawrence, the Ottawa River is no minor stream; it is, in fact, the largest tributary of the St. Lawrence and a river with many impressive tributaries of its own. The Ottawa is, without question, one of Canada's great waterways. Indeed, until the middle of the nineteenth century, it was equally well known as "La Grande Rivière." From its source in Lake Capamitchigama (directly north of the city of Ottawa) to its mouth at the St. Lawrence near Montreal, it runs west, then south, and finally east, forming a broad semi-circle 730 miles in length. In many places, the river is more accurately a chain of narrow lakes (Deschênes, Chats, Allumette, Timiskaming), long sheets of quiet water linked by short stretches of fast currents, rocky rapids, or abrupt waterfalls. Today many of the waterfalls have been swamped by twentieth-century hydroelectric dams such as those at Carillon, Chaudière, Chats, Chenaux, Bryson, and Des-Joachims. Above the dams, most of the rapids have been submerged, allowing pleasure boats to cruise leisurely in calm waters.

Two hundred years ago, before European settlers arrived, travel on the Ottawa River was far from pleasant, though the traffic could be heavy at times. The river was an important link in the great canoe route across the North American continent. Indians, voyageurs, explorers, missionaries, and fur traders regularly paddled large canoes full of freight up the Ottawa as far as the Mattawa River; a short portage from this river gave them access to the Great Lakes and the rich, fur-bearing lands of the Northwest. The difficulties and dangers of the Ottawa route were well known: in the section between the St. Lawrence and Lake Timiskaming, the river rises 572 feet, with a dozen major obstacles to manoeuvre. The first, going upstream from Montreal, were the Carillon, Chute-à-Blondeau, and Long Sault rapids, which required three portages in 12 miles. Beyond these white waters, the river was uninterrupted as far as Chaudière ("the boiling kettle") Falls; early travellers felt this cataract, forming about two-thirds of a circle and rising 34 feet in height, resembled a steaming cauldron. The Chaudière, combined with the Remic and Deschênes rapids just upstream, made for a total rise of 62 feet, necessitating an eight-mile portage (as far as the present town of Aylmer). Not much farther upriver lay another daunting challenge — Chats Falls, 38 feet in height. Then, between Chats Falls and Timiskaming, navigation was obstructed again at Chenaux, Portage-du-Fort, Calumet, Paquette, Culbute, Des-Joachims, Rocher Capitaine, Deux-Rivières, and the "Long Sault of the North." Beyond Lake Timiskaming the Ottawa looped north and east (through a series of larger lakes connected by more stretches of white water) for a further 300 miles. Two centuries ago, however, newcomers from Europe knew little of these far reaches of the river.

THE FIRST EUROPEAN SETTLERS

Surprisingly, the first European community in the Ottawa Valley was not planted on the Ottawa River but on the Rideau River. The newcomers, many of them from the United States, settled in Marlborough, Montague, and Wolford townships. Settlement began in the early 1790s, just after the area was surveyed, and 40 years before the Rideau Canal was completed. Stephen Burritt and William Merrick were among the first to arrive, giving birth to the villages of Burritts Rapids and Merrickville. The population was small at first but grew steadily. Merrick installed a small sawmill on his property at what was then called the Great Falls; although it served only a local market, this was, no doubt, the first mill in the Ottawa Valley to saw lumber. Burritt, Merrick, and their neighbours had reached the Rideau by trekking overland (and thus into the watershed of the Ottawa River) from Brockville on the St. Lawrence, following a primitive road cut through the bush.[1]

Philemon Wright, 1760-1839

The founding of Hull by Philemon Wright a few years later turned out to be more significant, especially as it drew attention to the vast potential of the Ottawa River and the forests that lined its banks. It was in February 1800 that Wright led a party of pioneers from Woburn, Massachusetts, up the Ottawa River to plant a settlement near Chaudière Falls. The party numbered more than 50 men, women, and children, including relatives, neighbours, and some hired labourers. These people were not United Empire Loyalists; indeed, Wright himself had taken up arms against King George III in the American Revolutionary War. He and his followers were American immigrants seeking to start new lives on new lands. Fortunately for them, British authorities at this time were seeking to populate the empty vastnesses of the Canadian colonies. To do so, they set up a program to arrange group settlements in Canada. By this plan, interim land grants were given to a leader and a number of associates; the associates were then expected to turn over some of their grant to the leader to compensate him for the trouble and expenses he had incurred (such as petitioning officials and surveying the land).[2] In the 1790s Philemon Wright made several visits to Lower Canada looking for good acreage and saw much potential in the uninhabited township of Hull. The government approved his application to found a group settlement, provided that every adult male swore an oath of allegiance to His Majesty.

On his earlier visits, Philemon Wright had reconnoitred the region, so he knew the difficulties of travel on the Ottawa River. Since the group was heavily encumbered with provisions, household goods, equipment, horses, and oxen, he chose to come in winter when the frozen river allowed a fairly smooth ride by sleigh. Europeans had long taken canoes up and down the Ottawa, but few had ever come this far up the river in winter. For the first days after leaving Montreal, Wright's caravan passed through areas that had been granted as seigneuries by the King of France in earlier centuries; by 1800 there were only a few people living on these seigneuries, but they had cut rough trails along the north bank of the Ottawa that Wright and his party were able to use. They occasionally came across a lone farm carved out of the forest, but after they reached the Long Sault rapids, there were no more trails or permanent habitations to be seen.

The Long Sault and its two adjacent rapids were impassable by sleigh, and the party had to spend three or four days cutting a track through the bush before returning to the river. Not knowing if the ice were rotten under the snow cover, they proceeded slowly, the men walking ahead of the heavy sleighs, testing the ice with axes. The only humans encountered on this stretch of the river were the members of an Indian family of three; the father volunteered to lead the way in checking the ice and stayed with them until they reached Chaudière Falls. The journey from Montreal took about two weeks. Most nights the women and children took shelter in the covered sleighs while the men slept in blankets around the fire. The party's arrival in Hull Township on 7 March 1800 marked the beginning of a settlement known first as Wrightstown and later as Hull.[3]

RECOGNIZING THE VALLEY'S ABUNDANCES

The Ottawa Valley might have been settled earlier, but potential pioneers may have worried that the rapids and waterfalls of its major river barred access to anything larger than a canoe. (Philemon Wright claimed that fur traders had actively worked to keep the Valley's abundances unknown to outsiders.) By 1800, however, where some people had once seen only difficulties, others now saw opportunity. These newcomers recognized the many ways in which the wild waters of the Ottawa River and its tributaries could be put to good use. The new-comers would bring in the new technology that was powering a great industrial revolution in Europe and North America. One example would be new advances in harnessing the energy of falling water. Mankind had long used water power to drive his machinery, but in the nineteenth century millwrights became more adept at capturing a greater portion of the energy potential of large waterfalls and making more efficient use of smaller ones. And then, later in the century, engi-neers found an even better use for falling water — generating electrical power. In the Ottawa Valley, Chelsea Falls, Rideau Falls, the Long Sault, and the Chaudière (especially) were all put to good use by lumbermen. At the same time, a third use of water to create energy — steam power — was brought nearer to perfection. Although steam had been exploit-ed for some time, rapid advances now brought it into wider use in both light and heavy industry. The Ottawa Valley certainly had the water resources needed by investors who hoped to bring the Industrial Revolution to Canada. It also had another valuable resource that would be useful — wood.

Many visitors to the Ottawa Valley marvelled at the majestic stands of timber they found stretching to the horizon on both sides of the river — to the Laurentian Mountains in the east and the Madawaska Highlands in the west. One veteran lumberman told of the Madawaska and Petawawa valleys he had beheld in the 1870s (when the area had already been logged for more than 40 years): he recalled that "the whole country was covered with an ocean of pine; as far as the eye could reach from any prominent height, nothing was to be seen but a mass of pine tops; in fact one could imagine that it would never be cut or used up."[4] Earlier travellers — explorers and fur traders — had not always been favourably impressed, however. The first man to record his impressions of the Ottawa Valley and its forests, Samuel de Champlain, had found nothing here to praise at all. Canoeing up the river in 1615, he had seen only a tedious, worthless, forsaken wilderness; for Champlain, it was "an ill-favoured region full of pines, birches and a few oaks."[5] He perceived neither beauty nor utility in the thick groves of pine he encountered. To be fair, Champlain was a man of his time: before Jean-Jacques Rousseau and the late eighteenth-century Romantics, few Europeans found beauty in Nature in any of its forms.

Nor is it surprising that Champlain saw no utility in the vast timberlands of the Valley. Any pines he saw as suitable for naval masts and spars were too distant from saltwater ports to be of any use. In any case, his plan was to establish a French colony based on agriculture: he was looking only for good farmland. For Champlain, if the land was going to be tilled, pines and birches were essentially a nuisance that had to be got rid of. Two hundred years later, when the first serious farming attempts were made in the Valley, circumstances were different and thinking had changed. Pioneer farmers in the Valley were fortunate to find a growing market for wood, and what would have been treated as a nuisance became an asset. The trees still had to be removed, but now there was a commercial outlet for them in the square-timber, lumber, and pulp-and-paper industries. Farmers were able to harvest trees as well as field crops.

Visiting in a later era, Champlain would no doubt have recognized the value and abundance of the Valley's forests, especially its pineries. While the Ottawa River created the Valley, it is the pine that should be the emblem or totem of those who live here. In the Valley, this tree can be found in profusion from river lowlands to mountain ridges. It is appropriate, too, that the approximate northern limit of the pine's habitat is also the northern limit of the Valley itself (that is, the height of land beyond which water drains towards James Bay). In some places, the forest was almost uniformly pine; with few other species to get in the way, harvesting was much easier.

The white pine (*Pinus strobus*) is the most prolific variety and was zealously sought by merchants across Canada, Britain, and the United States. The white pine is light in weight, easy to work, unlikely to warp, strong, and flexible, and in the Ottawa Valley it could be found growing to a great size. It was the mightiest tree in the forests of eastern North America. Some of the pines that once stood on what is now Parliament Hill were said to have measured 180 feet in height and 16 feet around.[6] Shipbuilders, particularly those of the Royal Navy, relied

Felling a large pine with axes. Axes were still being used to fell the big pines in the 1870s.

on the white pine for use as masts and ship framing, but it was also much in demand for furniture, housing, and heavy construction. The red pine *(Pinus resinosa)* is smaller, but since it is a little stronger, almost immune to dry rot, and not as abundant in the forest, it usually fetched higher prices.

Next in importance in the Valley was the spruce, which also came in two species. Ignored at first, white spruce *(Picea glauca)* came to be accepted by lumber buyers later in the nineteenth century as a suitable construction wood, especially when Valley pine supplies began to run out. Equally plentiful and also ignored at first was the black spruce *(Picea mariana)*. With its low pitch levels and good fibre content, it was perfect for the pulp-and-paper industry, which emerged at the end of the nineteenth century. Smaller quantities of other conifers were also brought to market: hemlock as cheap lumber, cedar for posts and poles, jack pine for railway ties, and balsam for pulp. Hardwoods such as oak, maple, ash, and elm could be found throughout the Valley, but although they could bring good prices, they were always of secondary interest. Because of their greater density, hardwoods could not float for very long and thus were difficult to get to mill or market.

After Champlain passed by, many people marvelled at the wondrous crop of trees Nature had sown in the Ottawa Valley, but it was a long time before anyone tried to harvest it. Philemon Wright was the first.

PHILEMON WRIGHT AND THE BEGINNING OF TIMBERING

When Philemon Wright came to Hull Township with the hope of establishing a community of independent farmers who would follow agrarian values and build better lives on new land, he had sold his properties in Massachusetts to finance his dreams. He later claimed that, in the first six years, he put $20,000 of his own money into the effort. From the outset, the crops he and his associates planted did passably well, but the community was not able to fully support itself. Provisions and manufactured goods had to be brought in from Montreal, and soon Wright had to look beyond farming to cover his expenses. When he was scouting for land to settle on, Wright had cho-sen Hull Township because he felt the rich timber groves he saw there were a sign of good farming soil, and in the first years he spent his time clearing trees to open the land for tilling. Soon he installed a small mill where he sawed the trees into boards and barrel staves, which were to supply community needs. By 1806, however, Wright was determined to harvest trees as a cash crop to be sold on the Quebec City commercial market. As he said, "it was time to look out for an export market to cover my imports."[7]

Philemon Wright's decision to try selling timber at Quebec City could not have been taken at a better time. Wright had undoubtedly heard that war had broken out with France in 1805 and that the British were seeking naval timber at Quebec because Napoleon Bonaparte was blockading their traditional source of supply on the Baltic Sea. The Royal Navy had always been crucial to Britain's survival in wartime, so it turned to its North American colonies, especially Canada and New Brunswick, for naval timbers. Hoping to develop a safe, new source of timber for shipbuilding, the British removed all tariff duties on wood from the colonies and raised the duties on foreign imports.

Wright's first shipment (most of it likely pine and oak) included a good stock of heavy timbers as well as over 9,000 boards and a quantity of staves. Baltic timbers were usually squared off on four sides so they could be more easily loaded into ships,[8] and Wright probably followed this practice in order to ensure his products would sell. Getting the wood to Quebec was a remarkable feat for it had to be achieved without benefit of roads or sailing vessels; the only way was to float it down the Ottawa River to Montreal and then along the St. Lawrence. Wright lashed the timbers together to form small rafts, known as "cribs." The cribs (there may have been as many as 19) were, in turn, fastened one to another to make an extended raft. The boards, staves, and oak that had been sawn at Wright's mill were then stacked on top of the cribs.

Wright took his 18-year-old son, Tiberius, and three other settlers (one of them a free Black from Massachusetts) with him on the journey. Setting out on 11 June 1806 from somewhere near the mouth of the Gatineau River, they floated easily with the current down the Ottawa until they arrived at the three sets of rapids that started at the Long Sault. Here began their greatest challenge, as the river fell 58 feet in a distance of 12 miles. Wright had travelled up and down the Ottawa for several years and must have been aware of the seasonal changes in water levels on the river. He likely knew that, on the stretch between the Chaudière and the Long Sault (in the years before dams were constructed), the water level could drop by 12 feet or more between the heights of spring and the lows of summer. North West Company fur traders were sending canoes regularly up and down the Ottawa in these years; they knew the river well, but there is no evidence Wright sought their advice. In any case, mid-June was probably the best time to try running these turbulent waters. In May, the river, swollen with the spring runoff, would have been rushing with such a force that it would be difficult for Wright and his inexperienced crew to control the tim-

ber cribs in the rapids. By mid-July, however, the water might have fall-
en too low to allow the cribs to float over even the slightest projecting
rocks. Although he had chosen the best time of year to run the three
rapids, Wright and his men still had to beach and dismantle the raft
and then carefully guide each crib singly through the white water
strewn with scouring boulders. Some of the cribs were torn apart as
they hit rocks on the way down and had to be reassembled; one was
totally lost. Although the distance covered was short, it took Wright
more than two weeks to get his timber through the three rapids. Fifteen
years later, he noted that, "having, from experience, learnt the manner
of coming down, we can now oftentimes come down them in twenty-
four hours."9

After passing the rapids, the cribs were assembled once again into
one large raft, which was then allowed to drift out into Lac-des-Deux-
Montagnes. Here the current was weaker, but strong winds pushed the
raft onto the north shore. The crew seems to have had only poles to
steer their course, and Wright now realized that he needed more men
to help out. From this point on, he periodically hired local people,
including three Indians from the Mohawk village of Kanasetake (at
Oka), to help him through the rough stretches. He also occasionally
stopped at communities along the way to sell a few boards and buy
provisions (including rum) for the crew.

Wright had scouted the lower reaches of the waterway the previous
spring and had seen the advantages of taking a northern route (Rivière-
des-Prairies) around the Island of Montreal. This route was shorter and
less dangerous than heading south and navigating the long, menacing
rapids at Lachine. Local residents said it would be impossible to take
his cribs through the narrow and shallow Rivière-des-Prairies, but
Wright proved it could be done, and for a century thereafter it was the
main route for rafting Ottawa Valley timber.

Once past Montreal, he found the voyage easier since there were no
rapids to overcome on the lower St. Lawrence. On Lac-St-Pierre, a
widening of the St. Lawrence, he may have hoisted some rudimentary
sails to speed the progress of his raft. Inexperienced as he was, Wright
was fortunate to enjoy good weather here for, over the next century,

many rafts were battered to pieces by heavy gales on this lake. In any case, the intrepid raftsman floated uneventfully for another 150 miles down to Quebec, where he sold his cargo.[10] Wright's pioneering rafting trip took two months to complete, he and his four crewmen spending most days and nights on the water. Within a few years, Wright and other timbermen who followed his example learned the ways of the river; soon they were able to bring larger rafts much more quickly through the Ottawa River rapids and down the Rivière-des-Prairies. Wright was probably not immediately aware of the significance of his accomplishment, but his sale of sawn lumber and square timber at Quebec in 1806 brought the Ottawa Valley into the world market economy (William Merrick's earlier lumbering efforts on the Rideau served only a small, local clientele).

In Hull Township, more families joined Philemon Wright's colony, but a few years passed before the government issued official land titles to him and nine associates (including two of his sons). Following their prearranged agreement, the associates turned over a substantial portion of their grants to Wright, who ended up controlling huge tracts of land in the township. Many other newcomers were not granted any land at all and had to live in semi-feudal conditions as tenants on Wright land or as employees of the family firm, P. Wright & Sons. For a number of years, Wrightstown was, in essence, a "company town" ruled by its founder. Wright diversified his interests, adding a distillery, brickworks, cement plant, steamboat, and foundry, as well as arranging contracts with Colonel John By in the construction of the Rideau Canal. Timbering, however, became his main preoccupation.

Although not highly educated and possessing few social graces, Philemon Wright was a shrewd and powerful personality, a man of high energy, vision, ambition, and determination. When his grist and lumber mills burned down in May 1808, he showed his strength of will by taking a raft all the way to Quebec, selling the timber quickly and hurrying home with the proceeds to rebuild the mills on a larger scale by autumn (and by this time he was already a grandfather). Besides being the largest landowner and employer, Wright, at one time or another, held many of the most important public offices in the district

— militia captain, justice of the peace, roads commissioner, government land agent, member of the Legislative Assembly. He was, beyond question, the most powerful individual in the community, wielding his influence in a paternalistic, though not usually oppressive, manner. Compared to his contemporary, Laird McNab, a pernicious despot who tried to build his own colony on the Madawaska River, Wright was a benevolent patriarch; if not exactly revered by the community, he was certainly respected. He and his children (he had eight) lived in the grandest houses in the area, but the family firm was perpetually in debt; the Wrights constantly struggled to pay off loans taken to finance their business ventures. More than once they hovered on the brink of bankruptcy, and in 1826 a Quebec merchant had Philemon's third son, Ruggles, already a prominent timberman, held in jail a few days for unpaid debts.[11]

The second and third generations of the family continued to be heavily involved in the square-timber and sawn-lumber trade (by the 1830s they were sending eight or nine rafts a year to Quebec). None of the later Wrights, however, grew truly rich from their influence or efforts; their long-term wealth was based on real-estate holdings. Throughout his life (he lived until 1839), Philemon Wright continued to profess the dream that "we can wean ourselves from the lumber business and follow agriculture." But, as so many other hopeful settlers found out, farming in the Ottawa Valley usually required involvement in the forest industries, in one way or another.[12]

Wright was not the first venturer to respond to Britain's efforts to cultivate a timber industry at Quebec; a few others got rafts there before him,[13] and many followed their example in ensuing years. Together they proved British authorities right in giving the colonies tariff advantages. Colonial timber exports were able to meet Britain's needs throughout the Napoleonic Wars and again during the War of 1812 with the United States. Square timber flowed across the Atlantic, a great deal of it originating in the Ottawa Valley. Philemon Wright's sale of a small stock of forest products at Quebec in the summer of 1806 was momentous as it gave birth to the square-timber industry in the Ottawa Valley, an industry that would flourish for more than a century and nourish settlement in the Valley.

The British were pleased with the stability that her British North American colonies provided during the war years and maintained preferential tariff policies until 1860. By this time, however, Canadians had learned the trade and were able to continue selling timber in Britain without tax privileges.[14] The Canadian forest industry got a further boost in 1854 with the negotiation of a reciprocity treaty that eliminated tariffs on wood and other natural products shipped between British North America and the United States. This agreement opened up a whole new export market for Ottawa Valley sawn lumber, an industry that grew and prospered for the next half century. The industrial revolution that was sweeping across the western world would not have been possible without a cheap and versatile construction material such as wood. It was Philemon Wright who showed the outside world that the remote Ottawa Valley could be a reliable source of high-quality wood products.

OTHER TIMBER PIONEERS

In the Ottawa Valley, Philemon Wright was the first to profit from the growing timber market at Quebec, but others soon followed. In 1808 Joseph Papineau began to develop his hitherto uninhabited seigneury at the Petite-Nation River. He contracted to supply a Quebec exporter with square timber cut on his land, and he brought in 20 axemen from the St. Lawrence Valley to hew the wood and raft it down the Ottawa. When Papineau sold it ten years later, there were about 300 people living on the land — two-thirds of them *habitants* from seigneuries in the Montreal area, the rest newcomers from New England. The settlers were not given title to their lots but rather held them (following French seigneurial custom) as concessions from the seigneur. They were tenant farmers and, to survive, many of them had to work as loggers in the winter and as river drivers in the spring. Unlike Philemon Wright, for whom timbering was initially a second choice, the Papineaus focused on harvesting the forests from the outset. After the 1808 venture, however, they did not directly engage in the trade themselves; instead, they leased sawmills and cutting rights to other entrepreneurs. Still, they did develop "la Petite-Nation," which was the only functioning seigneury in the Ottawa Valley. In 1817, Papineau sold the seigneury to his son Louis-Joseph, who later gained fame as the leader of the Lower Canada rebellions. After retiring from politics in the 1850s, Louis-Joseph Papineau devoted much of his time to the seigneury, including building a luxurious manor house, 'Montebello,' which still stands today.[15]

The third pioneers of the forest industry in the Ottawa Valley were David Pattee and Thomas Mears. About 1806 these recent immigrants from the United States, recognizing the water-power potential of the Long Sault rapids, built a mill near their head and began sawing lumber for sale at Quebec City. This mill was the first on the Ontario side of the Ottawa River and the first in the Ottawa Valley to produce sawn lumber for sale in outside markets. Mears and Pattee's investment was heavily mortgaged, however, and in a short time they had to sell out to the Hamilton brothers of Quebec. The Hamiltons stayed in the lumber business for two generations, but it was the Mears–Pattee mill that gave birth to Hawkesbury, a town that remained prominent in the forest industry for more than a century thereafter.[16]

Papineau, Pattee, and Mears proved that good profits could be made from the Valley's timber, and soon other entrepreneurs were sending logging gangs into the woods up the Ottawa and its tributaries. It is astonishing how quickly the edge of the forest frontier moved. The first logging campaigns were often high-grading operations that took only the choicest timber (red pine and oak, for example) in areas where access was easiest (especially along the shoreline of the Ottawa River). Other early operators moved up some of the tamer tributaries, such as the Nation River, where they stripped some areas, as far inland as Winchester Township, of the best timber. It was not long, however, before some entrepreneurs found that Chaudière Falls and Chats Falls were not as daunting as had been thought; they learned that it was possible (though with considerable effort) to take men, oxen, and logging supplies up the Ottawa River and bring square timber down safely through its roughest waters. By the 1820s, some operators were already logging up the Madawaska River, one of the wildest tributaries of the Ottawa. Within a few years, the logging frontier had moved as far as

Felling a large pine with saws. By the end of the nineteenth century, cross-cut saws had replaced axes in felling the mighty timbers.

Lake Timiskaming, fully 250 miles above the Chaudière: the McConnell family of Hull was rafting square timber from that lake by 1839 and perhaps even earlier. The next major milestone was the beginning of sawmilling above the Chaudière. In 1846 John Egan had the audacity to transport the workings of a small, but complete, sawmill up the Ottawa and install it at the mouth of the Quyon River; three years later he was sawing lumber at two more mills on the Bonnechère River.[17] Egan's output would have been only for local consumption, though, for there was no way to get lumber out to more distant markets until railways arrived in the 1850s.

The sudden opening of the square-timber industry surprised and annoyed the fur traders, who for nearly 200 years had had the Ottawa Valley to themselves. Now, other men were ascending the river seeking a different prize. The land swarmed with loggers carrying axes to level the forests. Logging began to destroy the habitat of the animals on which the traders depended. The rivers became clogged with floating timber. George Simpson, governor of the Hudson's Bay Company, also worried that the timbermen would hurt the fur trade by offering the local natives alternative employment as canoeists and camp hunters. His response was to jump into the timber trade and try to undercut the McConnells. He was prepared to bear short-term losses and drive them out of business. In the early 1840s, the Hudson's Bay Company cut and squared timber at Lake Timiskaming and Fort Coulonge and sent rafts to Quebec. The timber, however, was not of high quality and did not sell well. The losses proved too heavy and Simpson abandoned the scheme in 1845. Thereafter, the Company reconciled itself to a slow retreat up the Valley, closing its fur-trading posts at Fort Coulonge in 1844, at Fort William (opposite Allumette Island) in 1869, at Fort Timiskaming in 1902, and at Mattawa in 1909.[18]

POPULATING THE VALLEY

Long before the fur traders began retreating from the upper Ottawa, waves of settlers seeking farmland had been pouring into the lower reaches of the Valley. The first large-scale settlement began after the Napoleonic Wars ended in 1815. Facing post-war economic depression and rising unemployment in England, Scotland, and Ireland, the British government had begun to subsidize immigration to Canada. Particular attention was given to demobilized soldiers, landless rural people, and workers who had been replaced by machines. Many of the immigrants crossed the Atlantic on "timber ships," ships that had carried wood to Britain and were now returning to Canada to pick up another cargo. Britain gave the newcomers free ocean passage, provisions, tools, and land; many chose to take lots along the Rideau and

Mississippi rivers. After a decade or so, assisted immigration declined, and thereafter most newcomers arrived on their own.

From the outset, it was clear that the Valley would have a population diverse in both ethnicity and religion. The Irish were numerous from the beginning, especially among the veterans of the 99th Regiment, who were brought in to establish military settlements at Perth and Richmond in 1818. Many more came from Ireland later, fleeing the miseries of the potato famine of the 1840s. Francophone communities became conspicuous in the Valley by the middle of the century. They were established mainly by young *habitant* families who were unable to find land on crowded seigneuries along the St. Lawrence and were encouraged by the Catholic church to settle in groups on both sides of the Ottawa River. Immigrants from England also came to settle in the Valley but their numbers were never as prominent as in other areas of Ontario. The Scots came in two groups: those who came directly to the Valley and those who moved in from earlier-established Scottish communities in Glengarry County (a short distance away on the St. Lawrence). Among the earliest settlers were a significant number of people born in the Thirteen Colonies or the United States; these immigrants were prominent in founding such communities as Hull, Petite-Nation, Merrickville, and Burritts Rapids. Some settlers in the latter two towns were United Empire Loyalists, but, generally, Loyalists were not numerous for most had already taken lands elsewhere before the Ottawa Valley opened up to settlement.

The census of 1911 provides a good profile of the population of the Ottawa Valley in its maturity — that is, in the years after agricultural settlement and immigration had largely ceased. By this year there were about 405,000 people living in the Valley. Residents of French ancestry made up the largest group, with 42 percent. Those who claimed Irish ancestry numbered 26 percent, followed by the English with 12 per cent and the Scottish with 10 percent; American-born residents totalled only 1 percent. As for religion, 58 percent were Roman Catholic, 14 percent Presbyterian, 12 percent Anglican, and 9 percent Methodist. Even if one looks at only the Ontario side of the Valley, the census still shows a remarkably diverse population. There, inhabitants of French ancestry were still the largest group, with 30.5 percent, while the Irish made up 29.9 percent, the English 15 percent, and the Scots 12 percent. The religious profile on the Ontario side shows that 48 percent were Roman Catholic, while 17 percent were Presbyterian, 15 percent Anglican, and 11 percent Methodist.[19]

While some of those who settled in the Ottawa Valley in the nineteenth century may have come intending to find work in the forest industries, most probably arrived dreaming of new fertile land to farm. Unfortunately, many of the tens of thousands who took up farming here in the nineteenth century did not find prosperity. Most of those who were lucky enough to get lands on the Ontario side of the Ottawa River below the Mississippi did fairly well. But those who settled on the Canadian Shield in Lanark, Renfrew, Pontiac, and Gatineau counties often found little more than thin soil, rocky hills, and tangled swamps. Inevitably, farmers trying to clear and work marginal lands (and even some who had good lands) had to take seasonal employment in the forest industries in order to raise cash to get them through the difficult early years. For many, however, the temporary arrangement became a lasting tradition as their sons and grandsons also went into the bush every winter to help meet their families' continuing need for an outside income. Others gave up their dream of farming altogether and worked from season to season in the logging shanties, on the river-drives, the timber rafts, the log-sorting booms, the lumber barges, and in the Valley's many sawmills. Their broken dreams assured timbermen and lumbermen of a reliable supply of cheap labour. Thus, it is possible to say that a shortage of good farmland in the Ottawa Valley contributed to the growth and success of the forest industries.

Life in the Valley was certainly not ideal. The weather could be dismaying and the geography difficult. Good land was scarce, and the alternative — work in the forest industries — was not a perfect solution. It was arduous and dangerous. Some of the disappointed left for greener parts. Many stayed on, however, but not with bitterness. On the contrary, they chose to meet the hard realities of life in the Valley with humour, optimism, and high spirits. They got on with life, and their experiences in timbering and lumbering make for a fascinating story.

3

GOVERNMENTS AND THE OTTAWA VALLEY

People living in parts of Lanark and Renfrew counties in the nineteenth century would surely have been shocked to find that there were serious doubts about whether they had legal title to the land they thought they owned. Few people knew that the government's right to grant this land to settlers had been challenged by the Aboriginal inhabitants of the area. Clear title to these lands was not formalized until as late as 1923.

In 1791 a government surveyor, Theodore de Pencier, arrived on the Rideau River to conduct the first surveys in the area and establish the limits of Marlborough Township. In the course of his work, he encountered a party of Indians who told him that he was on their land and had no right to be there. Although one of his men was threatened with a gun, de Pencier carried on and ultimately completed his work. Three years later, William Fortune was sent up the Rideau to survey two more townships, Montague and Wolford, as settlers were expected to arrive in the area shortly. Fortune engaged a group of Indians to assist his expedition but discharged them after a short time, claiming they would not follow orders and even threatened his life. He also reported that the Indians accused the king of stealing their lands and offering them no payment in return.[1] The Crown went ahead and granted land to the incoming settlers, but the Aboriginal inhabitants continued to feel that the question of land title in the Ottawa Valley had not been fully settled. No other incidents of confrontations are known, though the

Indians periodically petitioned colonial authorities on the matter.
(Indeed, some First Nations are still pressing land claims in the Valley
in the twenty-first century.)

On the Lower Canada, or Quebec, side of the Ottawa River, the government has always insisted that Natives had no land rights at all.
Essentially, the government has maintained that the French king never
recognized Aboriginal title in New France and, with the conquest of
1763, the British Crown had acquired all French land rights without
qualification. Twice over the years, the Algonquin and Nipissing
Indians living in the Ottawa Valley requested that they be compensat-
ed in some way for the land the Crown had given to European settlers.
The government's response was that if any compensation were war-
ranted it had been satisfied in 1853 by the establishment of a reserve
at Maniwaki on the Gatineau River.[2]

On the Upper Canada, or Ontario, side, the land question remained
unsettled for a long time. In this province, the Crown was supposed to
get the Indians to relinquish all claims to land before it granted legal
title to anyone. At councils held in 1783 and 1784, the British government purchased a large tract of land, including the southernmost
reaches of the Ottawa Valley, from Iroquois and Algonquin First
Nations. The only payment for the land was a narrow strip of property
on the St. Lawrence River and a promise to clothe one chief and his
family for life. The government then went ahead with surveys and land
grants in the Valley, but put off further negotiations with the Indians
for another 35 years. It was this inaction that led the Indians to threat-
en the early surveyors.

Finally, in 1819, British officials met the Mississauga Indians near
Belleville and negotiated what became known as the "Rideau
Purchase," which included Carleton County and neighbouring areas.
In this case, the Indians surrendered nearly 2,500,000 acres of land in
return for less than £600 sterling. After this, the government once again
put the question of Aboriginal claims out of mind, this time for more
than a hundred years. It was not until after the First World War that the
federal government realized that serious doubts loomed over the legal
title to vast areas of Ontario, including parts of the Ottawa Valley. In

1923 it arranged the Williams Treaties, which finally formalized the title to all land north of the Rideau Purchase as far as the Mattawa River. In return for relinquishing their claims to 17,600 square miles of the Valley, the government paid each Indian $25, along with a lump sum to their bands.[3]

GOVERNMENT TIMBER REGULATION

Even though Aboriginal land claims were not fully extinguished until the twentieth century, British authorities never admitted any doubt that the Crown held ultimate title throughout the entire Ottawa Valley. After setting up colonial governments in Upper and Lower Canada in 1791, the British gave those bodies full responsibility to manage Crown land (i.e., land not yet granted to settlers). These governments were authorized to grant settlers full title to parcels of this land (William Merrick and Philemon Wright were early beneficiaries of this policy). These governments were also expected, however, to protect the Crown's assets on all ungranted land. In particular, they were expected to prevent trespassers from cutting timber that might be useful to the Royal Navy. When the Royal Navy offered to buy timber at Quebec in 1804, the government issued licences that, for the first time, allowed cutting on Crown land. Soon a huge new industry was born: harvesting timber for export.

Amazingly, in the early years much of the timber exported from Canada was illegally harvested. To no one's embarrassment (not the government's, not the timbermen's, not the buyers'), the new industry was based largely on outright theft. Some of the timber was stolen from privately held land (which had already been granted to settlers). The bulk, however, was brazenly pilfered from Crown land without a licence. In the early years, most timbermen simply did not bother to seek a licence; they just sauntered up the remote Ottawa Valley, cut wherever they fancied, and blithely rafted their timber to Quebec. Here, they found buyers eager to fill a growing, non-military market in Britain. A few timbermen, it is true, did obtain licences to supply wood to the Royal Navy, but it was obvious to everyone that they usually cut more timber than their licences authorized and sold the surplus on the open market.

Government officials in Upper and Lower Canada did little to try to stop the abuses. In 1809 Lieutenant-Governor Francis Gore issued a proclamation setting out severe penalties for cutting timber on Crown land without a licence. Contraband timber could be seized by magistrates and sold, with the proceeds going to the Crown. Those found guilty of illegal cutting were subject to fines, and a third conviction could bring deportation for seven years. These penalties were no more than token threats, however. For a number of reasons, the government simply ignored its own regulations. In these early days, the forests of Canada seemed inexhaustible, and timber poaching seemed to present no threat to government interests. Besides, Great Britain needed timber and Upper and Lower Canada needed the employment and revenue that the new industry generated. By 1812 the timber trade had surpassed the fur trade in the economy and was generating important new spinoff activities, such as the construction of ships to carry the timber across the Atlantic (and bring immigrants back). In any case, it seemed prohibitively expensive to prosecute cases of unlicensed cutting in remote forests. The difficulties of law enforcement in the Ottawa Valley were notorious. Distances were long and communications poor, and for a long time there were only three courts in the area, at Perth, Wrightstown, and L'Orignal (near Hawkesbury).[4]

It was not until 1819 that the government took its first serious steps to enforce the law, seizing some timber rafts on the Ottawa River as contraband. The government hoped these seizures would deter timbermen from further trespasses on the forests of the Crown, and for some, such as George Hamilton, the strategy worked. For unpaid loans and mortgages, Hamilton, an Irish-born Liverpool merchant, had taken over the lumber mill at Hawkesbury begun by Thomas Mears and David Pattee. The mill burned down, but Hamilton quickly rebuilt it on a larger scale. He was able to get some of the sawlogs (logs suitable for sawing into lumber) he needed for his business from local settlers as they cleared their lands, but he needed more and soon turned energetically to unlicensed logging. At the same time, however, Hamilton had also accepted positions as a justice of the peace and

judge of the district court. The result was that while he was supposed
to be serving the Crown as an officer of the court, he was also stealing
timber from the Crown. Pattee too was a justice of the peace and Mears
the district sheriff. Both men were embittered by the foreclosure on
their mill, and Hamilton feared they would take action against him. If
he wished to avoid the public embarrassment that would arise if officials of his own court confiscated his timber rafts, he knew he had to
stop poaching timber. Ultimately, Hamilton found he was able to survive by legal means and became a strong advocate of strict measures
against unlicensed logging.[5]

For most timbermen, however, the threat of confiscation did not
deter their thievery from Crown timberlands. Raft seizures increased,
but they were considered no more than a nuisance. When confiscated
timber was put up for sale by the Crown, timbermen would just agree
amongst themselves not to bid against one another; the man who had
cut the confiscated wood and rafted it down the Ottawa River would
then simply buy the raft back for a pittance. In the winter of 1823,
Sheriff John Powell of Perth, disgusted with the contempt for the law
he had seen, took it upon himself to take direct, extra-legal action.
Hearing that the timberman Alexander McDonell was cutting red pine
on the Mississippi River without a licence, he led a party of armed militia to confront him. Powell was expecting trouble as there had been
reports of violence in the bush between rival timber gangs, and appar-
ently McDonell had a reputation that gave the sheriff cause for concern. To his surprise, however, McDonell greeted him cordially and
entertained the militiamen at his timber shanty. The two men agreed
that McDonell would pay a fee or duty for the pine he had cut.[6]
Pleased with his success, Powell went on to use his new procedure elsewhere in the Valley. This improvisation, however, had no basis in law,
and the government soon ordered him to return to confiscating whenever he came across illegally cut timber.

Unfortunately, the reinstatement of raft seizures brought only further disdain for the rule of law in the Ottawa Valley. In the 1820s Capt.
John LeBreton, a retired Royal Army officer with a half-pay pension,
was living just above Deschênes Rapids on what is now known as

Britannia Bay. (He also owned much of what is now LeBreton Flats in Ottawa.) Many of the timber rafts coming downriver stopped in the bay, within sight of his house, where they were dismantled before descending Chaudière Falls. In 1823 LeBreton wrote to Lieutenant-Governor Sir Peregrine Maitland, denouncing the timbermen who, he charged, were cavalierly plundering Crown lands of the best trees. He claimed the Valley was in a state of total "insubordination for want of proper persons to enforce the laws" and that, even if the authorities identified the thieves, "they have only to cross the River into Lower Canada and bid defiance to our Laws." LeBreton was more than pleased when the lieutenant-governor invited him to report further on the subject. He replied that he reckoned the illegal cut of timber in the Ottawa Valley above the Chaudière in the previous year totalled as much as a million cubic feet. He estimated that, in the coming year (1824), the total figure could rise to one and a half million cubic feet. LeBreton also complained that thieves had poached timber from his own, privately held land, and that he could do nothing to stop them. He even claimed that "in the present state of this part of the country," he felt he was risking both "life and property" in reporting these disorders.[7]

The return to confiscating rafts sometimes led to violence. In one case, in 1825, deputy sheriff Alexander Matheson tried to seize a good-sized raft (69 cribs) belonging to Ruggles Wright that was anchored on the Upper Canada side of the Ottawa River above Chaudière Falls. Wright's foreman refused to let Matheson on board and took his raft across the river to the Lower Canada shore, where he felt the sheriff had no authority. Matheson held a different opinion, however, and the next morning assembled 20 armed militiamen and led them across the river. Wright's raftsmen tried to resist the militiamen, and four were injured in the skirmish that ensued. Matheson succeeded in seizing the raft but found it difficult to arrange a sale. As time passed, tensions rose to a dangerous height around the Chaudière. Indeed, the local justice of the peace feared mob rule and had to muster another armed party to prevent further trouble. In the end, Ruggles Wright succeeded in buying back his raft for a trifling price.[8]

The declining respect for law and the escalating violence in the Ottawa Valley finally prompted the government and some leading timbermen to seek better ways to regulate the timber trade. The government, for its part, began to see an advantage in charging duties for timber cut on Crown land. At a time when it was seeking new sources of revenue, it realized that tax revenue from this burgeoning industry could well exceed the costs of enforcing the law in remote corners of the Valley. It was at this propitious time that Ruggles Wright, Alexander McDonell, and a few other timbermen chose to ask the government to formalize the procedure tried earlier by Sheriff Powell.[9] Their petitions received a warm reception. In 1826 the lieutenant-governors of Upper and Lower Canada issued proclamations designed to bring order to the timber trade in the Ottawa Valley; the proclamations gave the government the authority to charge duties for timber cut on Crown lands.[10]

It was large-scale operators such as Hamilton, McDonell, and Wright who had undergone a change of mind about lawlessness in the timber trade. It was not a new-found reverence for the sanctity of the law, however, that had altered their thinking. Rather, they were concerned that timber poaching, if allowed to continue, would destabilize their businesses. The timber trade was a classic boom-and-bust industry: high prices regularly led to overproduction and, inevitably, to depressed prices. Timber barons worried that illegal timber cutting made it easier for small operators to compete in the trade, and this would increase the risk of overproduction. Men of capital, such as they, were better able to bear the expense of paying duties for cutting on Crown land; adding such charges would work to their benefit in the long run for small operators would be less able to compete. Thus, men who had profited by their disregard for government now turned to government for help in preserving their interests.

Another aim of these timbermen was to attain respectability in the communities where they lived. In the past they had shown no shame in poaching the king's trees and no reluctance to use violence in the bush. Some, such as Ruggles Wright, Alexander McDonell, and Peter Aylen (infamous for attacking the crews of rival timbermen), were unrefined and heavy-handed scofflaws. Others, such as George

Hamilton (and John Egan, a later timberman), were polished and gen-
teel scofflaws. Now they hoped that by becoming strong law-and-order
advocates, they could boost their social standing. In this they succeeded. Three went on to gain high positions in their local militia battalions. Hamilton kept his judicial posts. Wright was appointed postmaster and justice of the peace in Wrightsville. McDonell served for many
years as postmaster at Sand Point, Ontario. Aylen became a town coun-
cillor and justice of the peace in Aylmer, Quebec. Egan gained election
to the legislative assembly. Unlawful practices in the timber trade had
brought them financial success, and in the rough, frontier society of
the Ottawa Valley, it now brought them power and social acceptance.

The Ottawa Valley was the centre of the timber trade in the Canadas,
and it was here that the major principles of government regulation
were worked out; indeed, the proclamations of 1826 applied exclusively to the Valley, at first. These proclamations were a landmark
advance as they established Sheriff Powell's idea of charging duties
based on the quantity of wood cut on Crown land; over time, these
charges became known as "timber duties" or "timber dues." The government appointed agents to count the sawlogs and square timbers as
they floated down the Ottawa River and calculate the duties owing.

Further innovations followed over the next decade. First, the government decided that timbermen should not be licensed to cut anywhere
they wished; cutting licences were now limited to specific parcels of
Crown land. These parcels came to be known as "timber berths" or
"timber limits" (as they are still called to this day), while the licensees
became known as "limit-holders." To obtain a licence, the timberman
had to pay a fee based on the size of the limits. These annual charges
were known as "ground rent" or "stumpage" (terms still in use today).
Often, as the industry grew, several timbermen would apply for the
same timber limit, so the government decided to hold public auctions,
with the licence going to the highest bidder. This innovation provided
provincial treasuries with a further source of revenue; receipts from
auctions were called a "bonus."[11] The principles of charging timber
duties and 'ground rents' and holding auctions to finance the regulation of the timber trade were all initiated in the Ottawa Valley.[12] These

principles were later incorporated into the landmark Timber Act of 1849, a statute that applied to all of Canada. (By this time, several other areas, such as the valleys of the Richelieu, St. Maurice, Saguenay, and Trent rivers and the hinterlands of Lake Erie, had also become vigorous producers of timber.)

The 1849 Timber Act was the first piece of legislation designed to protect Crown timberlands and regulate the harvesting of their forest resources. Before drafting the act, the legislature sought the advice of a number of prominent timbermen, most of them from the Ottawa Valley; Alexander McDonell, Peter Aylen, Robert Conroy, Joseph Aumond, and Ruggles Wright all gave advice before a legislative committee.[13] The statute that emerged reflected the wishes and experiences of these men. One of the changes they got was the right to hold on to their timber limits as long as they kept up the payments; this allowed them to spread their harvesting over many years or even to leave their limits untouched, speculating that they would increase in value. The Act also made it easier to sell a timber limit (transfer the licence) to another timberman, a change that further encouraged speculation in timberlands. By simply holding on to a timber berth, a limit-holder could make a fortune over time. Timber baron William Mackey, for example, is said to have pocketed $665,000 by selling J.R. Booth (the greatest of all timber barons) a limit he had bought for $400 30 years earlier. (When timbermen talked of "buying" and "selling" a timber limit, they were really talking about buying and selling a licence to cut wood on the limit. They did not own the limit; it remained Crown land.) Later amendments to the Act tried to discourage speculation and non-exploitation of timber berths by charging a small duty even if no wood was cut. For major producers, these changes were no hardship, for they had the means to pay the extra charges; small-scale timbermen, on the other hand, found it more difficult to compete.[14]

GOVERNMENT TREASURY RECEIPTS

The Timber Act of 1849 remained the basis of timber regulation for over 50 years. Both Ontario and Quebec kept the Act in force into the twentieth century, though it was amended, extended, strengthened, and refined over the decades. Governments found the Act extremely useful in raising money to meet their spending needs. Certainly, the vigorous growth of the timber, lumber, and pulp-and-paper industries in the second half of the nineteenth century was one reason for the increase in government revenue. But the government itself also took initiatives to make the Act more remunerative. In particular, it boosted timber charges periodically and tightened its methods of collection.

Ground rents for timber limits were a major source of government revenue, especially after the rates were hiked several times. In Quebec, for example, these rents grew from $2 per square mile of limits to $8 per square mile (400 percent) in 60 years. Timber limits became even more remunerative when public auctions were made mandatory (Ontario, 1866, and Quebec, 1874). Still, the most lucrative source of government revenue was timber duties. In Quebec, they accounted for 70 percent of all money raised from the forest industry between 1867 and 1919. Different forest products (square timber, white pine sawlogs, spruce pulpwood, etc.) were charged at different rates, but these rates all underwent significant increases over the years, some rising as much as threefold.[15]

The most important step in raising revenue, however, was the government's crackdown on the evasion of timber duties. One trick that timbermen often pulled was trying to avoid the government agents who were posted at points along the Ottawa River to count the timber as it floated by. In two weeks in 1843, the agent at Carillon caught six timbermen, including Ruggles Wright, trying to sneak their timber cribs past his post, usually under the cover of night. Other timbermen resorted to a more subtle stratagem. For many years timbermen were notorious for contending that a great deal of the wood they floated down the Ottawa River had been not been cut on Crown land but rather on private properties held by settlers. It was, therefore, exempt from duties. For example, in 1844 John Egan claimed that he got more than four-fifths of his production from privately held land. However, most — if not all — of Egan's timber came from above Chaudière Falls, and in 1844 the number of settlers on the upper Ottawa River was not very large. Egan could not have had much private land to cut on. In

1849 W.W. Dawson, a veteran of the timber trade, told the legislative assembly that, in his estimation, nearly half of the timber cut in the Ottawa Valley in the previous three years had been "fraudulently obtained" — that is, cut on Crown land but said to have originated on settlers' farms. Dawson reckoned the loss to the government treasury at about £15,000 annually, though he opined that evasion of duties was probably less common in the Valley than in other parts of Canada. In 1849 the new Timber Act insisted that timbermen had to provide proof that any wood they claimed to be exempt from duty had originated on private land, as well as swear an oath that their annual declaration of timber cut on Crown timber limits was truthful. The new requirements had the desired effect: within a few years the proportion of Ottawa Valley timber exempted from duty declined sharply.[16]

Sworn declarations did not halt all the abuses, however. Government timber agents knew that lumber companies had several ways of evading payment. One common trick was to understate the size and number of sawlogs they cut on their limits. In 1888 a Quebec agent working in Hull decided to investigate the accuracy of the declarations submitted to his office. As a test, he placed an inspector in the mill of E.B. Eddy, and discovered that the great lumber king was sawing far more wood than he professed to have cut in the bush. The agent estimated that timber duties on the unreported sawlogs used at the Eddy mill would have amounted to at least $12,180 (more than $200,000 in today's money). There is no evidence that any legal action was taken on this matter or that the crusading public servant was able to pursue investigations of other firms.[17]

Still, within a few years both Ontario and Quebec took steps to tighten their collection systems. Since the 1860s they had been sending "rangers" into the woods to inspect the cutting operations. In the 1890s, the two provinces increased the numbers of these rangers and expanded their duties. They were now expected to visit each shanty in their districts two or three times a winter before the limit-holder prepared his annual declaration. They were to inspect the shanty account books, count and measure random piles of cut timber, and sometimes even count stumps. The new procedures made it much more difficult for limit-holders to understate the volume of wood they cut.[18]

  The tighter collection regimens implemented over the years yielded more and more revenue, and governments became increasingly dependent on timber duties and ground rents. The payments were never onerous (though limit-holders constantly complained about them), but they did add up. Between 1867 and 1900, taxes on the forest industry accounted for 20 percent to 30 percent of all money flowing into the treasuries of Ontario and Quebec; indeed, apart from federal government subsidies, they represented the largest single source of revenue in both provinces.[19] Not surprisingly, government records show that, for many years, more than half of the receipts generated by timber duties and ground rents came from the Ottawa Valley.[20] In Ontario, the Valley remained a leading supplier of treasury revenue into the 1880s. By that time, much of the best timber on its side of the Ottawa River had been harvested, and investors were shifting their attention to rich new timberlands around Georgian Bay, Lake Superior, and Rainy River. On the Quebec side of the Valley, however, there were still vast tracts of barely touched forest to exploit, particularly around Lac-des-Quinze and Lac Expanse (now Lac Simard), 370 miles above Ottawa.[21] As a result, the Ottawa Valley contributed more than half of all Quebec's timber duties and forest rents until the end of the nineteenth century. All in all, from the day in 1823 that Alexander McDonell paid the first timber duty until at least the end of the century, the Ottawa Valley proved to be a leading source of revenue for government treasuries.

  In addition to the revenue from timber duties, the treasuries of Ontario and Quebec collected hefty sums from the periodic auction of timber limits. For example, on 9 December 1903, about a hundred men gathered in the legislative chamber in Toronto to bid for 37 limits scattered across Ontario. Bidding was lively, and new records were set. In all, $3,687,300 was raised, surpassing the previous high of $2,315,000 set in 1892. Most of the timber limits auctioned were in the upper Great Lakes area, for by this time the lumber industry was declining in the Ottawa Valley. Nevertheless, there were still some good untouched timberlands left on the Ontario side of the Valley that could rouse a lumberman's interest. Indeed, one — a 3.75 square-mile limit at the headwaters of the Jocko River — was bought by Thomas Mackie for a record $31,500 per square mile (nearly $600,000 today). This sale beat the old Ontario record of $17,500 per square mile that the Gilmour Company had paid for another Ottawa Valley limit 11 years earlier.[22]

CANALS

After the War of 1812, merchants in the more populated areas of Upper and Lower Canada began to press governments to undertake a program of public works that would improve navigation on the Great Lakes and the St. Lawrence River. The merchants argued that opening this route to steamboats would stimulate economic growth in the two colonies. The merchants' campaign succeeded, and between 1824 and 1842 the government financed the construction of the Welland, Cornwall, Lachine, and Beauharnois canals. Understandably, other merchants soon pointed out that the Ottawa River could also benefit from such public works. With the river in its unimproved state, steamboats on the Ottawa were restricted to short runs between waterfalls. Steamers were in use both below and above Chaudière Falls by the 1830s (Philemon Wright built the first in 1819), but all passengers, freight, and mail had to be transshipped at each obstacle on the river. The first works to improve navigation in the Ottawa Valley, however, were not financed by Canadian money but rather by the Imperial treasury, when the British government took upon itself the expensive task of building canals on the lower Ottawa River and its tributary, the Rideau.

The Rideau and Ottawa river canals were not constructed to please businessmen, however, but rather to make the colony more secure in case of war. During the War of 1812, American military offensives showed that shipping on the St. Lawrence River between Montreal and Lake Ontario was vulnerable to attack. British military planners now looked for another way to move troops and supplies into the interior of the continent without going close to the American border. After some study, they decided to develop a triangular route between

Montreal and Lake Ontario, sending ships along the Ottawa, Rideau, and Cataraqui rivers and using canals to overcome the impediments of geography.

The Rideau and Ottawa river canal projects, then, were designed as two parts of an integrated scheme of military preparedness. The Rideau Canal was built between 1826 and 1832 under the direction of Col. John By of the Royal Engineers, and in 1827 his name was given to the settlement — Bytown — that grew up at the eastern entrance to the canal. By's marvellous engineering achievement, 123 miles in length, allowed shipping to move over a 300-foot height of land between the Ottawa River and Lake Ontario. As for the three Ottawa River canals, they were begun earlier (1819) and completed later (1834). These works allowed shipping to bypass the Long Sault, Chute-à-Blondeau, and Carillon rapids which blocked navigation between Montreal and Bytown. Together the two projects proved costly to the British treasury, totalling £1,135,000, and in hopes of defraying the annual cost of maintaining the canals, tolls were levied on commercial vessels as they passed through the locks, as well as on the passengers, freight, and timber they carried. As time passed, however, it became clear that the canals would never come close to paying their way. It also became clear to the British that the chance of attack from the United States had much abated. As a result, the British were happy, in 1856, to hand over both the Rideau and Ottawa River canals to the Province of Canada. In 1867 the new federal government assumed responsibility for these works and soon decided to rebuild the Ottawa River canals on a larger scale. By the 1880s, the three originals had become two – the Carillon and the Grenville canals. (These were reduced to one, even larger, work when the Carillon hydroelectric dam and lock were completed in 1963.)[23]

Although they were not intended to serve commercial purposes, the Rideau and Ottawa river canals proved to be a boon for Ottawa Valley timbermen from the outset. Timbering on the Rideau River was well underway before the canal was built; indeed, the Rideau was the first tributary of the Ottawa to have its timberlands harvested on a large scale. Oak found along the Rideau was considered the finest in Canada.

By the time the canal was completed, however, timbermen such as Philemon Wright had stripped most of this species, as well as the best white pine, from the lower stretches of the river.[24] At Rideau Falls the water drops about 40 feet, but the fall was abrupt and clean, so timbers could drop from that height into the Ottawa River without serious damage. However, after the Rideau Canal was completed, timbermen preferred to use the new facilities; the eight locks at the easternmost end of the canal (those beside the present Château Laurier) allowed timber to enter the Ottawa River gently and without disassembling the cribs. Besides being rafted down the canal to the Ottawa River and ultimately to Quebec, timber could go in the other direction as well — to Kingston and Lake Ontario. In fact, the largest single raft ever to pass through the Rideau Canal was one taken south (in 1899) to Kingston, where the timber was to be used in the dockyards; the raft, belonging to J. B. Grier of Ottawa, contained 550,000 cubic feet of wood.[25]

As for the Ottawa River canals, the main beneficiaries were undoubtedly the Valley's timbermen and lumbermen. From 1850 to the end of the First World War, forest products (mostly sawn lumber) accounted for more than 80 percent of the tonnage shipped through the Ottawa River canals. These canals played a key role in the prodigious growth of the lumber industry. Every year large fleets of barges pulled by steamboats carried hundreds of millions of board feet of lumber sawn in the Valley to markets in Montreal and the United States. The amount of tonnage carried on return trips upriver was lighter, but Valley timbermen and lumbermen benefitted here too, as the Ottawa River canals provided them with a cheap way to bring in the food, equipment, and machinery they needed to carry on their businesses.[26]

While they acknowledged the benefits that the British-built Rideau and Ottawa River canals brought them, Ottawa Valley timbermen wanted their own government to use some of the timber duties it collected to help their industry grow. After all, in the first 20 years of collecting duties (1826-1845), the government took in more than £235,000 just from timber cut on Crown land above Chaudière Falls. Valley timbermen maintained that when the duties were first instituted, Governor General George Dalhousie promised that his government would devote some of the receipts to improving navigation on the Ottawa,[27] and the next most obvious target for government improvements was at Chaudière Falls. The drop at the Chaudière was a little less than at Rideau Falls but much more hazardous. Before a twentieth-century hydroelectricity dam tamed its fury, most visitors were amazed by the volume of water that poured over the Chaudière's rocky ridges. The falls bristled with jagged ledges that threatened to damage any timbers that were allowed to "run the chute." The government did spend £2,000 deepening channels near the Chaudière in the late 1820s,[28] but timbermen preferred a canal, which would allow them to bring square timber safely downriver and take supplies upriver past the "boiling kettle." Construction costs would have been enormous, however, as any project to carry shipping around the Chaudière would have had to extend eight miles upstream to bypass the Remic and Deschênes rapids as well. Nevertheless, the benefits of a canal at the Chaudière were promoted as early as 1832,[29] and several schemes for a comprehensive navigation system up the Ottawa (even through to Georgian Bay) were proposed and studied over the next century. In the end, all were rejected as impracticable and impossibly expensive.[30]

Instead, the government put its efforts into other improvements at the Chaudière. In the 1850s it wanted to attract investors to exploit the water-power potential of the falls and establish flour and lumber mills there. As a result, it constructed an array of concrete diversion dams, bulkheads, and flumes at the falls to channel the river current more directly to the mill sites. Lumbermen did, indeed, come and install mills at the Chaudière but soon began to complain of unreliable river levels. The government sympathized with their complaints and over the ensuing decades raised and extended the dams. Even so, the problem of fluctuating water levels on the Ottawa River continued to worsen. As the forest cover was removed by logging, agricultural clearance, and fire, the Ottawa watershed became less able to moderate seasonal extremes in the water supply. High water levels in spring flooded sawmills, broke log booms and covered shipping piers; low levels in summer incapacitated sawmills, grounded shipping, and slowed the floating of timber and logs. After decades of discussion, several large dams were finally constructed on the Ottawa. The first, at the Chaudière (completed 1909), alleviated water shortages but could not mitigate difficulties caused by surplus water; this problem had to be resolved farther up the river. Accordingly, between 1911 and 1914, the government built reservoir dams to control water levels at Kipawa River, Lake Timiskaming, and Lac-des-Quinze.[31]

Earlier, while rejecting calls for a canal to bypass Chaudière Falls, the government had been persuaded to fund two curious public works farther upriver. In 1853 John Egan, in his capacity as a member of the Legislative Assembly, had prevailed on the government to construct a short canal with locks around Chats Falls and thereby open up a longer stretch of the upper Ottawa to steamboat service. Egan was at this time the dominant square-timber producer in all of Canada. Holding vast timber limits in Pontiac and Renfrew counties, he stood to benefit the most from navigational improvements in this part of the Valley. However, the project encountered labour shortages and excavation problems and was finally suspended four years later (though only after nearly a half million dollars had been spent). Then, in the 1870s, the federal government took on another venture: constructing a bypass around Calumet Rapids. This project, named the Culbute Canal, consisted of two locks and an impounding dam. The work was completed at a cost of only $235,000 (over four million in today's dollars) because the entire structure was built of timber taken from nearby forests. The Culbute Canal opened up a long stretch of the Ottawa River (from Chats Falls to des Joachims rapids) to steamboat navigation, but shortly after it was completed, the Canadian Pacific Railway line was extended to Pembroke and Mattawa. The upper Ottawa, now served by all-season rail, had less need for steamboats, and the canal was abandoned in 1889 after only 13 years of operation.[32]

TIMBER SLIDES AND OTHER PUBLIC WORKS

Valley merchants were unhappy that their governments would not agree to build canals on the Ottawa River and make it fully navigable. For a long time the people of the Valley had enjoyed little political clout; after all, they were few in number, were divided by a provincial border, and lived far from their provincial capitals. In 1841, however, their prospects brightened somewhat when Upper and Lower Canada were merged into the Province of Canada and the elected representatives of both sides of the Valley found themselves in the same legislature. Here they allied themselves with the representatives of the powerful merchants of Montreal and Quebec, men who saw potential for profit in the Ottawa Valley timber trade and wanted to help it grow. Building additional canals was unrealistic, but slides to carry timber around waterfalls had already been built on the Ottawa River and proven to be both feasible and useful. Within a short time the new government took on the responsibility of operating a network of slides and other works to facilitate the movement of timber and logs in the Valley.

The first step in the project was to purchase the facilities that local timbermen had already built. And, as the next step, the newly created Department of Public Works was directed to construct further slides and other river improvements throughout the Valley. By taking responsibility for these works, the government averted the possibility of a few timbermen owning all slides on the Ottawa and its tributaries and thus controlling the passage of all timber and logs; monopolies of this kind would have led to serious disputes and violence. Indeed, there had been skirmishes in the bush after Ruggles Wright, George Hamilton, and Peter Aylen temporarily gained monopoly control of the Gatineau River in the 1830s.[33] Ultimately, Valley timbermen were quite content with the government's intervention in their industry (though they were reluctant to admit it).

The timber slide was central to the whole scheme of improvements on the river. The world's first crib-sized timber slide had been conceived and constructed by Ruggles Wright in 1829. That summer he blasted a rough channel through rock on the north side of Chaudière Falls, deepening and extending a natural chasm on his family's property; inside the cut, he built a ramp, made of heavy planks and a timbered frame, to carry a sheet of water from the rushing river above the falls to the still water below. The ramp was designed to carry a full timber crib down the incline on the sheet of water, safely bypassing the falls. The slide measured about 26 feet across, wide enough to accom-

Timber crib about to enter the Chats Falls timber slide, 1899. Raftsmen had to take great care in steering the crib to the slide entrance for, if they missed, the river current would carry them over the falls.

modate most timber cribs of the day, and this became the standard minimum width for all slides built on the Ottawa River thereafter.

Wright's idea was a success from the outset. Before 1829, almost all timber rafts coming from the upper Ottawa River stopped just above Chaudière Falls and were disassembled into their component cribs. Some raft owners, those who were pressed for time, allowed their cribs to "run" over the falls, even though they knew some cribs would be torn apart and many timbers damaged or ruined in the descent. However, most owners, wishing to protect their investment, took the time to disassemble their cribs and carried everything around the falls by wagon.[34] Once back in calm waters, all timbers were reassembled into cribs and the cribs into larger rafts. It was a laborious, time-consuming, and expensive process. After 1829 rafts still had to be taken apart, but Ruggles Wright's invention now allowed complete timber cribs to bypass the cataract with speed and without damage. Wright charged five shillings for each crib that used his slide, and claimed that, while in the past some rafts took up to 20 days to get by Chaudière

Chaudière timber slide. In the background, one can see the original Parliament Buildings; in the middleground, the residence of lumber baron H.F. Bronson, demolished 1965.

Falls, five or six rafts could now pass in one day. Wright's claim was somewhat exaggerated; a neutral observer who inspected the slide said that while rafts were detained two or three weeks in the past, they could now get past the Chaudière in two or three days.[35] Whatever the case, the proof was in the use: timbermen were quite willing to pay a fee to take their cribs through Wright's slide.

Ruggles Wright had got the inspiration for his invention some years earlier while visiting the timber-producing regions of Norway and Sweden. During his trip, he noted the narrow wooden flumes, carrying rushing water, which Scandinavian timbermen employed to bring logs one piece at a time down steeply inclined streams.[36] Wright's great achievement was to redesign the flume to accommodate the width of a Canadian timber crib. The Scandinavian model also came to be used in the Ottawa Valley and other parts of Canada; it was known here as a "single-stick slide." By the second half of the nineteenth century, however, Wright's invention had become the hallmark, the distinguishing characteristic, of the Ottawa Valley timber trade as a whole.

Timber slides at the major cataracts of the Ottawa were nothing like the canals that timbermen would have preferred; though they allowed forest products to be floated downstream, slides were of no use in moving anything upriver. Nevertheless, there is no doubt that Wright's idea brought great economies to the timber trade. These slides reduced the incidence of damage to squared timbers, allowing the owners to deliver a higher-quality product to market. More important, though, timber cribs no longer had to be taken apart and put back together at each obstacle on the Ottawa River, bringing big savings in time and labour. In addition, as the timber frontier receded farther up the Valley, investors were able to exploit rich stands of pine in increasingly more remote areas but could still be confident of getting their rafts to the Quebec market the same year. In 1849 the Ottawa Valley's most famous raftsman, Joe Montferrand, was called before a committee of the legislature to give advice on the drafting of the new Timber Act. He was well qualified for, as he told the legislators, he had worked 24 years piloting rafts on the Ottawa River, after serving a six-year apprenticeship. Asked about the usefulness of timber slides, Montferrand testified that "Formerly, rafts taken from . . . [the Coulonge River], did not reach Quebec before the fall; now a raft gets to market from that place in June or July, about two months difference."[37]

The success of Ruggles Wright's invention led others to follow his example. In 1836, lumberman George Buchanan opened timber slides at both Chats Falls and the Chaudière on land leased from the Crown. The latter was installed in the channel between Chaudière Island and Albert and Victoria islands, all of which straddle the falls. It operated in competition with Wright's slide, and many timbermen came to prefer the Buchanan slide, feeling that its location made it easier for their cribs to enter than Wright's, especially on windy days. Wright responded by building another slide at the Chats to compete with Buchanan's, but it did not do well. Soon other investors opened two more slides farther up the Ottawa, at Portage-du-Fort and Calumet Island, just before the government decided to take over responsibility for river improvements. By 1849 the government had purchased all six slides for a total of about $48,000.[38]

Few construction details are known about the early, privately built crib slides on the Ottawa. However, an 1844 map of Wrightstown[39] and an 1855 drawing by American visitor W. S. Hunter suggest that Wright's slide had a rather steep pitch; that is, the slide appears to have been quite short in length relative to the drop in elevation at the Chaudière (34 feet). Timber cribs would have descended this slide with considerable velocity, and the resulting turbulence caused some to be shaken apart. Refinements introduced in 1845 addressed the problem of turbulence in the early slides.

In that year the Department of Public Works undertook its first active project on the Ottawa — closing Buchanan's Chaudière slide and building a new one in the channel between Victoria and Amelia islands, closer to the south shore of the river. Before starting construction, the department's engineer, F. P. Rubidge, took the advice of James Skead, a veteran of rafting on the river, and designed a work with multiple slides. Rather than one steeply pitched slide, he built four more gently inclined slides separated by stretches of level water; the whole work extended for more than a quarter of a mile. The effect was to slow the speed of cribs on their descent. Rubidge himself added a second refinement. He fitted the lowest slide with what he termed an "apron," which was hinged at one end to rise and sink with seasonal river fluctuations. Without accommodating for low water levels, cribs tended to dive into the still water at the bottom of the slide and were sometimes torn apart by the impact or by hitting the river bottom. Floating on the water, the apron allowed cribs to exit the slide in a more horizontal and gentle manner. The department faced similar problems (seasonal river fluctuations and the difficulty of maintaining a uniform flow of water down the ramp) at the entrance to the slide. Too much water caused turbulence that could wreck the crib and too little could deny it entry. Over the years, government engineers mastered these problems, installing sophisticated sluice gates at the slide entrances, with stop-logs to control the water flow; ideally, they tried to ensure there were 18 inches of water running in the slides as the cribs came down.[40]

After 1845 the government went on to erect a number of new timber slides and reconstruct the privately built works. By 1862 the Department of Public Works was operating crib-sized slides at Arnprior on the Madawaska River and at seven stations on the upper Ottawa River: des Joachims, Calumet, Mountain Chute, Portage-du-Fort, Chats Falls, Deschênes Rapids, and Chaudière Falls. In 1874 another slide was added at Rocher Capitaine Rapids, above Rapides-des-Joachims. The bypasses at the steeper falls — Calumet, des Joachims, and the two at the Chaudière — were constructed with multiple slides and hinged aprons (Ruggles Wright's original slide of 1829 was rebuilt in 1862).[41] In 1881-82 two final crib slides were added to the system. One was a small facility on the South Nation River near Plantagenet, built to ensure delivery of construction timber and fuel wood to Montreal. The second was installed on the lower Ottawa River beside the new Carillon Canal. Since Philemon Wright's first trip of 1806, raftsmen had become much more adept at taking timber cribs through the rapids of the lower Ottawa. Still, some summers the river level was too low to float cribs, and raftsmen had to resort to the Ottawa River canals. In 1882, when the government enlarged the Carillon Canal and constructed a dam across the river, it took the opportunity to add a timber slide. This last project consisted of a single, long (over 600 feet), gently inclined slide fitted with a hinged apron at its foot.[42]

Timber slides were only one part of an energetic program of improvements undertaken by the Department of Public Works after 1841. The government also agreed to take over a number of single-stick slides erected by private investors and to build new ones. By 1867 the department had erected 22 single-stick slides, all on tributaries of the Ottawa above the Chaudière: 14 on the Petawawa, five on the Madawaska, and one each on the Coulonge, Black (Noir), and Du Moine rivers. In profile, these structures were wider at the top (six feet across) than at the bottom (four to five feet). Most of them totalled several hundred feet in length, but the slide around The Third Chute of the Petawawa was 1,346 feet long and that around High Falls on the Coulonge was 2,956 feet long (more than half a mile!). During the log-driving season, the department tried to keep two to four feet of water

Single stick slide on the Petawawa River. Slides such as this were used to flush timbers and sawlogs around waterfalls and rapids, preventing log jams.

running through their single-stick slides. With this flow, the largest square timbers and sawlogs could be floated (one by one) around the highest and wildest falls and rapids on these rivers, thereby preventing log jams. After Confederation the department continued to add further single-stick slides in ever more remote areas. As late as 1914 they provided bypasses for sawlogs through the new dams at Lake Timiskaming, Lac-des-Quinze, and Kipawa River.[43]

ˋBesides building and maintaining timber slides, the government found additional ways to assist the floating of timber and logs in the Ottawa Valley. The Department of Public Works removed boulders, blasted shoals and straightened channels along the Ottawa River from the Quinze Rapids beyond Lake Temiskaming south to Rivière-des-Prairies at Montreal — a total of 440 miles. It constructed an array of bulk-heads, glance-walls, and piers to channel river currents towards timber slides and mill sites on the Ottawa. It built dams to control water flow through single-stick slides on the tributaries. And it installed miles and miles of booms along river shores to keep timbers and logs in the main stream.[44]

It was the timber slides, however, that brought distinction to the Valley. As early as 1837 Sir Francis Bond Head, lieutenant-governor of Upper Canada, rode a crib down one of the slides (probably Buchanan's). Thereafter, it became a tradition to invite visiting dignitaries to take a ceremonial ride, usually down the south-side slide at the Chaudière. The Prince of Wales (Queen Victoria's son, later King Edward VII) accepted the invitation during his 1860 visit to Canada. In 1883, his sister, Princess Louise, rode down the slide with her husband, the Marquess of Lorne, Governor-General of Canada, accompanied by their guest, Mark Twain. And in 1901, the Prince's son, the Duke of York, and Princess May (later King George V and Queen Mary) took the plunge, escorted by Sir Wilfrid and Lady Laurier. Several Governors General — including lords Dufferin and Minto and their wives — also took rides on the slide.[45]

No doubt, timbermen and government officials took care to ensure the dignitaries a safe passage, securing the cribs more tightly than usual and enlisting the best raftsmen to pilot them. Still, the cribs could reach impressive speeds in the descent — after all, the Ottawa River drops 34 feet at the Chaudière, and timber cribs could weigh several tons. The adventure would take a few minutes to complete, as the four slides were spread out over a distance of more than a quarter of a mile. In comparison to modern-day white-water rafting, the ride would have been smoother but carried out with less protective equipment. For people in the nineteenth century, the fastest speed anyone could ever experience would probably be on a railway coach but the speeds reached on the slides may have come close to those of the fastest trains. More important, though, the hills of a railway line were gentler than the abrupt drops of a timber slide (even Rubidge's more gently inclined slides had a pitch of at least 10 percent, which is much more precipitous than the steepest CPR gradient in the Rocky Mountains which was only 4.5 percent.)[46] And, besides, travelling in an enclosed railway coach would have been much more reassuring than riding in the open air, where danger was more easily felt. All in all, running a timber slide was an exhilarating — perhaps even an alarming — experience for many people.

Members of the general public were sometimes allowed to sample this experience. One was Rev. George M. Grant, principal of Queen's University, who has left a stirring account of his adventure, taken about 1880. He begins by telling of the anxiety he felt as the raftsman steered the crib towards the Chaudière slide entrance and the sluice gate was thrown open:

> the ladies gather up their garments as the crib, now beginning to feel the current, takes matters into its own hands; with rap-idly-quickening speed, the unwieldy craft passes under a bridge, and with a groan and a mighty cracking and splashing, plunges nose forward, and tail high in the air, over the first drop. Now she is in the slide proper, and the pace is exhilarat-ing; on, over the smooth timbers she glides swiftly. . . . Now comes a bigger drop than the last, and the water, as we go over, surges up through our timbers, and a shower of spray falls about us. . . . Another interval of smooth rush, and again a drop, and yet another. Ahead there is a gleam of tossed and tumbled water which shows the end of the descent; down still we rush, and with one last wild dip, which sends the water spurting up about our feet, we have reached the bottom, clev-erly caught on a floating platform of wood, called the "apron," which prevents our plunging into "full fathoms five." We have "run the slides."[47]

Back in the 1830s, word of the success of Ruggles Wright's invention had spread quickly, and when the government took on the responsibil-ity for all slides on the Ottawa River, timbermen operating on the Trent River asked for and got similar assistance. Indeed, the Department of Public Works went on to install ten crib-size slides in the Trent water-shed, as many as were erected in the Ottawa Valley. A little later, the gov-ernment also began building slides (single-stick) on the St. Maurice and Saguenay rivers. By the 1860s, the government had also provided these three regions with a wide array of ancillary services (dams, piers, booms, dredging), services similar to those found in the Ottawa Valley.[48] Although crib-size slides were well known beyond the Ottawa and the Trent, the idea was not exported elsewhere. New Brunswick, the other major producer of square timber, did not need them. All the major waterways in that colony were navigable well into the forests of the interior, free of the waterfalls and rapids that impeded rivers draining the Canadian Shield.

The government's program to assist the Ottawa Valley forest industry was an enormous undertaking, but, surprisingly, after the initial costs of construction were met, the works did not cost the taxpayer anything; in fact, tolls charged for the use of these improvements added funds to the government treasury. The Department of Public Works employed "slide masters" and "boom masters" to keep the works in repair, to oversee the passage of timbers and logs, and to count them as they passed so proper tolls could be calculated. Tolls were higher for square timber than for sawlogs and were greater on some rivers than others (the Petawawa's were the highest since it had the most slides and booms). Without exception, every year between 1845 (the first year of operation) and 1867, revenue from slides in the Valley exceeded all expenditures for salaries, management, and maintenance; over these 23 years, the government netted nearly $500,000 (about $8,500,000 in today's money). For the next 40 years or so after Confederation, when the federal government took responsibility for slides and booms, it too benefitted from the regular surpluses the tolls generated in the Ottawa Valley. The public works on the Saguenay, St-Maurice, and Trent rivers, on the other hand, usually operated at a deficit, both before and after Confederation.[49] The tolls that Ottawa Valley timbermen paid for the use of booms and slides were, of course, additional to the timber duties and ground rents they paid the provincial government. Timbermen everywhere grumbled about all the costs they had to bear, but perhaps those in the Valley could more rightfully complain that the surplus money they generated was being used to subsidize competitors on the Saguenay, St-Maurice, and Trent.

The government's decision to take over responsibility for facilitating the passage of square timber, sawlogs, and (later) pulpwood down rivers such as the Saguenay, St-Maurice, Trent, and Ottawa proved to be an enormous boon to the forest industry. Still, this industry did not receive special treatment. For centuries the Canadian economy has developed around the export of staples such as wheat, minerals, and forest products, and it has become a practice in this country to provide public support for them. Staple industries depend heavily on sales in world markets and are thus vulnerable to wide and chronic price fluctuations. Canada in the nineteenth century was a young country in which private investment capital was scarce, so staple exporters needed state assistance to succeed. Assistance often came in the form of publicly financed or subsidized transport facilities. For example, the government built the Welland, Cornwall, and Lachine canals to help get wheat to distant markets. Later, governments across Canada assisted the construction of roads and railways to provide access to remote mining areas and subsidized pipelines from oil and gas fields. The forest industry got similar treatment. In New Brunswick the province helped out by dredging the major rivers and installing a system of towpaths along river banks, allowing investors to exploit the local forests more efficiently. In Ontario and Quebec, the timber slides, booms, and dams provided by government lowered the cost of getting the provinces' wood products from remote forests to distant markets. In the end, government assistance to forest industries strengthened the whole economy.

4

SQUARE TIMBER

The success that Philemon Wright and others found selling timber to British buyers at Quebec sparked a timbering boom across Canada after 1806. Crowds of adventurers quickly began to seek out promising pine groves, not only along the Ottawa but along most major streams flowing into the St. Lawrence River and the Great Lakes. The square-timber trade grew and flourished along the Richelieu, St-Maurice, and Trent rivers, but it was the Ottawa Valley that led the industry throughout much of the nineteenth century. It was here that the art of squaring timber as well as driving and rafting it to market reached its highest form and fame.

When Wright floated his first raft to Quebec, it took him two months to make the journey, and it is likely that the timbers he brought with him were squared in only a rudimentary fashion. For the timber industry to succeed, Wright and his emulators had to learn a new set of skills, and it is surprising how quickly they succeeded in developing ways to pilot vast rafts of timber down the fast and tricky currents of the Ottawa and St. Lawrence rivers. Within a few years they were able to raft their timber from Hull to Quebec in two or three weeks. By the end of the War of 1812 they were floating scores of rafts every year to Quebec. From there the timber was shipped across the Atlantic to London, Liverpool, and other British ports. Turning out high-quality square timber, however, required a longer learning

Hewing timbers, Jocko River, Ontario. The master hewer is standing on the far side of the timber holding the broad hewing axe; he has already squared one side of the timber.

process; it took decades for shantymen to master the art of hewing huge pine trees into finely sculptured timbers.

The highest-quality square timbers were hewn perfectly flat on four sides, leaving a sharp edge on the corners. The sides did not have to be equal, and, indeed, many timbers did not show a square form in profile. Most of these timbers were massive in size. They were sold and taxed by the cubic foot, and, in the early years, specimens from the Ottawa Valley measured as much as 100 cubic feet in volume on the average. A Valley clergyman, J. L. Gourlay, claimed that, as a youth in 1844 he had personally helped square a timber 73 feet in length and 24 by 25 inches in girth (a total of 304 cubic feet) and that he had seen others that were larger. For tax purposes, however, one stick of squared white pine was deemed to contain 70 cubic feet of timber.[1]

Trees, of course, are cylindrical, so the process of hewing them square was shockingly wasteful: more than a third of the tree trunk was hewn away and discarded (and that is not counting branches and tops).[2] The squaring process left a great deal of perfectly sound wood on the ground to rot or, worse, to provide kindling for devastating forest fires. It was not until mid-century that Canada followed New Brunswick's example of allowing partially squared or "waney" timbers to be brought to market; these sticks were bevelled at the corners, giving them an octagonal shape in profile. The new process did not eliminate wastage, however; it only reduced it. An Ottawa Valley timberman, Daniel McLachlin, seems to have been the first in Canada to produce waney timber, delivering 50,000 cubic feet to Quebec in 1856. By 1900 exports of waney timber outnumbered fully squared sticks three to one.[3]

Almost all the square timber produced in British North America was shipped to Britain, where most was used as a heavy construction material for wharves, bridges, mining supports, and ship framing and decking (the decks of the gigantic ocean liners *Lusitania* and *Mauretania*, launched in 1906, are said to have been built of timbers supplied by J.R. Booth of Ottawa). Shippers preferred timber in squared form because it was easier to load into their vessels than raw, untrimmed logs. Importers preferred the timber unsawn because they feared that thin boards and planks would warp during the long ocean passage to Britain. Although hardwoods such as oak, elm, and ash fetched the best prices among British timber buyers, because of the difficulties in rafting them, Ottawa Valley exports were tiny; in 1858, for example, hardwoods made up less than one percent of all square timber produced in the Valley, and 30 years later almost none were turned out. Spruce was the most prolific tree, but it did not grow large enough to be squared. It was the pine, then, that got almost all the attention in the Ottawa Valley. Red pine predominated at first, but the larger and more plentiful white pine prevailed after 1850; by 1888 this species made up better than three-quarters of all square timber produced in the Valley.[4]

The venture of cutting down a large white pine standing in an Ottawa Valley forest, squaring it on the spot, and then delivering it to a buyer hundreds of miles away at Quebec could take nearly a year to complete. Timbering, like farming, followed a strict yearly cycle dictated by the seasons.

PREPARING FOR WORK IN THE BUSH

The cycle began with a timberman deciding where he wanted to cut in the coming year. If he did not already have a timber limit, he could either buy an existing limit from another timberman or obtain one at a provincial auction. If he chose the latter, the cost could be substantial for the bidding at auctions often drove prices to lofty heights: in 1907, for instance, J. R. Booth paid the Province of Ontario $300,000 (more than five million dollars today) for the right to cut timber along the Montreal River.[5] Understandably, then, it was important for investors to know as much as possible about the limits beforehand. When a number of limits on the upper Ottawa River were auctioned in 1880, a trade journal reported that most of the bidders "had either personally investigated the limits . . . or possessed confidential information from explorers employed by them."[6] As time passed and the best pine was removed from the more accessible parts of the Ottawa Valley, new timber limits offered at auction were located in increasingly remote areas, and it became difficult for timbermen to do the investigating themselves. As a result, they came to rely on expert evaluators, known as "timber cruisers."

Timbermen sometimes employed local Indians as cruisers but usually used experienced shanty foremen who knew the needs of the trade.[7] One veteran Ottawa Valley shantyman confided that, in the early days, cruising was not always considered necessary because, if a limit did not measure up to expectations, it was easy to simply poach wood on land somewhere nearby. Eventually, however, laws were more strictly enforced and timber evaluation became a more precise science. The veteran claimed that, by his time (the 1880s),

> often every tree is not only counted but an inspection is made of it so as to get an idea as to its soundness, by which a general average can be made of the whole lot on the limit; and so expert will some of the Bush Rangers become that, after examining a given territory, they can compute within a thousand feet, board measure, what it will cut out.[8]

The cruisers (two or three to a party) would usually set out in early spring when visibility was best (as the days grew longer, but before leaves appeared on the trees). Travelling on snowshoes and pulling toboggans, they would criss-cross the limits that were up for auction, shinnying up trees and clambering over hills, counting, measuring, and inspecting the standing timber. At the same time, they also drew rough maps noting the best groves of pine, the number of "floatable" streams, the preferred sites for shanties, and the most convenient routes for hauling trails. With this information, the limit-holder would try to calculate the costs of felling, squaring, and removing the merchantable wood. In effect, a timberman's future and fortune depended to a large degree on the estimates and advice of his cruisers. Even if a timberman did not begin cutting on his new limits immediately, the cruisers' report could remain useful for a long time.[9]

The next question a timberman faced was how much timber he should cut on his limits in the coming season. Ideally, he would like to have some idea of the price square timber might fetch the next year at Quebec and the cost of borrowing the money needed to cover his expenses. When facing these questions, however, most timbermen found themselves virtually helpless. Timber prices were highly volatile and nearly impossible to predict a year in advance. And given the chronic shortage of investment capital in Canada, borrowers usually found themselves at the mercy of a few merchants and moneylenders at Quebec. The costs of wages, provisions, equipment, and draught animals needed for squaring timber in the remote forests of the Ottawa Valley were notoriously high; it was estimated in the 1830s that some Valley timbermen were spending over £100,000 a year on their ventures. The only major Valley timberman who was able to supply his own capital was Allan Gilmour, whose family operated a multinational firm based in Scotland. Other timbermen essentially had two options: they could obtain supplies or advance payments from a merchant by contracting to deliver a minimum quantity of square timber to Quebec by a certain date, or they could arrange loans from middlemen, to be repaid after selling their timber rafts. Later in the century, when the banking system had matured, more investment capital was available and timbermen found it a little easier to raise money. In any case, most timbermen carried a heavy debt load.[10]

A timberman usually spent his summer months arranging to gather the provisions and equipment he would need for his upcoming bush and river operations. Although much could be delivered over the ice later in the year, he would have to have a considerable stock of supplies ready to go by early fall. In total, he needed enough supplies to feed and equip his men and animals for operations that could last as long as nine or ten months — from September, when the first shantymen were sent into the bush, until summer, when the timber rafts were sent down the Ottawa River. In 1851 John Egan claimed that his timbering operations required him to purchase, every year, "about six thousand barrels of Pork and ten thousand barrels of Flour" to feed the nearly 2,000 men he employed. He also claimed that he used "about sixteen hundred horses and oxen in the winter, which consume about 60,000 bushels [of] oats and provender, and twelve hundred tons of hay."[11] Egan's figures may be somewhat inflated (he was trying to show the legislature how important the timber trade was to the provincial econ- omy); still, he was the largest timber producer in the Valley. Twenty years later, James Little, timberman and forest expert, listed the sup- plies needed to operate a moderate-sized outfit in the Ottawa Valley[12]:

- 825 barrels of pork
- 900 barrels of flour
- 525 bushels of beans
- 3,650 gallons of syrup
- 37,000 bushels of oats

- 7,500 pounds of tea
- 1,875 pounds of soap
- 6,000 pounds of tobacco
- 900 pairs of blankets
- 300 tons of hay

In addition to these items, a timberman had to provide numerous other necessities — saws, shovels, axes, grindstones, and other logging tools; ropes and chains; pails, pots and pans, tin cups and tin plates; boots and clothing; tents, sleighs, canoes, and wagons.

Much of the equipment needed was manufactured outside the Valley, but as the years passed and farming became better established in the Valley, more and more of the food for the men and feed for the animals was supplied locally. Timbermen tried to buy or grow their hay and oats as close as possible to the shanties as these commodities are bulky in nature and thus costly to carry over long distances. Even the expense of transporting hay within the Valley was high due to poor roads: one observer estimated that it cost two to three times the purchase price to get hay to the shanties.[13] As for flour and other foodstuffs, records of cargoes shipped through the Ottawa River canals show that imports of these products declined after 1870,[14] indicating that the Valley was becoming more self-sufficient. John Egan boasted that his local purchases supported "hundreds of farmers in the Valley of the Ottawa," and his boast was probably accurate. Some farmers certainly benefitted from meeting the enormous needs of the timber trade, mostly those fortunate to have land in the southern, more fertile, parts of the Valley.

While arranging for his provisions, a timberman might also spend some of his summer checking out conditions at the "logging farms" he had established on his timber limits. The timberman undertook these investments hoping to supply some of his own agricultural needs and thus reduce his dependence on borrowed capital. Moreover, as the timber limits he harvested became more remote, the cost of supplying his shanties increased. It made sense for a timberman to try producing food and feed as close as possible to his logging operations. From the very first days of the timber trade, the Wright family had always supplied some of the agricultural provisions they needed for their bush work. The Wrights were not typical, however, for they owned 17,500 acres outright in Hull Township, much of it good farmland. Even so, they still saw the value of establishing farms on their timber limits in the back country as well. As early as the 1830s, they had opened several farms up the Gatineau River, including Victoria Farm, 45 miles north of Wrightstown, near the present Gracefield.

The use of logging farms spread quickly, and by the 1850s timbermen such as Alexander McDonell were cultivating land far up the rugged Petawawa and Madawaska rivers. By the 1880s others were reported growing root crops and even corn as far north as Lake Timiskaming. It was difficult to find arable pockets on the Canadian

Shield, but timbermen were able to establish enough logging farms to help them ease their supply difficulties. The farms they developed were, of course, located on patches of timber limits from which they had already stripped the forests. Some of the farms grew over the years to cover several hundreds of acres and included dwellings, barns, stables, blacksmithing facilities, and other workshops. Many of them also included storehouses, or "depots," to hold supplies for several shanties in the surrounding area. The farms were run by experienced agriculturists, who grew hay, oats, barley, buckwheat, beans, potatoes, and turnips and raised pigs, chickens, horses, and cows. Logging farms also served as summer pasture for the timberman's oxen and horses that hauled timber in the winter. Most of these farms have now returned to bush, but a few buildings still stand, such as those at the old Usborne Depot on the Coulonge River. A few logging farms became the nuclei of settlements that have lasted until today — for example, Eganville in Ontario and Labelle in Quebec.[15]

When September arrived, it was time for the timberman to start sending the men, animals, provisions, and equipment up to the limits where he intended to cut. Moving the huge volume of supplies he had assembled required a prodigious effort as transportation in the Ottawa Valley, whether by land or river, was always difficult. Roads in the Valley were neglected for many decades as the government directed most of its attention to improving the St. Lawrence transportation axis. The first major road in the Valley, the Richmond Road from Chaudière Falls to Perth, was constructed in 1818 by demobilized British soldiers brought to the area as settlers. About the same time Philemon Wright and others opened an eight-mile land link between Wrightstown and Aylmer, allowing wagons to portage goods around Chaudière Falls and Deschênes Rapids. By the middle of the nineteenth century, the government had built roads from Montreal up both sides of the Ottawa River — one as far as Wrightstown and the other through Bytown to Pembroke. (Parts of old Ontario Highway 17 followed the same route.) This road reached Mattawa by the 1860s and Lake Timiskaming by 1888. Another major government project was the Opeongo Road, an ill-advised effort in the 1850s to promote settlement in the Madawaska Valley.[16]

Lunch in the Bush, January 1903. Since there was no time for the men to return to the shanty for a noonday meal, they had to eat in the bush.

All these roads were quite rudimentary at first and, because bridges were often lacking, some sections were usable only in winter, when horses and sleighs could cross rivers on the ice. Land travel in the Valley was slow, unpleasant, and often dangerous: in 1821 Philemon Wright, Jr., died when his carriage overturned on a road near his home.[17] Apart from the Opeongo project, it was a long time before governments opened roads inland from the Ottawa River. Still, it was in these more remote, interior areas that the best stands of red and white pines grew. Government inaction did not deter the timbermen, however; they simply set about cutting their own "tote" roads (also called "cadge" roads) through the bush to reach their timber limits. Timbermen invested considerable money in these endeavours, which often necessitated costly bridge-building. Some of the roads up such tributaries as the Madawaska, Petawawa, and Gatineau, which today are part of the public highway system, were originally opened by timbermen to accommodate the horses, wagons, and sleighs supplying their shanties. The villages of Chelsea, Wakefield, Low, Kazabazua, and Gracefield on the Gatineau River began as overnight stopping places for teamsters and horses; they are all 12 or 13 miles apart, the distance a wagon generally travelled in a day.[18]

Throughout the nineteenth century, the Ottawa River was the true highway of the Valley, at least for ten or 11 months of the year. To be sure, for a few weeks in autumn when ice was forming and at breakup time in spring, the river was impassable by either steamboats or sleighs, but for the rest of the year it was alive with traffic. Despite the many rapids and falls on the river, steamboats succeeded in moving goods, mail, passengers, and even oxen and horses up and down the river between Montreal and Lake Timiskaming. Not surprisingly, it was timbermen who took up the challenge of providing shipping services on the Ottawa; they had the most to gain, but the whole population benefitted. And again, Philemon Wright was the pioneer. In 1819 he built the SS *Union* at Grenville, above the Long Sault rapids, to run between there and Wrightstown.

Strangely, steamboats did not sail on the lowest reaches of the Ottawa River until 1826, when service was initiated between Montreal Island and the Long Sault. Shipping on the river received its biggest boost with the construction of the Ottawa River canals in the 1830s; these works opened the whole river between Montreal and Wrightstown to steamboats. At the latter, however, all freight and passengers had to be carried around the Chaudière–Deschênes barrier on the Wrightstown-to-Aylmer road and reloaded onto boats that serviced Lac Deschênes. Steamboating on this lake began in the 1830s but was much enhanced when the timbermen Joseph Aumond, John Egan, and Ruggles Wright launched a daily service in the 1840s. Their vessels ran between Aylmer and a landing on the Pontiac shore near Chats Falls. Here they installed an ingenious, three-mile, horse-drawn rail service to carry everything around the falls to the navigable waters above. This is where Egan persuaded the government to begin its misguided canal project. Above Chats Lake, however, travellers and freight were able, by the 1870s, to use the Culbute Canal to bypass the Calumet Rapids. Decade by decade, water transport was extended farther and farther up the river. By 1882, steamboating reached lakes Timiskaming and Kipawa, a seven-mile rail line having been built to carry goods and passengers around the rapids on the Ottawa River between Mattawa and Lake Timiskaming. The steamboat services were initiated by Olivier Latour, who was soon bought out by another timberman, Alex Lumsden. Despite the number of times freight and passengers had to be unloaded and reloaded — from steamer to wagon or rail car then back to steamer — shipping on the Ottawa worked remarkably well, from spring to autumn. By the end of the century, however, the Canadian Pacific Railway, which afforded year-round service, was carrying most of the people and freight travelling up and down the Ottawa Valley.[19]

The first consignment of supplies a timberman would send into the bush usually consisted only of basic provisions and equipment. They were carried by an advance party of men, dispatched with a few oxen or horses, to prepare his timber limits for the coming season. On arriving, the men spent a few days harvesting wild hay in nearby "beaver meadows" (marshes); this hay, though not of good quality, would sustain their animals until better provender could be brought in. If the area had been worked the previous year, the men would also check on the equipment and unused supplies that had been stored in the depots and "keepovers" (temporary storehouses erected in the spring). From the foreman's report, the timberman could gauge what supplies should be sent in his next shipment. Generally, two major deliveries of provisions and equipment were made thereafter. The first was in October, when the main party of shantymen were arriving for the season's work, and the second in winter after the rivers froze.

The October delivery began with fleets of steamboats launched from Aylmer to carry goods up the Ottawa towards the timber limits. The steamers would land their cargoes at one of the burgeoning new villages along the river — Arnprior, Fort Coulonge, Pembroke, Mattawa. From these forwarding centres, the supplies were sent inland to the shanties. Timbermen used two methods for inland delivery, both fraught with difficulty. Heavy and bulky freight, such as equipment and blankets and hay and oats, was usually carried overland by horse-drawn wagon. For the teamsters, it was long, tiresome work, driving horses across muddy river fords and along narrow trails barely hacked out of the bush. The work could be dangerous, too, especially when the

men had to goad struggling animals up slippery slopes and guide heavily laden wagons down rocky tote roads. Smaller and lighter goods,
such as flour, beans, and pork, were often taken inland by birchbark
canoe, but this method was also risky, for Ottawa River tributaries were
notoriously turbulent. The canoes had to be portaged, paddled, and
poled upstream, through strong currents, rocky shoals, and swirling
eddies. In the process, some cargoes were inevitably lost when these
frail vessels, heavily laden with goods, capsized.[20]

For the winter delivery of supplies, the Ottawa River again served as
the main avenue of transport. As soon as the ice on the river was judged
safe, hundreds of freight-bearing sleighs were put into action. By the
middle of the nineteenth century, it was common to see as many as 20
sleighs a day leave Bytown for the shanties upriver. It was said that on
clear days one could see clouds of steam from the horses' nostrils miles
away in the freezing air. The season generally lasted from mid-
December to mid-March, and in those three months sleighs could
make two return trips between Bytown and Lake Timiskaming. Horse-
drawn sleighs could carry hefty loads of provisions and equipment on
the winter ice much faster than could horse-drawn wagons stumbling
along the Valley's wretched roads in the fall. And unlike steamboats
and canoes, freight did not have to be unloaded from sleighs and carried around falls and rapids; the teamsters simply steered their sleighs
from the river onto land and followed the portage routes, now covered
with snow. Timbermen were able to transport an immense volume of
provisions and equipment to their remote shanties in the wintertime.
The system was efficient but not without risk: on one occasion a team
of 14 horses bringing supplies to the Hurdman family's timber limits
fell through the ice of the Ottawa River and drowned.[21]

WORKING IN THE BUSH

At the timber limits, the advance force sent ahead in September (generally six or seven men, including a foreman and a cook) had been
busy preparing a camp for the next season's work. If buildings
remained from a previous year, they were cleaned and repaired. If not,
the men's first task was to erect a shanty, stables, and a privy before the

rest of the men arrived. In choosing a site for the camp, the foreman had to consider several matters. Most important, of course, the site had to be close to the pine groves where the men would be cutting over the winter. Another consideration was proximity to a reliable source of drinking water for men and horses. At the same time, the camp had to be on high, well-drained ground, where the water could not be contaminated by faecal waste. Finally, it had to be convenient to land or water supply routes. The men lived in tents until the shanty was completed. That accomplished, they hurried to their next task — improving the "floatability" of nearby streams before they froze up. Here they removed boulders, straightened channels, and built small dams to raise water levels; this work would make it easier for the men to drive, or float, the timber down to the main river in the spring. Finally, before the snow got too deep, the men cut a network of rough trails from the pine groves to the drive streams; these trails had to be made passable for teamsters to "skid" (drag) timbers from the stump to the water's edge.

The main force of shantymen usually arrived sometime in midautumn, as temperatures dropped and sap stopped running in the trees, making them easier to cut down. In the early days, many timbering endeavours were small ventures consisting of family members and a few neighbours, most of whom were expected to do a variety of jobs. Later, large-scale operations became more common, with some employing as many as 70 men (this being about the maximum the largest shanty could accommodate). These outfits would consist of several gangs of five or six men, each of whom performed a specialized task in the timber-making process — felling, lining, scoring, hewing, and hauling. As well, the large operators often employed a clerk and a blacksmith to work at the shanty. The men were paid according to a hierarchy of skills, ranging from hewers at the top to road-makers and general labourers at the bottom.[22]

The job of felling trees was crucial to the timber-making process, a job requiring proven experience. "Fellers" (the term "faller," used elsewhere in North America, was seldom heard in the Valley) were expected to cut trees so they would drop in the most favourable direction —

that is, where they would not hang up on other trees, sustain damage from rock outcrops, were in the best position for squaring and hauling, and, if possible, landed on a bed of brush to cushion the fall. For most of the nineteenth century, fellers relied on long-handled, double-bit axes weighing six or seven pounds to do the work; saws were employed only for simple tasks such as trimming branches. The two-man cross-cut saw was not used to bring down trees until the 1870s, when a number of technical advances were introduced — raking-teeth that removed sawdust from the cut, coal oil that washed sticky resin away from the teeth, and wedges that prevented blades from jamming in the cut. Still, as late as 1885, a government official noted that axes were still being used for felling purposes in the Ottawa Valley. By 1903, however, the *Canada Lumberman* was claiming that this practice was virtually confined to the maritime provinces.[23]

It was usually the hewer who decided which trees were suitable for squaring. He looked for pines with a straight trunk, large girth, few branches, and no outward signs of rot or disease. The hewer, as the senior man in the gang, then sat back while others felled the trees and prepared them for squaring. Once on the ground, the trees were "topped off" at a point where the taper became too pronounced to allow squaring. After the branches and some of the bark were removed, the "liner" stepped in. Using a cord coated with soot or chalk, he marked the line along which the timber should be hewn. In effect, it was the liner who determined the dimensions of the finished timber. He was followed by "scorers," who performed the preliminary hewing, chopping the side flat within an inch or two of the line. It was at this point that the hewer took over. With his many years of experience and his ten- to 12-pound broadaxe (sharpened every night to a razor's edge), he finished the job. The hewer was the prideful, master artist, who, like the great sculptors and surgeons, had others do the preliminary work. At the same time, however, he alone had to bear ultimate responsibility for the quality of the product. The best hewers were able to carve a perfectly smooth surface along the entire length of the chalk line. After he performed his artistry on two flanks, the gang rolled the huge timber over and he repeated the process on the other two sides. As a final step, the men

Hauling timbers by sled. This photo shows how much a single sled could carry; some of these timbers would weigh over a ton.

chopped each end of the squared timber to a pyramid point in order to ease its long passage to Quebec through the rocks and shoals of rivers without damaging the wood.[24]

Each gang in the shanty was expected to produce five to seven square timbers a day in good weather.[25] Quality was also important, since poorly dressed timber brought lower prices at Quebec. Certainly quality was low in the early years, and the merchants at Quebec constantly pressed timbermen to improve their production standards. The settlers whom Philemon Wright brought with him from New England and the French *habitants* who moved to the Valley from parishes on the St. Lawrence knew a little about the art of squaring timber; living in frontier communities, they had had some familiarity with hewing large logs into roughly squared timbers for use as posts and beams in the construction of houses and barns. But although they were experienced woodsmen, they were not necessarily adept at high-precision axemanship. As for newcomers arriving directly from Scotland or Ireland, they knew almost nothing about felling trees (let alone hewing timber), and many were injured and even died while clearing their lands and building houses.[26] It took a generation or more for the Ottawa Valley to develop a reliable corps of men who could take the art of hewing timber to its highest level.

Skidding logs, 1871. Rough terrain and snow could make work dangerous for shantymen when skidding logs as shown here.

In December, another contingent of men would arrive at the limits: teamsters hired to haul timbers from the stump where they had been squared to rivers and lakes nearby. Here the timbers were laid on the ice to await the spring breakup and the journey to Quebec. Timbermen often encouraged the teamsters to bring their own oxen or horses with them, an arrangement that benefitted both parties. For the teamsters, usually Valley farmers, it meant cash earnings and free fodder for the winter. For the timberman, it meant fewer animals of his own to feed year round. In the early years, oxen were more commonly used to haul timber than horses. Oxen could pull heavier loads, withstand rougher treatment, and live on coarser feed; they could also be slaughtered to feed the shantymen. Horses were easier to handle, moved faster, and ate less, however, and ultimately displaced oxen in the bush. The Wrights were using horses by the 1830s and the McLachlins by the 1840s. In 1873 Allan Gilmour had 80 yokes of oxen and 250 spans of horses at work on his Gatineau limits; seven years later he was using only horses.[27]

Horses were also more adaptable to pulling the sleds that became more common in hauling timber. At first, the teamsters simply roped or chained one end of a timber to a low-lying bobsled (actually just a bare frame connecting a set of two short runners) and had the oxen or horses skid the stick along a forest trail (also called a "skid road"). Dragging often damaged the timber, however, and eventually most operators turned to a double bobsled (two sets of short runners), which could carry both ends safely above the rocks and snags of the trail; it could also carry more than one timber at once. Some authorities credit the interrelated Fraser family of Cumberland and the Hurdmans of Aylmer for introducing the double bobsled. Timbering traditions could linger long in the Ottawa Valley, though, even if they were inefficient. George M. Grant saw both single and double bobsleds in use in 1881, and timber was still being dragged behind single bobs in the Jocko River area in the early twentieth century.[28]

While oxen and horses could be depended on to move timbers over a distance, it still took human muscle to turn and roll the huge sticks, to lift and shift them in the first place. Three generations of prying tools were employed to do the work. The first, known as the "pike-pole" or "handspike," was really no more than a hardwood pole used as a simple lever. By the mid-1800s, timbermen were equipping their shantymen with "cant-hooks," shorter poles fitted with a metal hook to grip the timbers. A later improvement was the "peavey," which was rigged with a hinged, adjustable hook and a sharp spike on the end.[29]

Skidding trails had already been cut through the forest by the advance party sent ahead in September. The shanty foreman was expected to find the easiest and shortest land routes to water so the timber could be floated to market. Most timbermen felt that it was

Loading logs on a sled, 1871. The men are using cant-hooks to manoeuvre the heavy logs which they then chain to the double bobsled.

uneconomical to skid the heavy timbers much more than three miles overland, though Peter White of Pembroke is said to have hauled them as far as 18 miles on his limits back of Deux Rivières.[30] In the early years of timbering, skid roads were simply rough pathways hacked through the forest. They required little work to prepare: a few logs were laid corduroy-fashion to fill in hollows and swampy areas, and some shovel work was done to level any uneven terrain. They had only to be wide and flat enough to accommodate a two-horse bobsled. In later years, especially after lumbermen began to take sawlogs out of the Valley's forests, more elaborate, heavy-duty hauling roads were cut through the bush to carry bigger sled loads. In any case, the teamster's job was to get the squared timbers from the stump to a frozen lake or river, where they were piled on the ice to await the spring drive.

One more task remained before the winter ended and the ice gave way: the shantymen had to stamp every stick of timber with the limit-holder's identification mark so he could prove ownership when they floated downriver. The major tributaries of the Ottawa River were usually worked by several timbermen, and they would all send their season's cut down the river at about the same time. On some rivers they formed cooperatives to share the expense of installing such things as slides and dams and agreed on how to sort the logs and timbers. Still, theft and disagreement were inevitable, so ultimately they lobbied the government to help them. In 1870 Alonzo Wright, a former Gatineau River lumberman and now Member of Parliament for the Hull area (and grandson of Philemon), introduced legislation that brought long-lasting order to the timber industry (as well as the lumber industry) across all of Canada. The Timber Marking Act compelled anyone who floated timbers or logs on the inland waters of Canada to select and register a particular mark, which had to be conspicuously placed on each stick of wood. The marks were recorded in an official registry, which remained active for more than a century thereafter. By marking the timbers, each owner was able to identify his products in the river (much like cattle branding on the western plains). Over the years, timbermen displayed an imaginative sense of artistry in designing these marks; they included a wide range of initials and numerals, as well as figures such as hearts, crowns, stars, leaves, and various combinations thereof. Out on the ice, the shantymen were furnished with a heavy, embossed hammer to stamp the owner's mark on the timber, though sometimes a scribing knife was used.[31]

THE SPRING RIVER-DRIVE

Bush activities usually petered out as winter came to an end, for timber could be hauled only as long as there was snow on the trails. Some of the shantymen, especially those who had farms to attend to, left at this time. The others, who were staying on for the spring drive, were then able to enjoy a little relaxation as they waited for the river ice to break up and the spring freshets to carry the timber downstream. For a week or two there was little to do but prepare for the drive and make sure the dams they had installed on nearby streams the previous fall were still in good form. The dams, built with timbers deemed unsuitable for squaring, were intended to catch the runoff of melting snow and thus improve a stream's floatability. First, by raising water levels upstream, dams lifted the timbers above rocks and shallows, allowing the wood to float unimpeded on the current. At the same time, dams

Spring river drive, Almond creak Ontario, 1902. It was not unusual for drivers to work hip-deep in the icy waters of the spring runoff.

lowered levels downstream, allowing the men to improve the channels by moving or blasting boulders out of the way. Finally, when the flood-gates of a dam were opened, the surging water created a strong flush-ing action, carrying the timbers on a great tide that overcame any remaining obstructions downstream (thus, they were often called "splash dams"). Many streams had a series of splash dams that were opened one after the other along the way.

The job of the "river men" or "drivers" (*draveurs* in French) was to keep the mass of timber moving down the small streams to larger trib-utary rivers such as the Gatineau, Madawaska, Coulonge, and, ulti-mately, to the Ottawa, where they would be banded together into cribs and rafts. Speed was imperative, for the work had to be done during the short period of the spring runoff. If the weather did not cooperate, river levels could fall too quickly, leaving the winter's cut stranded on the shoreline until the next year's drive. The drivers spent most of their days walking along the shores or wading in the icy waters using cant-hooks or peaveys to keep the timbers moving.[32] Most of the time they were kept busy "sweeping" — that is, pushing timbers caught up on

Rouge River, Quebec, 1863. A river drivers' camp. Note the canoe; pointer boats had yet to be invented.

rocks, in shallows, and overhanging bushes back into the main stream. Occasionally, the drivers were called upon to use their skill and daring to break up log-jams that formed in narrow gorges along the tributaries (see Chapter Seven).

When the drivers succeeded in getting the timbers to the larger tributaries, the traffic became heavier: here their timbers (and often sawlogs destined for lumber mills) met timbers that had come down other streams. It was difficult to keep the assorted wood from mixing. At the same time, however, the drivers' work could become a little easier for many of the larger rivers had single-stick slides to take the timber past the most irksome gorges. As mentioned earlier, slides, dams, and booms that had been privately erected by timbermen on five Ottawa River tributaries were taken over and extended by the government in the 1840s. Soon, however, timbermen began installing additional private works farther up these tributaries and on others elsewhere in the Valley; they often financed these improvements through cooperative organizations (see Chapter Five). On some tributaries, the timbers might be driven for over a hundred miles before reaching the "rafting grounds" of the Ottawa River. If the winter snowfall and spring rains were adequate, the river drive could be completed in a few weeks, but, regardless of weather conditions, water levels usually fell off considerably by the end of May, ending the river-driving season. When the logs arrived at the Ottawa River, some work remained to be done, however — identifying and bringing together each limit-holder's timbers so they could be assembled into rafts. When these tasks were completed, some of the drivers were paid off and left for home, while others stayed on to work as raftsmen, who would take the timber all the way to Quebec.

RAFTING ON THE OTTAWA

Philemon Wright's first rafting voyage down the Ottawa River in 1806 was, perforce, a learning experience. Wright and his men would have had little background in rafting for this art was not widely practised back in New England. In the previous century, however, French colonists had periodically rafted square timber down the Richelieu and St. Lawrence rivers to Quebec for export to France.[33] In the journal of his inaugural rafting trip, Wright occasionally noted that he engaged the help of French settlers living along the Ottawa. These men may have had at least some traditional knowledge of rafting on large rivers. It is also possible that some of these settlers had worked as voyageurs in the fur trade and thus knew the best channels to take on the Ottawa. In a memoir written years later, Wright claimed there were men around who knew the Long Sault rapids well, but he said he could not afford to pay for their help.[34] In any case, with good luck, Wright and his men managed to get their timber to Quebec without major mishap. Over the years, Philemon and his sons took many timber rafts to Quebec, but Anglophone raftsmen never became numerous in the Ottawa Valley. For the most part, Francophones dominated timber rafting over the next hundred years. Building on their old traditions, they mastered the skill of raft-making, learned the quirks of navigation on the Ottawa River, and picked up the tricks of piloting these cumbersome crafts all the way to Quebec.

The work of assembling rafts was supervised by a "pilot" (foreman)

Men rowing a timber raft down the Ottawa River. Rafstmen would often resort to rowing when contrary winds or currents threatened to take them off course. Note the number of hardwood pins used to hold the cribs together.

hired by the owner. The pilot's responsibilities were heavy, for he was entrusted with getting the cargo, which could be worth $100,000 or more, safely to Quebec. He had to make crucial decisions along the route, balancing the safety of the payload and the welfare of his crew with the need to minimize the owner's expenses. He was expected to be well informed about water conditions on the Ottawa River, conditions that could change from week to week. Without a good pilot, the timberman could lose a whole year's investment.

The pilot's first task at the rafting grounds was to supervise the construction of the timber cribs. It is not known exactly how Philemon Wright went about making his first raft, how he fastened his square timbers together into 19 or so cribs and then formed those into a large raft. Within a few years, however, Valley raftsmen developed a standard and distinctive way of making rafts designed for conditions on the Ottawa. The length of a crib was variable as the timbers could range from 20 to 70 or more feet; the width of the crib, however, was standardized by the 1830s at a maximum 24 feet so it could fit the river's timber slides. To fashion a crib, the pilot would choose two lengthy "floats" to form the long sides of a frame. Then two, twenty-four-foot "traverses" were fastened to the ends of the floats by means of hardwood pins driven into auger holes. (The floats and traverses were generally made of squared or half-squared timbers of lesser quality, which would be difficult to sell at Quebec.) Next, as many marketable timbers as possible were squeezed into the inside of the frame. On lengthy cribs, extra traverses might be added to restrain the movement of the timbers floating inside the frame. After this, two or three "loading sticks" were attached lengthwise by pins to the traverses to stabilize the frame. Finally, another layer of wood products was sometimes stacked on top — sawn lumber, staves, or hardwood timbers (which were difficult to float).

Once a number of cribs had been put together, the pilot began to assemble them into an extended raft. Unlike the making of cribs, wooden pins were not used to hold a raft together: instead, the cribs were fastened one to another by ropes, chains, or withes (thin saplings of willow or birch twisted into what became, in effect, a wooden rope of great pliability and strength). These more flexible bindings allowed rafts to be taken apart quickly when the time came for the cribs to run the rapids or descend the timber slides one by one. To reduce the strain on a large, unwieldy raft, a little slack was allowed in the fastenings to afford each crib some freedom of motion in rough water. By the middle of the nineteenth century, rafts could be immense in size, some containing over 200 cribs and covering an acre or more; as late as 1896, when the timber industry was past its peak, a raft totalling 257 cribs was sent down the Ottawa from the Coulonge River. The largest rafts carried as many as 80 crewmen. The men worked, ate, and slept on the rafts, each one of which was outfitted with crude shelters and a cookhouse to serve their needs during the long trip to Quebec.[35]

Square timber was rafted from as far north as the foot of the Quinze rapids (the head of Lake Timiskaming), more than 600 miles from Quebec. By the 1880s, after the last timber slide was installed on the Ottawa, a journey of this length might be completed in as few as eight weeks. A rafting trip of this brevity would be exceptional, however, for

Timber raft on the Ottawa River, c. 1890. Some rafts could contain over 100 timber cribs and cover more than an acre of the river.

so many things could go wrong — storms, contrary winds, accidents, heavy traffic at the slides, and especially low water levels (a problem that worsened as the century progressed). Normally, raftsmen setting out from Lake Timiskaming could expect to be on the river for three to four months. Some years, water levels on the Ottawa fell so low by August that rafting was no longer possible; if a raft had not reached the St. Lawrence by this time, it had to be beached somewhere along the Ottawa for the winter. The delay would be costly to the owner for he would get no money until the timber reached Quebec the following year, but had to pay off the raftsmen at this point.[36]

A raft put together on Lake Timiskaming might have to be disassembled and reassembled more than a dozen times along the Ottawa — at rapids such as Long Sault of the North, Deux-Rivières, Allumettes, Paquette, Calumet, and Chenaux, as well as at the eight government-run timber slides. If weather and water conditions were ideal, the pilot of the raft might choose not to disassemble all the cribs but to run the rapids in "bands" of two or more. Only single cribs could descend the slides, however, so to use this bypass the whole raft had to be taken apart. At the Long Sault, Blondeau, and Carillon rapids below Ottawa, pilots had three choices. Many pilots chose to run all three rapids, a few cribs at a time. But when river levels were low, some would take their cribs through the government canal (for which, of course, the raft's owner would be charged lockage fees). After 1882, when a slide was installed adjacent to the new Carillon canal, pilots could use this bypass (though they would have to pay slideage tolls).[37]

Running a rapids saved the raft owner time and money (avoiding tolls and fees). It was a dangerous practice, however, and many lives and payloads were lost when pilots misjudged the risks. Taking cribs through the slides was safer, but accidents could happen here too. On one occasion at the Chaudière, for example, a crib hit the bottom of the first slide and became stuck (possibly because there was too little water flowing down the ramp); the two raftsmen on board crawled out and climbed back to the top of the slide just as another crib was about to enter; if they had not arrived on time to warn the two men on board to jump off and get ashore, they would have been crushed to death when their crib hit the first and was smashed to pieces.[38]

Whether they were being run through a rapids, descending a slide, or being poled through a canal, all cribs had to be manned: at least two raftsmen were required to navigate a single crib, while ten or more might be needed on a band of cribs. The men used oars to negotiate the best approach to a rapids, slide, or canal, and, once underway, they could also use pike poles for steering. After completing their descent, the men would moor the cribs along shore and return upstream to bring another one down. Sometimes they walked back and sometimes they were carried in wagons; at the Long Sault, they could take a modest rail line that had been built in 1854 to supplement the canal. Getting timber cribs past the numerous navigational obstacles along the Ottawa was tedious work; at some obstacles, the men could make no more than two trips a day.[39]

Out on the open water the rafts drifted downriver with the current, but the pilots could employ a number of tactics to hasten the voyage. Sometimes, for example, they hoisted lugsails on 12- to 15-foot masts, but sails were useful only on wider stretches of the Ottawa, such as lakes Timiskaming, Chats, and Deschênes. On narrower stretches, the raftsmen often had to row, pulling on long (up to 30 feet), heavy oars to keep the ungainly craft on course (oarlocks were fitted on the outermost cribs). Sometimes the winds blew too strongly and the crew had to throw anchors overboard to prevent the raft from being swept into a deep bay, where it could be trapped for days or weeks. The most important advance in rafting was the decision to use steamboats to tow the timber downriver. Raft-towing began as early as the 1830s on the lower Ottawa, and by 1882 the practice had reached Lake Timiskaming. Still, many timbermen were not willing to pay the additional cost of towing, preferring to rely on sails, river currents, and muscle power to get their timber to market. One (albeit minor) route where steamboat towing was used more routinely, however, was the Rideau Canal. Square timber was rafted along this waterway in its very first year of operation, and the practice continued for 90 years, much of it in cribs towed by steamers.[40]

In the last decades of the industry, some timbermen experimented with carrying their product part of the way to market by rail. The first attempt was made in 1881, when timber was rafted down the Ottawa River to Aylmer. There it was loaded on flatcars of the Quebec, Montreal, Ottawa & Occident Railway, which had been completed three years earlier. More than 700 carloads of square timber were carried to Quebec, and the experiment was declared a success. A few timbermen followed this strategy in following years, but it never became routine. In 1904, J.R. Booth reversed the process, sending timber first by rail from his Madawaska limits to Coteau Landing on the St. Lawrence River and from there rafting it down to Quebec.[41] Rail conveyance was more expensive, but it allowed timbermen like Booth to avoid the increasing problems of unreliable water levels on the Ottawa. These experiments proved to be valuable: when rafting on the Ottawa River ended forever in 1908, rail became the only means of getting square timber out of the Valley.

Most, but not all, of the square timber produced in the Ottawa Valley went to Quebec for export to Britain. As has been seen, some timber was rafted through the Rideau Canal to Kingston, where it

Mealtime on a timber raft, c. 1880. A camboose kitchen can be seen in the
background. The man at the farthest right may be the raft's pilot.

would be used in the dockyards. Indeed, small amounts of timber were
still being rafted down the canal as late as 1921.[42] In addition, after the
Richelieu Canal was completed in 1844, a considerable amount of val-
ley timber was rafted down the Ottawa and St. Lawrence rivers to Sorel,
and from there the cribs were then towed by steamboats up the
Richelieu River and across Lake Champlain to markets in Vermont and
New York; a good deal of this timber was used to build the wharves of
New York City.[43]

   The timber rafts of the Ottawa Valley were a familiar and impressive
sight on the local riverscape for a long time. Some years in the nineteenth century, 300 or more rafts, large and small, would drift down
the Ottawa; when several arrived at once they could fill the river from
shore to shore. Ottawa River rafts were notably distinctive from those
found in other parts of the country. For example, the rafts that were
used to bring square timber down the St. Lawrence from Lake Ontario
and Lake Erie were made up of fewer, and larger, cribs (known as
"drams"). In New Brunswick, the cribs (there called "joints") were

looser in form; they did not require rigid, heavy-duty frames because the rafting rivers of this province had few stretches of rough water.[44] The distinctive Ottawa River raft could evoke a variety of images. At long range, the raft might give the appearance of a floating island or village, complete with cabins, cookhouse, and its own population of workers. In rough waters, it could resemble a vast blanket woven of timber, bobbing and heaving on the waves. In quieter waters, it might look like a patchwork quilt stitched together by lace. The picturesque (though not always tidy looking) Ottawa raft proved to be a true hallmark of the square timber industry.

TIMBERING: FROM DOMINANCE TO DEMISE

In 1867 A. J. Russell, collector of Crown timber dues in the Ottawa Valley, advised the government to avoid any policies that might harm the timber trade in his area, for as he pointed out, the Valley was "the principal site of that trade," and its well-being was important to all of Canada.[45] Although square timbering prospered in many parts of Canada, there is no doubt that the Ottawa Valley was the "principal site" of the industry throughout most of the nineteenth century. Comparative figures of square timber output for the early years of the trade are difficult to find, but statistics kept by provincial governments show that, in the 1840s, the Ottawa Valley was producing more than all other areas of Canada combined. By the 1850s the Valley accounted for more than 90 percent of the red and white pine timber produced in what is now Ontario and Quebec.[46] Later figures show that the Valley dominated the timber trade into the 1890s; although its share of total output in the two provinces had fallen, the Valley was still performing far ahead of all other areas taken individually — areas such as Lake Erie, Georgian Bay, and the St. Maurice and Trent rivers.[47] Ottawa Valley production exceeded even the output of the entire province of New Brunswick. Britain considered this province, with its rich pine forests along the St. John, Miramichi, and St. Croix rivers, an essential source of timber. In 1845, however, the Ottawa Valley turned out more than twice as much square pine as New Brunswick. It is true that the New Brunswick square-timber industry was in decline by the 1840s, but even in its best year, 1821, its output was lower than the Ottawa Valley's in 1845.[48]

Still, by the beginning of the twentieth century, the square-timber industry, so long accustomed to swaggering through the Ottawa Valley, was now staggering towards its demise. In July 1908, J.R. Booth sent the last raft, 150 cribs of white pine timber, down the Ottawa River from his limits on the Coulonge. That summer, a large, new hydro-electric dam was under construction at Chaudière Falls, and everyone knew this would bring an end to rafting on the Ottawa. When completed the next year, the dam raised water levels above the falls by ten feet, making it difficult for timber cribs to gain access to the slide. When Booth's raft arrived at the Chaudière, crowds of people gathered to watch the cribs run the slide — so many that police had to be called to prevent them from trying to jump aboard.

The new dam may have ended rafting, but there is no doubt the timber trade itself was almost finished anyhow. In the previous year, only 24 cribs had passed through the Chaudière slide.[49] After a century of diligent cutting (not to mention numerous forest fires), Valley timbermen were finding it nearly impossible to locate accessible stands of pines of the size and quality they used to harvest. As a result, they had to settle for smaller trees, and the dimensions of square timber taken down the Ottawa declined noticeably. In the early years of the trade, Ottawa Valley timbers had averaged more than 20 inches square and as much as 100 cubic feet in volume; by 1908 they averaged less than 17 inches and only a few reached 40 cubic feet in volume.[50]

Although rafting ceased in 1908, timbering lingered on for about five more years, the products being carried to Quebec by rail. By this time the market for square timber was disappearing, as steel came to replace wood in large construction projects. The industry was revived briefly in 1925 and 1930 when the British Admiralty asked J.R. Booth's company if it could fill an order for waney timbers to be used as decking on its warships; fortunately, the firm was able to find enough old scorers and hewers to carry out the job.[51]

5

LUMBER

In the 1850s, square timbers floating down the Ottawa River were joined by a valuable new forest product: sawlogs destined for large-scale lumber mills. As we have seen, lumber had been sawn in the Ottawa Valley from the earliest days of European settlement, but the output was always small and little was sold outside the Valley. A number of hard realities had long hindered the development of a large-scale lumber industry, especially one based on export: a scarcity of investment capital to finance the building of heavy-duty sawmills; the remoteness of the Valley from outside markets; and, indeed, the lack of any reliable markets outside the Valley. With happy timing, however,

Sawing a thick log into lengths, c. 1900. Sawlogs were usually cut into 12 to 16 foot lengths.

these difficulties were overcome within a few years in the early 1850s. First, the government made the best water-power sites on the Ottawa River (those at Chaudière Falls) available for development, a move that induced well-funded American entrepreneurs to invest money in lumbering. Shortly after, profitable new markets for lumber opened up in the United States. And, finally, the Valley gained a long-needed rail connection to the outside world.

Most of the natural products that Canada produced in its early years — codfish, furs, wheat, square timber — were shipped to European markets. The 1850s brought a major change in course. The determination of investors to build sawmills in the Ottawa Valley and sell lumber in the United States marks one of the first moves to a North-South trade that has only recently culminated in the North American Free Trade Agreement.

THE VALLEY AT MID-CENTURY

In 1846 most of Canada was seized by a frenzy much like what would be seen in the California Gold Rush three years later or in the Klondike at the end of the century. A booming British economy led thousands of Canadians to seek their fortunes in timber. Battalions of men — farmers with little experience along with veteran shantymen — rushed into the woods and spent the winter hewing trees into square timber. That year the woods were alive with the sound of axes and a record 20.5 million cubic feet of pine timber were cut in the Ottawa Valley alone. The British market, however, could not absorb the supply, and prices plummeted. By 1848 nearly 26 million cubic feet of timber lay unsold at the port of Quebec; that year, few men went into the woods, and Ottawa Valley output fell to 8.9 million feet. A number of timbermen, including William Stewart, member of the Legislative Assembly for Bytown, suffered ruinous losses in the depression and were forced out of the trade.[1]

The square-timber trade began to recover in 1850 and later went on to set new production records. Still, many timbermen were troubled by the declining imperial tariff preference and the volatile nature of the trade (they had seen other booms and crashes in the past); they had large annual payments to make for their timber limits and now began to seek other ways to profit from the wood they cut on those limits. The most obvious choice would be to move into lumbering. Like timbering, the lumber trade was also subject to boom-and-bust cycles, but it had several advantages. First, by sawing trees into boards and planks, the lumberman wasted far less wood than if he hewed them square. Moreover, he could be less choosy when cutting trees on his limits: now he could harvest smaller, poorer-quality pines and could take the prolific white spruce as well. In addition, lumbering provided the limit-holder wider opportunities for profit: sawn lumber was a more finished product (and thus had more value added) than hewn timber; and sometimes the lumberman was also able to participate in the lucrative wholesale end of the trade. Manufacturing lumber was obviously an attractive alternative, but it required expensive machinery for which few timbermen had the capital, especially after the years of depression. Banks were of little help to early lumbermen; indeed, the mayor of Bytown described banking services in the Valley in the 1850s as "primitive."[2] In the end, very few timbermen succeeded in expanding into lumbering on a large scale; those who did succeed, men like Allan Gilmour and Robert Hurdman, needed outside financial help.

Lumbering was, of course, not new to the Ottawa Valley: William Merrick was sawing lumber on the Rideau River as early as 1795. As the population grew, sawmills seem to sprout up almost everywhere there was a waterfall to power them. In fact, the census of 1851 shows 118 sawmills scattered around the Valley, many of them incorporating flour and woollen mills in the same building. Almost all operated on a small scale (the 118 sawmills employed only 158 men) and sawed lumber only a few months a year. Most of the mills were powered by water taken from the river above a falls and channelled down a flume, after which it dropped into the buckets of a water wheel. The weight of the water filling the buckets turned the wheel, which then activated the machinery inside the mill. The water wheel was mounted vertically on the side of the mill and was sometimes enclosed to protect it from ice buildups (it could not function in winter, however). Most mills relied on a single upright, or "muley," saw; moving slowly up and down, it

could take half an hour to slice one board off a large sawlog. Despite
the slow pace and winter dormancy, these mills had some strong
points. They were not expensive to build or maintain. The mechanics
were easy for the miller to understand, making repairs manageable.
And they could operate on streams with low water flows. Still, the output of these Valley mills was small, even in the aggregate, and most of
the lumber was sold locally.[3]

One exception stands out, the Hamilton family's mill at
Hawkesbury, powered by the rushing waters of the Long Sault rapids.
This establishment specialized in sawing pine deals — thick (at least
three-inch) slabs of wood that found eager buyers in Britain (and practically nowhere else). In the 1820s, the mill was said to be equipped
with nearly forty saws. By the 1830s George Hamilton was among the
three leading deal exporters in Canada. Most of his competitors were
located close to the seaport of Quebec, whence the wood was shipped
across the Atlantic. Hawkesbury, however, was nearly 200 miles inland,
so Hamilton had to bear higher costs of delivery. Most of his deal production he floated, in timber-crib fashion, down the Ottawa and St.
Lawrence rivers to Quebec. Exposure to water, however, discoloured
the wood, lowering its value, so Hamilton had to maintain a cleansing
operation at the port. A smaller share of his production he shipped to
Quebec by barge. This way he could preserve his deals from damage,
but, of course, the costs were higher. Nevertheless, Hamilton managed
to expand his business. In 1855 the Hawkesbury mill, now operated as
Hamilton Brothers (George's sons John and George Jr.), was turning
out a hefty 750,000 deals (about 20,000,000 board feet) a year.[4]

Operating at Hawkesbury, the Hamiltons may have had to bear
high costs of delivery, but at least they did not have to worry about
waterfalls or rapids; they had direct water access to Quebec.
Lumbermen sawing wood in mills farther up the Ottawa River and
hoping to sell it outside the Valley faced even higher delivery costs for
they had to contend with the Long Sault rapids that blocked the river
route. Unlike square timber, deals could not be floated over the rapid,
since they were more susceptible to damage from the scouring rocks.
And, of course, lumber in any of its forms was too bulky and heavy to

be transported long distances by wagon or sleigh. Nevertheless, before the arrival of railways, the only feasible way to export lumber manufactured above Hawkesbury was to ship it out along the Ottawa River. The completion of the Ottawa River canals in 1834 made this possible by overcoming the blockage at the Long Sault. Bytown and Hull replaced Hawkesbury as the head of navigation on the Ottawa, but lumbermen using the canals would have to pay costly lockage fees to get their product out.

Before 1850, only two lumbermen with mills above Hawkesbury are known to have made serious efforts to saw wood for sale outside the Valley. The first attempt was an enterprise begun by Julius Caesar Blasdell at Chelsea Falls on the Gatineau River in 1847. Blasdell did not have the capital resources to complete his sawmill, however, and it was taken over by Allan Gilmour, who expanded its operations. The Chelsea mill had a capacity greater than the local market could absorb, and the surplus was sold outside the Ottawa Valley.[5] The other pioneer of the export lumber trade was Thomas McKay, who had become wealthy as a contractor in the construction of the Rideau Canal. (Later he built Rideau Hall, now the residence of the governor general.) In 1848, with the help of his son-in-law, John McKinnon, McKay expanded his sawmill at Rideau Falls. Not all his increased output could be sold locally, so he too had to find new customers. He arranged for American shippers to carry his surplus lumber down the Ottawa River, down the St. Lawrence to Sorel, up the Richelieu, and then along the Champlain-Hudson canal; this route gave him access to the busy markets of New York and New England. Transport would have been costly, as the lumber had to pay tolls on four or more canals, but the experiment seems to have been a success. In 1849 McKay is reported to have shipped 2.4 million board feet of lumber along this route.[6] By mid-century, then, a few, modest attempts had been made to sell lumber sawn in the Ottawa Valley in American markets.

OPENING UP THE CHAUDIÈRE

Travellers on the Ottawa River had long noted the great water-power potential of the Chaudière Falls. With a huge volume of water falling

30 to 33 feet (depending on the season), the Chaudière offered the best industrial site in all of the Ottawa Valley. From the beginning of settlement the Crown had recognized the strategic value of the area, but it issued no land grants for the four islands that straddled the falls; the Crown preferred to retain control of Chaudière, Victoria, Albert, and Amelia islands, perhaps in the hope that a canal with locks might someday be built to carry shipping around the cataract. In 1850 there were, however, a couple of small mills sawing lumber and milling flour on the mainland beside the falls. These belonged to Daniel McLachlin (who soon moved his operations to Arnprior) and Philip Thompson (part of whose establishment survives today as The Mill Restaurant).[7] The Wright family, who owned the shoreline on the Hull side of the river, seems to have had little success with milling at the Chaudière; they concentrated their efforts on the lower Gatineau River. In reality, the immense force of the water power at the Chaudière may have been too great for McLachlin, Thompson, and the Wrights to harness; the Chaudière sites were more suited to large-scale mills, and they lacked the capital to finance such costly works.

The Crown could not ignore the Chaudière for long, however. The four islands were the ideal location to build bridges to span the Ottawa River, providing a link between Upper and Lower Canada. Colonel By had used the islands to bridge the river, but the main span between Chaudière Island and the mainland was torn out by spring ice within a few years. In 1844 the provincial government replaced the span with a stone suspension bridge that would last 45 years. This more robust structure only added to the industrial potential of the Chaudière, and soon entrepreneurs were pressing the government to open the islands for sale or lease.[8] Accordingly, in 1851-52 the government surveyed the islands and announced that it would hold auctions to open them for industrial development. More than 60 building lots in the interior of the islands (lots with no access to water power) were offered for sale. More important, 26 hydraulic lots (shoreline locations giving access to water power) were also opened for auction — but for lease only, because, as a navigable stream, the water power of the Ottawa River had to remain in the control of the Crown. The hydraulic lots were leased to the highest bidders on 21-year terms. In return for the payments, the government built diversion dams and flumes to direct water to the hydraulic lots, making it possible for the lessees to generate power.[9]

The government advertised its intention to open up the Chaudière in newspapers throughout Canada and the northeastern United States. At the first auction, held in Bytown on 1 October 1852, 13 of the hydraulic lots were auctioned away to four bidders — three local investors and one American. John J. Harris, the American, ended up with six of the lots yet paid less than half as much as the others.[10] Several explanations have been offered for how Harris gained this preferential treatment. Richard Scott, mayor of Bytown at the time, later claimed that he wanted to encourage Harris, with his strong capital base, to invest in the Chaudière; Scott says he threw a banquet for Harris and promised that no one would bid against him for the lots he wanted. On the other hand, an Ottawa newspaper reported that Harris did it all alone: that he was visiting Bytown on business, recognized the value of the Chaudière water power, and negotiated a deal with the government himself. There may be some truth in this story, for it turns out that Harris and his partner, Henry F. Bronson, had purchased timber limits on the upper Ottawa River the year before.[11]

During the 1850s, the government held three further auctions, selling and leasing lots on the islands at Chaudière Falls.[12] Dozens of aspiring industrialists, some from the Bytown area and some from the United States, invested in mill sites. Within a few years, however, most had given up their dreams of sawing lumber or milling grain, realizing they lacked the capital needed to exploit the sites effectively. By 1870 most of the Chaudière Falls area was dominated by a handful of "lumber kings," who were using its great water power to operate large-scale, export-driven sawmills.

Several of those who rose to dominance at the Chaudière were of American origin. John Harris was from New York State, where he ran a lumber business in partnership with Bronson. Harris kept his residence in New York, but Bronson moved to Bytown and became one of the leading lumbermen in Canada. Harris withdrew after a few years, and

Bronson formed a new firm with his son Erskine H. and another non-resident American partner, Abijah Weston. The firm Bronsons and Weston Lumber Co. manufactured lumber at its large Chaudière sawmills for the rest of the century. Another firm obtaining land at the Chaudière in the early 1850s was that of William G. Perley and Gordon B. Pattee, New Hampshire lumber merchants. The two men took up residence in Bytown and quickly made their sawmill a giant of the lumber industry. Two other Americans, Levi Young and Alanson H. Baldwin, also arrived at this time and established big-time lumbering operations. These four firms were the core of what came to be known as the "American community," which jump-started the export lumber trade at the Chaudière Falls. The Americans had access to the extensive capital needed to obtain the most up-to-date technology — the heavy-duty hydraulic gear that was required to harness the Chaudière water power and the sophisticated mill equipment needed for large-scale lumber production. Some of them had direct experience in both saw-ing lumber and selling it to wholesalers; they knew the American lumber market, what kinds of lumber were preferred in which areas. Others had been involved in shipping and knew the intricacies of transport on the inland waterways of New England and New York, knowledge that was useful in getting the lumber to market.[13]

Three other entrepreneurs, however, showed that it was possible to succeed at the Chaudière without the advantages that the four early-established firms possessed. Two of them arrived in the area around 1854, with no money, started small, and went on to build huge enter-prises. Ezra Butler Eddy, a native of Vermont, began by making match-es, pails, and wash tubs from the scraps of nearby mills. Within 20 years he had a large sawmill on the Hull shoreline of the Chaudière and was one of the leading lumber manufacturers in the Ottawa Valley. John Rudolphus Booth was born in the Eastern Townships of Quebec; he rented a small mill at the Chaudière for a few years before acquir-ing hydraulic lots of his own. By the 1890s Booth was acknowledged the premier lumberman of the Ottawa Valley. By this time Young and Baldwin were out of business, but a new lumberman had joined the Chaudière group. Robert Hurdman was a native of Hull Township who had toiled in his family's square-timber business for decades. In 1879 he moved into lumbering at the Chaudière, and within a few years had joined the ranks of the Valley's lumber kings. Hurdman did not have enough capital to do it alone, though; he succeeded only with the help of outside partners.[14]

The first lumber kings of the Ottawa Valley were, of course, the Hamilton family of Hawkesbury, and they had reigned alone for a long time. But within 20 years of the opening of the Chaudière, two or three of the firms there were already turning out more lumber than the Hamiltons.[15] The locus of the Valley's lumber industry had moved upriver. The small, cramped area around Chaudière Falls was quickly covered with bustling sawmills and crammed with acres of lumber piles. Almost every inch of the islands was devoted to lumber. The water power of the falls made it possible to establish a large-scale industry, producing sawn lumber for export (mainly to American markets). Although the number of firms active at the Chaudière became fewer over the years, the falls would remain the hub of lumber manufacturing in the Ottawa Valley well into the twentieth century.[16]

OPENING UP AN AMERICAN MARKET

By the middle of the nineteenth century, the lumber trade in the northeastern United States was beginning to feel the effects of several decades of vigorous population and industrial growth. Lumber, the universal building material, was in short supply, and prices were rising quickly. As it became apparent that the best forests of Vermont, New Hampshire, and New York were being logged out, local lumbermen began seeking new sources in Canada. To men such as Harris, Bronson, Perley, and Pattee, the Ottawa Valley was an obvious place to look. Bronson, indeed, had travelled up the Ottawa River as early as 1848 scouting for new timberlands to harvest, perhaps inspecting the timber limits he and Harris obtained three years later; in 1853 the pair began erecting a large sawmill at the Chaudière.

The very next year the two Americans received exciting news: the United States and Great Britain had negotiated a reciprocity treaty that removed customs duties on all natural products passing between the

United States and Britain's North American colonies. The negotiators for the British colonies were hoping that free trade in natural products would open new markets at a time when the colonies were losing their preferential tariff advantages in Britain. As for the Americans, shortage of lumber was only a minor consideration in the negotiations, but after the treaty took effect, Canadian lumber found eager buyers in the United States, and Ottawa Valley producers became major suppliers. For the Ottawa Valley, the treaty gave a powerful boost to investors hoping to make better use of its rich timber and water-power resources; it gave hope to a young industry seeking to expand export sales. Before the treaty came into force, the costs of transport, combined with customs duties, had made it difficult to sell lumber even in nearby New York State. Removing the duties made all the difference. Now Valley lumbermen could feel confident of making a profit. Bronson and Perley were soon selling lumber they manufactured at the Chaudière to their old customers back in the United States. Census comparisons show a huge jump in Ottawa Valley lumbering activity in a nine-year period. The censuses include no production figures, but they do show that employment in Valley sawmills rose from 158 hands in 1852 to more than 2,300 in 1861.[17]

The United States cancelled the reciprocity treaty after only 12 years, but Ottawa Valley lumbermen suffered little immediate harm when customs duties were reimposed on their exports.[18] Demand for building materials continued to grow in the United States after its Civil War ended, and Valley lumber producers now had the sawmill capacity and technical expertise to sell their output, despite renewed customs barriers. In only a dozen years, a robust and dynamic industry had been established throughout all of Canada. Although the lumber trade suffered from the international economic depression of the 1870s, exports to the United States followed a general upward course for another 20 or more years. Still, the trade was risky and some large Valley producers, men like A. H. Baldwin, J. M. Currier, and James Skead, did go bankrupt in the 1870s; if they had not had to pay duties, they might have survived the depression years. J. R. Booth, H. F. Bronson, and other lumber kings spent the next decades longing for the days of free

trade and urging the Canadian government to seek a new treaty.[19]
More than a century would pass before free trade was renewed between
Canada and the United States, but the short time the Reciprocity Treaty
lasted (from 1854 to 1866) proved to be enough to open up a reliable
American market for Canadian lumber and sustain a large-scale lum-
ber industry in the Ottawa Valley.

OPENING A RAILWAY CONNECTION

Opening the Chaudière water-power sites for development provided
investors with the capacity to saw lumber on a large scale, and the
Reciprocity Treaty provided a market for the lumber produced. To
reach its full potential, however, the Ottawa Valley lumber industry
needed rail service; railways would allow lumbermen to exploit timberlands far away from their Ottawa River sawmills and get lumber
from those mills to distant markets.

The 1850s were years of intensive railway construction in Canada.
At this time, railways, like canals, were widely regarded as the best
way to boost economic development. Canals were never seen as
money-makers in themselves and were built entirely with public
funds. Railways, on the other hand, were expected to generate exciting profits and thus attracted private investment. Still, railway
investors did not hesitate to ask governments to help them out by, for
example, purchasing shares in their companies, guaranteeing loans,
or granting outright cash subsidies. Ottawa Valley lumbermen had
much to gain from railways, and they made sure they were not left
out of the action. They invested some of their own money in railways
and prevailed on governments to do so as well.

As early as 1848 a group of citizens met in Bytown to discuss constructing a rail line to Prescott, 60 miles to the south. Two years later
the group received a government charter to begin the Bytown and
Prescott Railway (B&PR).[20] Bytown had been incorporated as a town
only in 1847 and had a population of only about 7,000 people, but the
possibility of gaining a railway and a large-scale lumber industry
emboldened the community. Ottawa Valley limit-holders energetically
promoted the project. Joseph Aumond and John Egan, for example,

helped recruit Walter Shanly, a Canadian engineer who had gained a reputation building the Ogdensburg and Lake Champlain Railroad, to supervise construction. John McKinnon served as president of the railway. Aumond and Egan sat on the board of directors, along with such other lumbermen as Daniel McLachlin and Nicholas Sparks.[21] McKinnon and the board succeeded in convincing investors in Massachusetts and Britain to finance most of the railway's capital needs. The municipal council of Bytown helped out by purchasing £15,000 worth of stock, as well as loaning the company £50,000 (the mayor at the time was Richard Scott, who as we have seen was a strong ally of the lumber trade).[22]

A rail link to Prescott would connect Bytown with the outside world in several directions. The B&PR would provide a connection to the east-west Grand Trunk Railway (GTR), then under construction between Montreal and Toronto. It would also provide a southern connection with Ogdensburg, New York, across the river from Prescott, a town that was becoming a hub for several American railroads. Indeed, investors in the B&PR decided that the Ogdensburg linkage was more important, for they chose to match their track gauge (width between the rails) with the American standard rather than the Grand Trunk's. As a result, B&PR rail cars, ferried across the river by steamboat, could continue their journey on U.S. tracks, while goods destined for Canadian markets had to be transferred to GTR rail cars. Less important but still significant, the B&PR also gave Bytowners access to the port of Prescott and the St. Lawrence; the river, with its newly completed canals, was now bustling with commercial shipping.

When, on Christmas Day 1854, the first B&PR locomotive steamed into town, it brought much jubilation to the community. This was the first of three milestone events that Bytowners would celebrate in three years. One week later, on 1 January 1855, their town was elevated to city status and renamed Ottawa. The elevation gave its citizenry more municipal authority, not to mention greater public esteem. The name change resulted in the new rail line being rechartered as the Ottawa and Prescott Railway (O&PR). The third milestone was the announcement, on 31 December 1857, that Queen Victoria had chosen Ottawa to be the capital of the Province of Canada. (With Confederation in 1867, it became the capital of the Dominion of Canada.) The City of Ottawa had to compete with Toronto, Hamilton, Kingston, Montreal, and Quebec City for the distinction, and there is little doubt it would not have succeeded without the railway: the O&PR was an important part of the arguments the queen used to justify her decision.[23] Ottawa's new status as capital also brought a new industry to the Valley — public service. Both the public-service and large-scale lumbering industries began in the same decade, with the former ultimately outlasting the latter.

Though vigorously championed by the rising lumber interests, the O&PR did not live up to their expectations at first. The major problem was the choice of Rideau Falls as the rail terminus. This was convenient to the sawmills owned by Thomas McKay and John McKinnon (as president of the railway, McKinnon no doubt influenced the choice), but the growth area for the Ottawa Valley lumber trade was at Chaudière Falls. If a Chaudière mill owner wanted to ship his lumber out by rail, he first had to carry it across town. To help alleviate the problem, W.G. Perley organized Ottawa's first urban transit service. Though it consisted simply of horses pulling trams along rail tracks, it could carry both passengers and lumber from the Chaudière to the railway station.[24] Still, the extra handling reduced the benefits brought by the railway. It was not until 1870 that the O&PR rectified the problem by building a branch line around Dow's Lake to the Chaudière. The awkward location of the rail terminus caused Chaudière lumbermen to ship much of their production to market by water for many years (on barges towed down the Ottawa River by steam-powered tugs).

Despite its shortcomings, however, the O&PR still proved valuable to the lumber industry — lumber could now be taken to market in winter. And if speedy delivery were important at any time of year, even this flawed railway could get lumber to distant markets quicker than barges. The O&PR also provided an alternative route by which to bring in equipment and supplies needed in the lumber trade. And, further, the line made commercial communications easier and more reliable — business travel and mail delivery were important considerations in the new industrial economy. During summer in the 1850s one could travel by steamer from Ottawa to Montreal in one day. In winter, though, it took two days for sleighs to cover the distance on the frozen Ottawa River, and in spring and fall, when the river could not be used, the Valley's notoriously poor roads made travel unpredictable, unpleasant, and time-consuming.[25] With the railway, though, one could now get to Montreal (changing trains in Prescott) in less than a day, no matter the season. Clearly, the Ottawa Valley lumber industry would not have taken off so explosively in the 1850s without the Ottawa and Prescott Railway, imperfect though it was.

LATER RAILWAYS

For a number of years the Ottawa and Prescott Railway failed to generate the volume of traffic expected. This disappointment, however, did not deter the construction of additional lines in the Ottawa Valley. Over the next 70 years, another dozen or so railways were cut through the farmlands and forests of the Valley; a few are still operating today, though with different names. Several new lines were constructed into the city of Ottawa, including two from Montreal. Just as important, though, were the rail projects that opened up the hinterlands beyond Ottawa to the outside world.

The first of the new lines was the Brockville and Ottawa Railway, completed as far as Carleton Place in 1859. Its arrival in the Mississippi River town opened up whole new tracts of forests for export-minded lumbermen because now, for the first time, lumber sawn in the country upriver from Chaudière Falls could be shipped out of the Valley. The new railway allowed the local industry to grow by providing an outlet for the area's surplus lumber capacity, and within a few years Carleton Place became a major producer. Bankruptcy interrupted plans to extend the B&OR farther, but the project was revived when it was taken over by the Canada Central Railway (CCR). Several of the initial shareholders in this line, men like James Skead and J. M. Currier, were well-known Valley lumber kings. Within ten years the CCR was pushed up the Valley and new sawmills followed its progress. As in Carleton Place, the arrival of the CCR at villages along the route had an energizing effect on the lumber industry. It was as if the train had brought fertiliser up the track and dumped it at Arnprior, Braeside, and Pembroke. In these villages, small mills sawing lumber for local use soon flowered into large-scale export establishments. It was the CCR that made the fortunes of lumber kings such as Boyd Caldwell, Peter McLaren, Daniel McLachlin, the Gillies brothers, and Andrew and Peter White.[26]

Another rail project that had a huge impact on Ottawa Valley lumbering was the Canada Atlantic Railway (CAR), conceived and built largely by J. R. Booth. This venture was completed in three stages, the first beginning in 1880. By that year J. R. Booth had become the largest manufacturer of sawn lumber in the Valley. He was selling much of his output in the northeastern United States and felt he needed his own railway in order to secure and expand his sales there. Two other investors, including Chaudière lumberman W.G. Perley, contributed capital to the endeavour, but Booth was the leading force in the project. Within two years he had laid track from the Chaudière to Côteau Landing on the St. Lawrence, and from there a ferry carried rail cars across the river to connect with American lines. It has been claimed that Booth built the CAR without any government assistance,[27] a feat that would have been rare in Canada. It is more accurate to say that he built the first stage of the line without any assurance that subsidies would be granted. W.G. Perley was a political friend of Sir John A. Macdonald and asked him for a subsidy; the prime minister, however, was reluctant to approve federal help at first, fearing the CAR would take business away from the Canadian Pacific Railway, which was being built at the same time. After the first stage was completed, however, Perley managed to convince the government to grant the CAR a modest subsidy (below the average for federal rail bounties at the time).[28]

In the second stage of the project, Booth built a bridge three-quarters of a mile long across the St. Lawrence at Côteau Landing and extended the CAR across southwestern Quebec all the way to northern Vermont. Hoping to gain public assistance for these new works, Booth got 14 Valley lumber firms to support his cause. They petitioned the federal government, maintaining that the CAR was "most important" to the lumber industry as a whole and, thus, deserved financial aid. Among the petitioners was W.G. Perley, soon to be elected an MP for Macdonald's Conservative Party. This time the government was more amenable, and Booth won substantial assistance for his railway extension.[29] When the second stage was completed in 1895, the CAR had track totalling 163 miles, stretching from Ottawa to Vermont.

The third stage, completed in 1896, was a line that was operated as a separate company in its early years — the Ottawa, Arnprior & Parry Sound Railway (OA&PSR).[30] W.G. Perley died in 1890, so this time Booth took Claude McLachlin (son of Daniel) as a partner, though he controlled the company. The OA&PSR, with 264 miles of track, ran from Chaudière Falls in Ottawa to Depot Harbour on Georgian Bay (near Parry Sound). On the way, it passed through the upper Madawaska Valley, where both McLachlin and Booth had extensive timber limits. For the owners, the new line was intended to serve two main purposes: first, it was to carry sawlogs to their mills at Arnprior and Ottawa, where they would be sawn into boards and planks; second, it was to bring some of this lumber back up the line to Depot Harbour. Here, Booth kept a small fleet of ships to carry that lumber across the Great Lakes to Chicago and other booming markets in the American Midwest. Shipping lumber from Ottawa to Chicago by way of the St. Lawrence and the lower lakes would be 800 miles longer. Once again government heard an appeal for public assistance in building a private railway. This time Booth called on another Chaudière lumberman, Erskine H. Bronson (son of the late H.F.). Bronson was a cabinet minister in the Ontario government, as well as head of the family business. His influence proved helpful in gaining a hefty subsidy from the provincial government.[31]

The OA&PSR, which was absorbed by the CAR shortly after completion, helped Booth's lumbering business in many ways. First, it reduced the costs of getting supplies to his shanties in a remote, upland area. More important, the option of taking sawlogs out by rail was often cheaper than driving them down the wild and difficult Madawaska River. As well, rail delivery allowed him to harvest stands of hardwoods that had been left untouched because they could not survive a river drive. Finally, the railway also assured Booth that his sawmill need never be idle for want of sawlogs. This assurance meant he would be able to saw lumber even in winter, at least in years when market demand was high and the weather not too cold. In 1904, for example, he had a hundred carloads of logs arriving at Chaudière Falls every day, keeping his sawmill operating through the month of January. Two years earlier, Booth boasted that, with the railway, he could now cut down pine trees on his Madawaska limits one day and saw them into lumber at his Chaudière mill the next — from trees to boards in 24 hours. Quick delivery brought savings by reducing the time Booth had to wait to sell his product and get a return on the money invested in bush operations. By 1905 the CAR had become the largest sector in Booth's business empire, employing twice as many men as worked in his lumber and pulp mills combined. However, even though the CAR was still useful to his lumbering activities, he sold the line (and the shipping fleet) to the Grand Trunk Railway that year. Although the CAR had shown acceptable profits, Booth knew the lumber industry was in decline; it was time to sell.[32]

The Canadian Atlantic Railway was not a private railway, having received government subsidies, so Booth could not prevent other lumbermen from using the line. Indeed, the last stage of construction opened opportunities for new investors to enter the lumber trade. The most notable example was the St. Anthony's Lumber Co., which erected a huge, steam-powered sawmill in the wilderness of the upper Madawaska River in the year the railway was completed. The company got its sawlogs from timber limits bought from the estate of W.G. Perley, limits that were rich in pine but, before the railway, too remote to be harvested. St. Anthony's was the only major sawmill ever to operate in the higher-altitude, Canadian Shield regions of the Ottawa Valley. All other large-scale mills were built on the flat lowlands, on or near the Ottawa River. No other major mill was able to operate at such a short distance from its timber limits, and this advantage meant great savings in moving logs from stump to saw. In its very first year of production, the mill turned out twenty million board feet of boards and planks. Most of the output was taken west on the CAR to Depot

Harbour, and from there ships carried it to Chicago and other American cities. The St. Anthony's sawmill gave birth to the town of Whitney, which grew to 2,000 people within a few decades.[33]

The Canada Central and Canada Atlantic railways were only moderately profitable, but investors saw further potential in the Ottawa Valley, especially for rail lines that served the lumber trade. A new wave of rail construction ensued before long, with projects that opened up wide new areas of the Valley to lumbering. One example was a Canadian Pacific branch line, completed to Lake Timiskaming in 1896, that gave access to the rich forests of the Kipawa region in Quebec. Another CPR project that proved useful was a branch line completed from Hull to Maniwaki in 1903, making it easier for lumbermen to manage their logging operations far up the Gatineau River. Similarly, the Temiskaming and Northern Ontario Railway, built around the same time by the government of Ontario, gave access to the vast Temagami region north of North Bay. Another example was the Thurso & Nation River Railway, the last major rail project undertaken in the Valley. This line, completed in 1926, opened up a valuable forest of hardwoods that had never been cut because of the difficulty in floating the wood down rivers. The T&NRR, which ran 56 miles northward from Thurso, Quebec, was constructed by the Singer Sewing Machine Co. of New York to get the cabinetry wood it needed to manufacture its sewing devices. The line was later bought by the James Maclaren Company to carry pulpwood to its mill at Thurso.[34]

For lumbermen, the new railways helped conquer geography. They opened up great expanses of lush timberlands not yet visited by the shantyman and his axe. Some of the limits opened up by lumbermen were even more remote than those used by timbermen. Lake Timiskaming was the northern limit of square-timber operations. Beyond there, it took too long for timber rafts to get to Quebec, and in any case, the pines found farther north were seldom large enough to be squared. Still, the areas around Lac Kipawa, Lac-des-Quinze, and Lac Expanse (now Lac Simard) in Quebec and the Temagami region of Ontario held grand stands of pine and spruce waiting to be cut for lumber. The trees may not have been as big as those found on the

Coulonge or Bonnechere, but lumbermen were eager to take them out. By the 1870s they were buying up limits in these more northerly latitudes to supply sawlogs to their mills far down the Ottawa.[35] Not all lumbermen went to the far north, though; some chose to go hundreds of miles up tributaries such as the Madawaska and Gatineau rivers in pursuit of sawlogs. In either case, however, the distance between the supply centres and the shanties was stretched even farther than it was before. It was the railways that made it all possible; by overcoming geography, they allowed the lumber industry to grow by exploiting ever-more-remote timberlands. Trains helped conquer the long distances: they could carry men, supplies, horses, and farm animals at least part of the way to the shanties, and they could do it more smoothly, more quickly, and in any season. It was the steam locomotive that allowed the lumber industry to grow by exploiting ever more remote timberlands.

Besides the many obvious benefits, railways helped the lumber industry in another important way — ending the isolation of the Ottawa Valley. (It is true, though, that telegraphic service, which began in 1851,[36] helped too.) The trains that carried bulging car-loads of lumber out of the Valley brought back the latest advances in sawmill technology and, at the same time, put everyone in closer touch with the great changes in political and commercial ideas sweeping through the western world.

THE SEASONAL ROUND: BUSH AND RIVER OPERATIONS

Although there were differences in details, the general structure of the lumber business was much the same as the square-timber trade. As noted earlier, only two Ottawa Valley timber barons went on to become successful lumbermen. Most of the successful lumbermen, on the other hand, chose to engage in both timbering and lumbering at the same time (hoping to spread the risks of loss); only a few lumber kings, men such as E. B. Eddy and W. C. Edwards, eschewed timbering to concentrate solely on sawing lumber. Those who were active in both endeavours usually maintained separate shanties for hewing timbers and cutting sawlogs, but the routines followed in each were quite similar. Just as for the timberman, the lumberman's seasonal round began in the summer, when he would assemble the food, fodder, equipment, and horses he needed for the upcoming months of logging. When fall arrived, he would begin sending these necessities to his timber limits up the Valley.

Work in lumbering shanties was different, however. Cutting gangs here usually numbered only three men each — a "notcher" (the head man) and two sawyers; they were expected to cut at least 180 sawlogs a day in the autumn before the trees froze (and became harder to cut) and about 135 a day in the winter. Gangs in lumbering shanties differed from those in timbering in that they had no highly skilled specialists such as liners, scorers, and hewers. Lumbering gangs simply felled the trees, trimmed the branches, and cut the trunks into the desired length (usually 12 or 16 feet, with a few extra inches, called "broomage," to allow for damage on the river drive).[37] In lumber shanties, strength and stamina were more important than artistry. The skilled work required to produce lumber was performed at the sawmill, not in the bush.

For lumbermen, skidding and hauling sawlogs through the bush was a more elaborate process than it was for timbermen. As a first stage, horses dragged sawlogs singly or in pairs along skid roads to the main hauling road. Here they were piled high on "skidways" (platforms), either by men using muscle and peaveys or by horses with block and tackle. It was usually at this point that the logs were stamped with the limit-holder's identification mark. When winter snows came, the second stage could begin — hauling the logs to a driveable stream, where they were piled on the ice or on a "rollway" (platform) by the shore (from which they would be released into the water in the spring). This could be a long haul, however. Since sawlogs tended to be smaller than timbers and could withstand rougher treatment, they were easier to move over land. As a result, lumbermen were able to cut pine and spruce farther away from the drive streams, and hauling roads became longer and longer. At the same time, lumbermen could not resist the urge to haul larger and larger loads, sometimes as many as 25 to 30 logs at once. To do this they needed larger and sturdier sleds. They also

needed to provide wide, heavy-duty roads to accommodate the hulk-
ing vehicles, roads carefully levelled to prevent the top-heavy loads
from overturning. Lumbermen paid as much attention to maintaining
roads for hauling sawlogs out of the bush as they paid to the tote roads
they built to bring supplies in. In the fall, special gangs of road-makers
(also called "swampers") hurried to clear and grade the trails before the
frosts came. And after winter set in there was still work to be done: on
flat sections the men sometimes iced the surfaces with crude water-
sprinklers to speed the movement of the sleds; on steep hills they
would spread cinders and sand or used winches and chains to slow
them down. Although it required careful planning, road-making
involved more bull work than skill. While one veteran lumberman
preached that "it pays to make good roads," road-makers were among
the lowest paid of his shantymen.[38] Of course, if a lumberman was
squaring timber in the same area, he would not hesitate to use these
good roads to get his timber to a driveable stream.

The growing use of steam-powered machinery in heavy industry led
some lumbermen to dream about adapting this technology to their
bush operations; after all, replacing horses with machinery could bring
great savings. Not only could machines do more work, they did not
have to be fed when not working. For most Valley firms, however, the
use of steam power for log hauling remained only a dream, though the
Perley, Pattee Co. may have been the first in Canada to use the Glover
Steam Logger (in 1890). This four-wheeled vehicle, moving on cater-
pillar treads, was capable of hauling a chain of sleds carrying several
thousand logs at a time. Most lumbermen, however, found steam-powered log-haulers expensive and prone to breakdown, and they were
never widely used in the Valley. A second way lumbermen tried to
mechanize log-hauling was to invest in logging railways to connect
their timber limits to an existing main line. By 1902 both J. R. Booth
and St. Anthony's had built short rail spurs into their Madawaska limits, allowing them to carry logs almost directly from the stump to the
main line of the CAR. These rail projects proved successful for they not
only reduced hauling costs, but also enabled the firms to take sawlogs
out of the bush in any season. Still, logging railways were expensive,

and most firms did not see enough benefit in them. In the end, it was not steam but rather the internal-combustion engine that replaced horse power in the bush. The first gasoline-powered tractors and trucks arrived in the bush in the 1920s, though horses continued to be used on some limits for decades after.[39]

When spring arrived and the river ice broke up, the winter's harvest of sawlogs was let loose to float down the Valley's tributaries. However, as time passed, lumbermen found that their growing industry was generating more and more traffic on the tributaries; lumbermen were competing with timbermen, and with other lumbermen, for room on the rivers. Some individuals spent a lot of money building dams, slides, and "glance booms" (strings of partially squared timbers chained together to keep logs in the main channel) to get their winter's cut past the gorges, falls, and rapids that could impede the spring drive. They charged others for the use of their improvements, but quarrels arose over the size of the tolls and over which drive gangs should have priority in using the works. To lessen the possibility of violence, in the 1840s the government bought out the existing drive improvements on several tributaries (see Chapter 2) and operated them as public works. Government, however, did not take control everywhere in the Valley. In the stretches farther upriver from the publicly operated works, and on other tributaries where the government was not involved, timbermen and lumbermen had no choice but to install their own improvements. The new, private works did not bring peace, though, for the rivers remained crowded with competing drive gangs, all impatient to move their logs downstream at the same time.

After a while, many limit-holders came to see that by pooling their resources and working cooperatively, they could reduce expenses and avoid conflict. The Province of Canada provided the means by enacting legislation authorizing companies to build works to facilitate the passage of timber and logs down rivers and streams. Valley lumbermen quickly seized the opportunity and created joint stock companies to oversee and coordinate the drive on a number of Ottawa River tributaries. Private improvements on the river were amalgamated, and new works built; a standard fee was charged for every sawlog and stick of timber passing through. Agencies such as the Madawaska River Improvement Co., the Rivière-du-Moine Boom and Slide Co., and the Gatineau River Drive Co. brought efficiency and order to the tributaries, allowing the lumber industry to grow and prosper.[40]

The experiences of lumbermen operating on two rivers — the Lièvre and the Mississippi — show how lack of cooperation could harm the industry. In the 1830s and 1840s two lumbermen built sawmills on opposite sides of the Lièvre River, harvesting timberlands farther up the watershed. The two men quarrelled constantly and, while matters never came to violence, they were unable to agree how to share the costs of constructing and maintaining improvements on the river. The valley of the Lièvre was rich in timber, but without an efficient means of getting their sawlogs to their mills, both businesses failed in the end.[41]

Events on the Mississippi River in 1875 led to legal action that dragged on for nine years. The two leading lumbermen on the river were Boyd Caldwell and Peter McLaren, both of whom had a sawmill at Carleton Place. In the spring of 1875 Caldwell was bringing a drive of 18,000 sawlogs down the Mississippi when he was blocked by a dam that McLaren had erected at High Falls. McLaren had installed a bypass around the dam to allow passage of his own logs, but it was on his private property, and he refused to let Caldwell use it. The latter responded by having his men cut an opening through the dam and move his logs downriver. Provincial law had long guaranteed the free passage of timber and sawlogs down Ontario rivers, but McLaren claimed that this right did not apply to waterways that had been "improved" by privately financed facilities. The court case proceeded through several levels of appeal until the British Privy Council ruled in Caldwell's favour. In the meantime, the Ontario Legislature passed a Rivers and Streams Act which affirmed that the owner of improvements on any river could not refuse access to others as long as they paid reasonable tolls. The legislation had to be enacted three times as the federal government kept disallowing it on the grounds that it infringed upon private property rights, which are a federal responsibility. The matter was not settled until 1884, when the Privy Council upheld the Ontario legislation. The case, *McLaren v Caldwell*, has since been recognized as an important landmark in Canadian constitutional law.[42] In the end, the bad feelings and legal costs raised by this long-drawn-out case seem to have had a salutary effect on local lumbermen for a Mississippi River Improvement Company was ultimately organized to coordinate operations on the river.[43]

Events on the Gatineau River in 1900 showed how working together allowed lumbermen to invest in the latest technology to handle the huge flow of sawlogs that came down the river every year. The major lumber companies (W.C. Edwards and Gilmour–Hughson) operating on the river formed the Gatineau Drive Company to move their logs along the hundred-mile stretch between Maniwaki and Hull. They turned over responsibility for the drive to a contractor, Samuel Bingham, a veteran of many years in the business (also mayor of Ottawa, 1897-98). Before hydroelectric dams were erected, the Gatineau was a notoriously wild river with eight major falls and rapids in 100 miles.[44] The Drive Company took care to provide Bingham with ample facilities and equipment to do his job, including an extensive system of glance booms, some anchored to massive, rock-filled piers 100 feet square and 96 feet high. He had a steam-powered tugboat to work with and employed 350 men between May and October. In 1900, however, he had to face an extraordinary situation. That spring, sudden changes in water levels allowed a minor log-jam at The Cascades (a waterfall a few miles south of Wakefield) to grow into a gigantic entanglement: 500,000 sawlogs jammed into a pile 30 feet high in places, stretching from shore to shore and backed up for half a mile. Bingham could not use dynamite to break up the jam because the explosions would damage the sawlogs (with pulpwood this would not matter). Normally, he would have put large teams of men to work removing key pieces from the jam with pike poles and cant hooks; the work would have been extremely dangerous and probably would have taken the entire season to complete. This year, however, he brought in a 60-horsepower steam crane and fixed it to a floating platform measuring 36 feet by 120 feet. Using hooks and tongs attached to a long cable, the crane was able to pull the salient pieces out of the mess easily and safely,

A pointer boat shooting a rapids, c. 1910. This Ottawa Valley invention was used across Canada in navigating whitewater rapids.

thereby releasing the rest of the logs. With only nine men and an engineer, he succeeded in dislodging the massive jam in six weeks. Pleased with his experiment, Bingham kept the steam-powered crane in service on the Gatineau thereafter.[45] Drive cooperatives, then, not only helped avert conflict on rivers, they made it possible to invest in up-to-date, heavy-duty (and costly) technology.

Apart from the use of tugs and steam-powered cranes, there was little opportunity for mechanization on river drives. Still, lumbering did see one great advance in managing turbulent, log-filled rivers — the "pointer" boat. In the early years, timbermen often employed birchbark canoes on Ottawa River tributaries, but while they were light and easy to handle, they were inherently fragile. In the 1860s, however, John Cockburn, a recent immigrant from England, designed a rugged, stable rowboat specifically for the log drive; this new craft quickly replaced the canoe. With their flaring sides, pointers were famously responsive and nimble, easy to move in any direction. With their upswept, pointed bows and sterns (hence the name), they could ride over floating logs with ease. With their shallow draft (as little as four inches), it was said they could "float on a heavy dew." And with their sturdy construction, they could be run through rocky rapids or dragged around them. On the spring drive, pointers were employed to carry the drivers' tents, blankets, cooking equipment, and provisions downriver. They also allowed the men to reach hard-to-get-at corners of the river, to "sweep" them clean of stranded logs, and even to tow the logs into the mainstream. A Tom Thomson painting, *The Pointers*, shows the boat towing a barge carrying men and horses along the Petawawa River in 1916. In the autumn, pointers showed their versatility by carrying supplies up tributary rivers to the shanties; the 50-foot model, rowed with six oars, could carry two tons of freight. No matter how nimble they were, however, rowing these boats with a heavy load required a great deal of muscle power. As a result, some log-drivers were happy to equip their pointers with outboard motors when they became available; this adaptation was seen as early as 1918 on the Kipawa River.[46] Still, rowing remained the main means of propulsion as long as pointers were used.

John Cockburn began his boat-building career in Ottawa but in 1869 moved to Pembroke, where he set up a plant by the shore of the Ottawa River. From here, he and his family faithfully supplied lumbermen far beyond the Ottawa Valley. In some years they turned out 200 pointers, and this distinctive rowboat, brick red in colour, became the aquatic workhorse of the lumber industry (it was used by pulp-and-paper and mining companies as well). By 1969, however, trucks were carrying much of the industry's sawlogs to the mills, and river-drives were coming to an end; that year, 100 years after John Cockburn moved to Pembroke, his grandson, John A., retired and closed the business. The Cockburns never took out a patent on their versatile craft, and other manufacturers, such as Alexander Lumsden at Lake Kipawa, sold copies under the generic name "pointer." No matter who made them, though, this hallmark of the Ottawa Valley became a familiar sight on rivers across eastern Canada.[47]

John Cockburn may have initially designed the pointer for use on tributary rivers, but the boat soon proved its worth on the more extensive Ottawa River log-drive as well. After driving their sawlogs down the tributaries, the final stage of the lumberman's seasonal round was to get the winter's cut down the Ottawa to his sawmill. Over a number of years, Valley lumbermen worked out a meticulous system of driving, sweeping, booming, sorting, and towing their logs down the Ottawa. Because of all the waterfalls on the river, sawlogs floating from Lake Timiskaming to the Chaudière could be individually handled many times on the journey (logs sometimes took two years to reach the sawmill). All the log handling was done on the water, and Ottawa River drivers came to rely on Cockburn's pointer boat to do it.

In the early days of the lumber industry, each lumberman drove his own sawlogs down the Ottawa. Often one gang followed another along the same stretch of river within a few days of each other. Some lumbermen installed their own drive improvements along the route, but, working alone, they found it hard to protect these investments. Again, the benefits of cooperation became obvious, and in 1863 several of them combined to form the Upper Ottawa Drive Association to take charge of all logs coming down the river. Five years later, the venture was chartered as the Upper Ottawa Improvement Company, popularly known as ICO. The founding shareholders in this joint stock company were the seven leading lumbermen of the day — John Hamilton, A.H. Baldwin, Levi Young, H. F. Bronson, E. B. Eddy, W.G. Perley, and J.R. Booth. At first ICO handled all the booming and driving of logs between Des-Joachims and the Chaudière but paid contractors to tow the "bag booms" downriver (these booms were amorphous loops of timbers chained together, corralling the logs so they could be towed). In 1876 the company added log-sorting to its duties. In 1888 it took over responsibility for towing, and soon it had a fleet of a dozen steam-powered, paddle-wheel tugboats operating on the river. That same year ICO extended its drive operations farther north to the mouth of the Quinze River at the head of Lake Timiskaming, and in 1910 it began driving pulpwood down the river in addition to sawlogs. Lumbermen reckoned that, in its first ten years of service, ICO cut the cost of moving sawlogs downriver in half. The company continued in business until 1990, the last year that logs were driven, towed, and boomed down the Ottawa River.[48]

For over a hundred years the log drive on the Ottawa River followed

Sawlogs coming down the Ottawa River were sorted here at Chenaux Boom to separate those going to the Gillies and McLachlin mills in Braeside and Amprior from those destined for sawmills further downriver.

a complex routine that changed very little (though some refinements were introduced after hydroelectric dams were installed in the twentieth century). After a lumberman's sawlogs had been driven down a tributary and reached the Ottawa River, ICO collected them into bag booms, which it towed downstream by tugboat. When a boom arrived at a waterfall, the company's men would open it, releasing the logs to run freely through the white water; the logs were then collected once again into booms in the still water below the falls. The releasing and booming procedures would be repeated at each waterfall encountered along the Ottawa. When the logs reached Chenaux or Quyon, they were channelled into "sorting booms" (chains of timber permanently anchored to rock-filled cribs), where the men checked the timber mark of each piece to determine its owner. At this point, logs intended for the Gillies and McLachlin sawmills were removed from the pack and towed the short distance to Braeside and Arnprior. As for logs heading farther downstream, those owned by lumbermen with mills on the Ontario side of the river were separated from those destined for mills on the Quebec side. They were then put back in booms and towed

These booms, towed by tugboats, have been assembled below Chaudière Falls and are heading to mills farther down the Ottawa River.

downriver to a second sorting ground just above Chaudière Falls, where they were sorted according to the individual mill owner. (In 1893 spring floods caused a sorting boom to break and 70,000 sawlogs went crashing over Chaudière Falls, rendering many of them useless for lumber.) Most logs went directly to millponds at the Chaudière, but some were intended for sawmills even farther downriver, particularly the mills of W.C. Edwards at Rockland and the Hamilton Brothers at Hawkesbury. To get their logs safely past Chaudière Falls, these lumbermen often chose to send them down the government timber slide (for which, of course, they would have to pay a fee); indeed, after 1873 the north slide at Hull was reserved exclusively for the passage of sawlogs. Once below Chaudière Falls, these logs were boomed for the last time and towed, by non-ICO steamers, to Rockland or Hawkesbury.[49]

The work of driving sawlogs down long stretches of the Ottawa River (it was more than 300 miles from the Quinze River to Chaudière Falls) was immensely labour-intensive. Some bag booms could cover several acres of the river, and each sawlog might be boomed and released as many as seven or eight times in its passage down the river. In 1885 ICO handled more than 2,750,000 logs and employed 300 to 400 men through the summer season to do the work. By 1911 it had over 1,000 workers on its payroll. Still, ICO proved to be an effective, efficient operation. It charged a standard fee each time it handled a log (the fees had to be approved by the government), and the company was usually able to pay an annual dividend to its stockholders. Most of the stockholders were mill owners, and they were quite satisfied with the services provided. They were especially happy that, once they got their season's harvest into the Ottawa River, ICO took over full responsibility for the logs until they arrived at the mill. ICO was the only company in Ontario that provided such comprehensive log-driving services.[50]

MANUFACTURING LUMBER

For the western world, the nineteenth century was the great age of migration, and North America was the main destination as millions of Europeans crossed the Atlantic, hoping to build better lives for themselves. To build, however, one must have a reliable building material. In the nineteenth century, wood was still the all-purpose building material. Accommodating such a large number of newcomers would have been impossible without an abundant and low-priced supply of wood. Fortunately, the forests of eastern North America proved abundant enough to supply the lumber to build the houses, factories, wharves, bridges, and ships required to meet the needs of a surging population, as well as to export significant volumes for sale abroad. North America came to depend on large-scale sawmills such as those erected in the Ottawa Valley.

Fortuitously, as the tides of European migration swelled, major technological improvements were coming into use, allowing wood to be sawn more efficiently and making lumber available at affordable prices. Unlike the logging end of the lumber business, which remained dependent on muscle power, hand tools, and horses, sawmilling benefited from rapid advances in mechanization. Ottawa Valley lumber kings always took care to keep their mills equipped with the latest improvements in technology, but almost everything was imported. No important advances in sawmill design or lumber manufacturing were developed in the Valley, and only minor components were made here.

Lumber is wood that has been sawn into forms best suited for building purposes. In nineteenth-century Canada, three broad groups of lumber were offered for sale: deals; dimension timber; and boards, planks, and scantling. (Laths and shingles were also manufactured at sawmills but were not usually considered lumber.) After it is sawed into lengths and widths, lumber can be further improved (and thereby have more value added) in a number of ways: by drying or seasoning it to make the material more workable; by "dressing" (planing) it to provide a smoother surface; and by "edging" it to produce tongue-and-groove or ship-lapped sides for tighter construction purposes. Usually, all these processes were done at a sawmill. Ottawa Valley mills turned out all three forms of lumber and, indeed, for several decades produced more than any other region in Canada; a large portion of the Valley's output was sold rough or undressed, however.

Deal production was the first attempt by Canadian timbermen to add more value to the timber they were selling abroad. Instead of shipping square timber across the ocean, where some might be sawn up into boards in British mills, a few Canadians insisted on doing some preliminary sawing at home by cutting logs into thick slabs or deals. On arrival in Britain the deals were often sawn again into smaller boards, though many were used unaltered for heavy flooring or ship decking. Generally speaking, deals were three inches thick and 12 feet long. They could be of any breadth beyond seven inches, and, indeed, in 1898 the Gilmour–Hughson mill at Hull was reported to have produced a shipment of pine deals two feet and more in width. Deals with these dimensions were highly exceptional, however, especially by this time when there were few pines of this size left in the Valley; the shipment was said to have made up "one of the finest piles of lumber ever seen in Canada."[51] From its beginnings early in the nineteenth century, the Hamilton family's sawmill at Hawkesbury stood out as one of the leading deal manufacturers in Canada. The Hamiltons' early competitors were located near Quebec City, but output in that area dwindled in the second half of the nineteenth century. At this time, however, many of the new sawmillers in the Ottawa Valley — Gilmour, Booth, Perley,

Eddy, Maclaren — joined the trade. Along with the Hamiltons, the new-comers made the Valley the centre of deal manufacturing in Canada. Canadian deal exports rose until the First World War and then dropped off rapidly. Large pines became harder to find, and lower-priced spruce deals became increasingly more common in Canadian shipments. Spruce deals brought less profit, however, and most lumbermen decided to focus on turning out ordinary boards and planks. Still, J. R. Booth and W. C. Edwards continued to manufacture deals into the 1920s.[52]

Dimension timber was lumber sawn to make the thick beams and joists used in heavy construction projects; they usually measured five or more inches on the smallest side. Dimension timber was a specialty product, and only a few sawmills participated in the trade (in 1885 it represented only about 4 percent of the total lumber output in the Ottawa Valley). As with deals, the trade began when some investors realized they could earn greater profits by sawing large pines into timbers rather than hewing them square by axe. The best known manufacturer of dimension timber in the Valley was the Pembroke Lumber Co., controlled by the White family of that town. It was this firm that supplied the timbers for the decking of the new interprovincial Alexandra Bridge, which was constructed between Ottawa and Hull in 1901. As the twentieth century progressed, Ottawa Valley production declined as larger British Columbia fir timbers became available in eastern Canada and structural steel beams came more into favour.[53]

While deals and dimension timber sold well, the greatest growth in lumber sales was in boards, planks, and scantling. Planks were usually considered to be thick boards, while scantling referred mainly to two-by-four-inch studs used for framing. The driving force behind the surge in demand for lumber after 1850 was the adoption of "balloon framing," a new method of construction, used particularly in house-building. The traditional European method, "timber framing" (or "post and beam"), relied on a few heavy timbers to bear the weight of a building; since it required complicated joinery work, construction could be slow and costly. In contrast, with the new technique, framing was lighter: the building was held up by walls made of numerous studs fastened together by nails. The technique required no fancy joinery, needed less skilled labour, and was quicker and cheaper to complete. With these advantages, balloon framing ultimately revolutionized construction methods. And, important for the Ottawa Valley, the new method required great quantities of planks, boards, and scantling precisely sawn to standard measurements.[54]

Rapid advances in mechanization made it possible for large-scale sawmills to meet the demand for quantity and precision in lumber production; machinery was introduced into every possible step in the manufacturing process. Lumbermen wanted to cut more wood, more quickly, and more perfectly, with fewer men and less waste. Mechanizing was the obvious way to go about it. Ottawa Valley lumber kings designed their mills with mechanization in mind. Large-scale sawmills in the Valley were typically broad, barn-like structures, featuring wood as the primary building material. A framework of dimension timbers held up the works (balloon framing was unsuitable in such large buildings), walls were clad with boards, and roofs were covered with wooden shingles. The mills had full basements, and the foundations were usually of thick masonry to support the weight of the machinery and to withstand the intense vibrations generated by them. The mills as a whole had to be spacious enough to accommodate a wide array of machines and the gear-works, shafts, and belting needed to run them. In the early years, some lumbermen operated flour and woollen mills alongside their sawmills.

By the early 1870s, large-scale sawmilling was well established in the Ottawa Valley. Even though it was barely 15 years old, this new, export-oriented industry could boast at least nine large, sophisticated sawmills. The mills belonging to Perley & Pattee, Booth, Bronsons & Weston, Eddy, Young, Baldwin, Gilmour, Hamilton Brothers and Wright, Batson & Currier were known for their high production levels, commitment to diversification, and reliance on mechanization. These lumbermen built huge sawmills designed for large-scale production: by the early 1870s they were each turning out between twenty and forty million board feet of lumber a year. Diversification was aimed at reducing wastage, making maximum use of the wood they cut, and adding value to their products. E.B. Eddy, for example, sal-

Perley & Pattee Co. sawmill, 1872. Sawlogs are lying in the mill pond waiting for the men to steer them onto the jackladders, which will take them up to the mill deck to be sawn into lumber.

vaged leftover "butts" and "edgings" (board ends and sides) to manufacture matches, pails, and tubs, while others used mill scraps to make laths and shingles; A.H. Baldwin installed planing and moulding machinery to refine his lumber products.[55]

As for mechanization, the new technology had become indispensable to large-scale Valley sawmills by the early 1870s, despite the high costs involved. The mill operated by W.G. Perley and G. B. Pattee was typical. This installation, located on Chaudière Island beside the falls, consisted of a large central building with several wings, covering fully 18,400 square feet. The roof of one wing was supported by an immense hewn beam, 80 feet long and 21 inches square, undoubtedly a product of the firm's timbering operations. In some years this sawmill produced as much as forty million board feet of pine lumber. A look at its operations in the early 1870s shows that the Perley & Pattee mill was already heavily mechanized. Mechanization began with hauling the sawlogs out of the Ottawa River. To do this, workmen standing on the booms of the millpond steered the 12 to 16 foot logs onto a "jackladder" (an inclined trough), where an endless chain pulled them up to the mill deck. Here, the wet logs were clamped securely to a mechanized "carriage," which took them through the saws.

The mechanics of sawing had undergone considerable evolution in the previous 50 years. The traditional upright saws, cutting only on the downstroke, were maddeningly slow, so lumbermen were quick to welcome two major innovations — the circular saw and the "gang-saw." The latter combined multiple upright saws in a frame that moved rapidly up and down as a whole, allowing mills to cut a log into many boards at once. By 1850 the Hamilton Brothers and Thomas McKay were using both circular saws and gang uprights in their mills,[56] and by the early 1870s these saws were essential features in all large-scale Valley mills. In the Perley & Pattee mill, the mechanized carriage first pushed the logs through a "slabber gate-saw" which removed the outer slabs from each side of the log. Then, the large remaining "cant" (central core) was turned over on its flat side and run through a "stock" gang-saw; this engineering marvel had as many as 40 upright blades that could be spaced at one-, two-, or three-inch intervals to cut boards to the thickness desired. The process was not swift — it could take up to eight minutes for a stock gang-saw to eat its way through the length of a 16-foot cant — but at least it turned out a multiplicity of boards.

In the next step, "live rollers" (mechanically rotating cylinders) carried the rough lumber to a "double-edger" to have the sides trimmed square; this device had two circular saws, one fixed in place and the other adjustable to the width desired. Then, the boards were carried to a "double-butter" where the butts (ends) were cut off to produce boards of the desired length. Lastly, more live rollers hustled the freshly cut lumber and wood scraps right out of the mill, clearing space for more sawing. Perley and Pattee had a double production line, with two sets of all saws, carriages, and rollers, and thus could run two sawing operations at once in the same building. The high degree of mechanisation seen in their sawmill could be found in all large scale Valley

Inside the Wright, Batson, Currier sawmill, 1872. A large sawlog has had its sides removed by a "slabber saw" and is about to be pushed through a "gang" of upright saws which will cut it into many boards at once.

mills by the early 1870s. By this time, Valley lumbermen were fully committed to mechanisation.[57]

Of the nine large-scale sawmills operating in the Ottawa Valley in the early 1870s, eight were powered by water and only one by steam (Wright, Batson & Currier). Mills relying on energy generated by steam had a few minor advantages over those powered by water. While steam mills needed only enough water to keep their boilers filled, water-powered mills required large and consistent volumes of falling water. And while work at water-powered mills could be halted by winter ice or too-high or too-low water levels, steam-driven mills were able to function nearly the year round. However, burning fuel to produce steam made these sawmills susceptible to fire, resulting in insurance premiums that were three to four times higher. More important, the expense of equipping and operating a sawmill run on steam power was much higher than one run on water power. In the Ottawa Valley, an area with a plethora of good hydraulic sites, the advantages of steam were less meaningful.

Elsewhere in Canada, steam was common in sawmills, but along the Ottawa River and its tributaries, cheaper water power prevailed.[58]

Still, after the best hydraulic sites were taken, some Valley lumbermen did invest in steam-driven sawmills (all at locations that lacked falling water) and some prospered. The first such mill is believed to have been erected in 1849 by J. C. Blasdell on the Ottawa River near the outlet of MacKay Lake, but it was small and never a significant lumber producer. The large Wright, Batson & Currier mill was built in Hull (near the present Alexandra Bridge) in 1868; it was destroyed by fire ten years later. The Gilmour Company built a large, steam-powered mill a little farther downstream (where Brewery Creek rejoins the Ottawa River); it burned down twice in ten years but was rebuilt each time. In Arnprior the McLachlins used both forms of motive power: their operations near the mouth of the Madawaska River were powered by water, while those on the shore of Chats Lake relied on steam (this mill also burned down and had to be rebuilt). Other steam-driven sawmills include those of Senator James Skead in the present Westboro (burned and rebuilt), William Mason in Mechanicsville, W.C. Edwards at Rockland, Gillies Brothers at Braeside, White Brothers at Pembroke, and St. Anthony's at Whitney. Although at times there might be a half-dozen large-scale steam-driven mills sawing lumber in the Valley, their share of the total output was not high. In 1895, for example, only about 29 percent of the lumber produced in the Valley came from sawmills powered by steam.[59]

In the Ottawa Valley, both steam-powered and water-powered sawmills operated in similar-looking two-storey buildings constructed with heavy timber framing. From a distance, though, steam-powered mills were easily distinguishable by the lofty smokestacks standing nearby. Because of the danger of fire, steam was generated in a boiler plant built of brick or stone and located away from the mill; pipes took the steam to engines in the basement of the sawmill. The steam plant might hold as many as a dozen large boilers, which were heated by furnaces using mainly mill scraps as fuel. In contrast, water-driven sawmills were more integrated units, the power usually being generated inside the building.

By the 1870s, large-scale mills no longer relied on the traditional water-wheel (though these continued to be used in small country mills into the twentieth century).[60] In the large, new, highly mechanized sawmills, falling water was channelled down a "penstock" (flume) to the basement of the building, where it hit a horizontally placed iron turbine; the impact caused the turbine to turn and generate power. Turbines proved to be a major advance in sawmill technology, enabling production on a large scale. They generated far more energy from the falling water than the old water wheels and took up much less space (while turbines might measure as much as seven feet in diameter, some water wheels could stand 30 feet high). As well, enclosed inside the mill, turbines were less affected by ice and, thus, could operate in the milder days of winter.

On the main floor, where the saws and other machinery were located, steam-driven and water-driven mills looked much the same. They both used a complex system of shafts and rubber or leather belts to transmit power from the steam engines or water turbines in the basement to the machines on the floor above. In the 1890s companies such as Perley & Pattee replaced belting with wire-rope transmission as it could convey more power over longer distances.[61]

In the nineteenth century, few structures were more susceptible to fires than sawmills, water-powered as well as steam-powered. Today, "heritage" sawmills are a rarity. Wooden buildings littered with mill scraps, bark, and sawdust and surrounded by great piles of lumber supplied perfect fuel for a blaze. Heat generated by fast-moving belts, wire ropes, pulleys, and machinery could provide the spark. Pipe-smoking mill workers could be a hazard, too. Philemon Wright's first mill burned down in 1808, only a few years after construction, and many more were destroyed in the Valley over the next century. Sawmills were generally under-insured because premiums were understandably costly. Firefighting and prevention were difficult, but lumbermen did try to protect their investments. In the 1870s, Messrs. Perley and Pattee had their Chaudière sawmill outfitted with the latest in hoses and water-pumping equipment, the latter powered by its own water turbine. In 1882, when E. B. Eddy rebuilt his sawmill after a grievous fire, he used fire-resistant materials — thick masonry walls and galvanized iron roofing — as much as possible; this decision saved the building from destruction in the great Ottawa-Hull fire of 1900, and the mill still stands in Hull today. The St. Anthony's mill at Whitney, built in 1896, was also roofed in metal, even though it was a major producer of wooden shingles. Rejecting wood in sawmill construction may have been a poor endorsement for the future of the lumber industry, but by the end of the century, most new, large-scale mills in the Ottawa Valley were built with flame-proof materials.[62]

Sawmill technology continued to change rapidly in the late 1800s as lumbermen sought new ways to improve their efficiency. One major step was to replace their slow-cutting upright saws with high velocity circulars. Circular saws had been used for some time for cross-cutting purposes, but now they were adapted to cut logs lengthwise into boards. But though they could cut wood much faster, circulars had a few shortcomings. The lumber they turned out was often rough on the surface, though this could be acceptable for lower grade boards and dimension timber. Circular saws could also not cut logs larger than half their diameter, a problem which was resolved by placing one circular saw above another. In 1883, E.B. Eddy installed a 42-inch circular above a 60-incher in his new mill. And 20 years later, J.R. Booth used a similar arrangement to cut what may have been the largest sawlog ever brought to a mill in all of eastern Canada: this specimen, carried to Ottawa by rail from the Madawasaka, measured seven feet across at one end and 51 inches at the other. The most serious shortcoming of the circular saw was that its thick blades produced "kerfs" (the width of the cut made by a saw) sometimes of more than a quarter of an inch, resulting in an enormous amount of wood wasted as sawdust. Despite the problems, the speedy new saws were widely used in the Valley, some lumbermen even using them in gangs.[63] Soon, though, another technological advance arrived to change sawing methods yet again.

The new advance was the "band saw," a seamless, toothed ribbon of steel running on two wheels. Small band saws had been used for some time in woodworking, but adapting them to cut huge logs was a big step. Band saws had many advantages: though they could cut as fast as circular saws, they required less power to operate, and the blades had a longer sawing life. They could also turn out smoother, higher-quality lumber. More important, band saws cut a significantly narrower kerf; some lumbermen claimed that while a circular could cut 19 one-inch boards from a particular log, a band saw could produce 21 boards. In a large-scale operation, the savings were immense, so band saws were quickly accepted. Band saws designed for lumber mills became available in 1886, and both W. C. Edwards and Bronsons & Weston were using them at their establishments shortly after. When J. R. Booth installed 13 band saws in his mill in 1891, it was claimed that this was more than anywhere else in the world. The old upright saws were not immediately displaced by the new technology, however. Some Valley lumbermen continued to use them alongside their circular and band saws well into the twentieth century. Although they were slow, upright gang-saws remained economical for some tasks as they did not require many men to run them. In the 1920s, the McLachlin Brothers were still running two gangs (with 29 and 35 uprights) in their Arnprior mill; the blades were made in the firm's machine shop from "used" band saws.[64]

Another landmark change in sawmilling was the arrival of electricity. The first use of this new power source anywhere in the Ottawa Valley occurred on the night of 14 June 1881, when E. B. Eddy switched on 40 lights that he had installed to illuminate the interiors of his factories, workshops, and sawmill, as well as his lumberyards outside. This would have been a big event in any town, and the people of Hull turned out en masse to mark it. Eddy closed down the machinery in his sawmill and opened the building for public visitation. The town's band played on the streets for two hours as the people celebrated the new marvel. Eddy had recognized the hydroelectric potential of Chaudière Falls and put it to use by installing a water-driven turbine in an old stone building near his match factory. His initiative was one of the first industrial uses of incandescent electric lighting in Canada and came only a year after Thomas Edison's first successes in the United States. Some lumbermen had earlier tried using oil-burning lamps to illuminate their mills so their men could work at night during the busy summer season; this was risky, though, due to the possibility of fire. Electric lighting was much safer and allowed lumbermen to run their saws whenever they pleased. Soon J. R. Booth, Levi Young, and other Valley lumbermen followed Eddy's lead, generating their own electrical power to illuminate their mills and yards.[65]

It took another 20 years before technology progressed enough to allow electricity to be used to run machinery in sawmills and other heavy industries. For lumbermen, the advantages of the new motive power were obvious. With electricity, wiring could carry power over a long distance, so a sawmill and its energy source did not have to be in close proximity. Inside the mill, electrical wiring took up a minuscule space compared to the cumbersome profusion of belts, shafts, and gears that lumbermen had been using; switching to electricity would provide more efficiency in the layout of machinery and improve working conditions. W.C. Edwards was the first major Valley lumberman to convert. After his lumber business at Rideau Falls was destroyed by fire in 1907, he built a large new sawmill and planing mill there, harnessing the hydro energy of the site. It was a bigger step to switch an existing mill to electricity, however, and J. R. Booth waited until 1909 to build his own generating plant at Chaudière Falls. For 50 years he had relied on a number of penstocks (chutes) dispersed around his property to bring water from the falls to the turbines of his mills. Now, with one electrical generating plant, he was able to concentrate all his hydro power at a single point and, from there, simply rely on wiring to bring power to his sawmill, workshops, and pulp mill.[66]

It was the great technological advances of the late nineteenth century that allowed Ottawa Valley lumbermen to produce deals, dimension timber, boards, and planks on a grand scale. These advances also made it possible for them to reduce their manpower needs, speed up the sawing process, reduce wastage in the kerfs, and improve the quality of their product. No one put the new technology to better use than J. R. Booth. In the early 1870s he had been turning out 26 to 30 million board feet of lumber a year at his Chaudière mill, but within twenty years he had raised that figure to 90 million and by 1897 to an amazing 130 million board feet.[67] With these achievements in the 1890s, he came to be considered "the largest lumberman in the world."[68] Booth continued to lead the world until 1905, when a mill in Washington State surpassed his output[69] (but, of course, that mill had the advantage of working with much larger rain-forest trees). Even so, Booth had made the Ottawa Valley known around the world.

WORKING IN THE SAWMILLS

The large-scale lumber mills of the Ottawa Valley were major industrial operations, employing great numbers of workers during the sawing season. In 1888 it was estimated that the six lumber firms operating at the Chaudière had nearly 6,000 men on their payrolls. Sawmills of this size ran complex production lines, necessitating a wide variety of specialized jobs. In the early 1920s the McLachlin mill at Arnprior listed 33 different job titles on its payroll (of 529 workers), and each job was paid according to a hierarchy of importance. At the top of the pay scale were the sawyers, highly skilled technicians who, by manipulating a set of levers, controlled the whole sawing process. They had to make quick decisions on how best to cut each sawlog, and their judgement was crucial to the firm's financial health. Sawyers received triple the pay of those at the bottom of the scale — labourers and boys (aged 14 to 16), who performed general, unskilled tasks around the mill. Surprisingly, "white collar" workers in the office, eight clerks and one stenographer (the only female on site), were among the lowest paid on the McLachlin payroll.[70]

Work in sawmills anywhere could be bewildering, frightening, and dangerous, and Ottawa Valley mills were no different. When a sawmill was operating full out, the heavy machinery made the whole building shake and rattle. The iron turbine in the basement thundered and growled as it gyrated to generate power. A jungle of fast-moving shafts and belts (some of them two feet wide) rose from the basement and criss-crossed the ground floor to serve a maze of machines scattered about the work area. The mechanized jackladder jangled and grated as it dragged sawlogs into the building from the mill pond. The massive logs, clamped to a heavy-duty metal carriage, screeched defiantly as they were forced into the teeth of the gang-saws. Rough-cut boards and planks tumbled out the other side, falling onto rollers that carried them away to the edging and butting saws, and then outside the building to be sorted and piled. Throngs of workers served the machines while coping with hazards everywhere. The noise of the machinery was deafening and distracting (the gang-saws could be heard blocks away). Sawdust blew around the building, impairing breathing and vision. Lighting was poor, especially on night shifts, when lanterns provided the only illumination. Openings cut in the floor so mill refuse could be dumped into the river were a constant safety threat. Footing was uncertain when the floor became slippery with water sprayed from the saws as they cut through the wet logs. The work pressure was intense, for the men knew a slowdown anywhere in the mill upset the whole production line. Serious accidents were inevitable.

Young boys working on the mill floor were especially prone to accident, and provincial governments passed factory acts in 1884 and 1885, setting minimum conditions for their employment. In Ontario no one under 14 years old could work in a factory or mill, while in Quebec the age limit was 12; no child could work more than 60 hours a week, but even then, exceptions were allowed in emergencies. Enforcement was poor in any case (Ontario had only three inspectors to cover the whole province). Years after these rules were made law, a royal commission heard testimony from underage boys who had lost limbs in accidents at Chaudière sawmills. One witness who particularly moved the commissioners was a boy who had lost both an arm and a leg when he was 12 years old; he testified that the lumber firm (unnamed) had given him $10 for his suffering but his fellow workers had raised another $25 for him. Despite the dangers and the legislation, however, underage boys continued to work in Valley sawmills as mill owners and their foremen paid little attention to the factory acts. Indeed, as late as 1913 an 11-year-old boy was killed at W.C. Edwards's Rockland mill.[71]

Experienced adults were not immune either, and over the years many were maimed and killed in Ottawa Valley sawmills. In 1893 a newspaper reported a fatality at the Gilmour mill in Hull in which

William Marquell, an expert band sawyer, had his body literally cut in two pieces. A very large sawlog was being flipped on the carriage when a knot sticking out on it caught the endless chain, which drags the logs into the mill from the pond below. The log was given a jerk forward and struck with considerable force against the unfortunate sawyer's right shoulder. He fell forward on his hands against the moving carriage and the saw cut his arm off below the elbow. It was done in a moment, and the severed arm let his body fall on the moving carriage. He caught the band saw, and the rapidly moving strip of steel ripped him in two before a word could be said or any action taken to prevent the accident.[72]

STORING, SORTING, SHIPPING, AND SELLING LUMBER

As technological advances allowed mill owners to saw more lumber more quickly, they had to find new, labour-saving ways to move the increased output to their piling yards. By the early 1870s Allan Gilmour had installed an elaborate wooden flume to float freshly sawn lumber from his mill at Chelsea Falls to his yards three miles farther down the Gatineau River. At the same time, Messrs. Perley and Pattee and other Chaudière lumbermen had laid miles of railway tracks across their properties to link their mills, yards, and shipping docks; horses were used as the motive force to haul tramcars full of lumber along the tracks. In the twentieth century, some firms brought in steam locomotives to help in their extensive yards. The Gillies Brothers piling yards at Braeside covered 150 acres and could accommodate up to 50 million board feet of lumber; the brothers needed eight miles of track and a 30-ton locomotive to serve their yards.[73] Locomotives and tramcars, however, only moved lumber around the yards; they were no help in stacking the piles or loading and unloading cars. In this work, all boards and planks had to be handled piece by piece; it was tedious, labour-intensive drudgery that was difficult to mechanize.

In the 1880s it would not be unusual to find as much as 125 million board feet of lumber stocked in piling yards around the Ottawa-Hull area. Some of this stock was lumber waiting for sale or delivery to buyers outside the Valley. Most of it, however, was lumber piled for seasoning and not yet ready for sale. Seasoning (air drying) reduced the moisture content of the wood, making it less likely to warp or exude gum, resulting in a higher price.. It also made the wood lighter and, thus, cheaper to ship by rail or barge. The air-drying process could take two to six months depending on the weather, the species of tree, and how green the wood was when sawn; some sawlogs, having spent more than a year in the water (on the river drive and in the mill pond), were already partially seasoned on arriving at the saw. In the yards, the lumber was kept off the ground and piled carefully to catch the prevailing winds; room left for fire-fighting lanes and railway tracks also helped enhance air circulation.[74] In Ottawa-Hull, hundreds of acres around the Chaudière were covered with lumber stacked high above the heads of the yard workers. Visitors seldom failed to remark on the magnitude and fragrance of the yards. In 1884 one visitor exclaimed that

> A great part of the city of Ottawa is a city without residents, a
> city of lumber. Here are piles of lumber — square, quadruple,
> diagonal — built tier on tier high in the air, lumber for all
> intents and purposes; acres of inch boards, mountains unend-
> ing of joists, beams, sheeting, streets of lumber, blocks of lum-
> ber, miles on miles of lumber. . . . Fast as the great mills build
> the city up, so fast great railway trains and multitudes of
> immense barges pull it down and carry it away. The air is redo-
> lent with the smell of lumber. You breathe pine and resin at
> every step.[75]

In large-scale lumber operations, wood was sorted and piled according to species, size, degree of dressing and edging, and quality. It was easy for buyers and sellers to agree on the first three, but, except for deal exports, attempts to establish quality standards proved impossible. For deals, the government legislated that all exports had to be classified into three grades before export; the criteria used were rather arcane, but few disputes occurred. The government did not impose grading on other forms of lumber, however, and buyers and sellers were never able to agree on a uniform system. Most large buyers sent agents into Valley lumberyards to inspect the wood for cracks, dry rot, worm holes, gum deposits, stains, warps, wanes, excessive knots, and surface roughness. After some bargaining, the agents and the lumbermen would agree on grading for that particular purchase. Occasionally, Valley lumbermen would get together, hoping to agree on fixed standards and put up a common front against buyers. These attempts always failed, perhaps because the task was hopeless in the first place. In practice, the strength or weakness of the market determined whether certain boards were of first- or second-class quality; as a result, grading standards differed from yard to yard, from year to year. British buyers insisted on high-quality lumber (which could better bear the costs of transatlantic delivery), while Americans and Canadians were more willing to accept lower grades.[76]

Before 1850 the only lumber exported from the Ottawa Valley was the pine deals sent to Britain by the Hamilton family of Hawkesbury. Before the end of the century, however, the Valley was sawing a wide variety of lumber for markets around the world. In 1888 one-quarter of the lumber produced in the Valley was sold in Ontario and Quebec; the remainder was exported abroad: 34 percent to the United States, 25 percent to Britain, and 16 percent to South America, the West Indies, and elsewhere.[77] When exporting to the United States, many Valley lumbermen sold their output direct to wholesalers based in New England and the Midwest. Indeed, the McLachlin Brothers sometimes sold their entire season's cut to a single buyer: in 1894, for instance, they sold 60 million board feet of lumber to one firm for $900,000 (more than $15,000,000 in today's money). In years of strong demand, lumber was often sold long before it was sawn — indeed, even before the trees were felled in the forest. A few of the more aggressive lumbermen strove to gain additional profits by doing their own wholesaling below the border; J. R. Booth, E. H. Bronson, and W. C. Edwards, for example, maintained large lumber yards and sales outlets at Burlington, Vermont.[78] British sales were largely handled by exporting firms with offices in Quebec and Montreal; they bought the lumber (which now included small shipments of boards and planks as well as deals) and resold it in Britain. One exception was the lumber exported by Allan Gilmour, who was able to use family connections to arrange his own sales in Britain. As for South America and the West Indies, they became useful markets for Valley lumber surprisingly early; Messrs. Perley and Pattee were sending boards and planks to these faraway markets by the early 1870s. Indeed, in later years, lumber from the Valley was reportedly being shipped as far as South Africa and Australia. Sales to these markets were also handled by international exporting firms operating in Canada. Some of the lumber sold to these distant customers was taken by ships sailing out of Montreal. Most, however, was carried, "in bond," by barge or rail to Boston or New York and shipped out of those ports.[79]

Most lumber-exporting firms in the Ottawa Valley had two choices in getting their output to outside markets: they could send it overland by rail or ship it out by barge. The exceptions, of course, were those with mills located above Chaudière Falls; firms such as McLachlin Brothers, Gillies Brothers, the Pembroke Lumber Co., and St. Anthony's were totally dependent on rail transport to supply customers beyond the Valley. Railways were faster and could run in any season; water transport, however, was cheaper and, in the early years of the industry at least, Valley lumbermen preferred to ship their goods out. The Ottawa River near Chaudière Falls became crowded with fleets of lumber barges towed by noisy, steam-powered tugboats. In summertime, Ottawa, and especially Hull, became bustling river ports, with hundreds of men employed in shipping services. In winter, the ports were strikingly quiet, the waterfront lined with vessels hibernating in the ice. Lumber exporters benefited from a crowd of shipping firms that clamoured to carry their products to market. Nevertheless, some mill owners chose to maintain their own fleets of tugboats and barges: Bronsons & Weston, for example, operated four tugs and 39 barges, employing 222 men for 6 months of the year. A. H. Baldwin and J. R. Booth even established shipyards to build and service their vessels.[80]

The barges that carried the pine and spruce lumber out of the Valley were built in two maximum sizes, each as large as would fit in the canals they intended to navigate. The larger barges travelled down the Ottawa River, with some of them sailing on to Quebec City while others headed up the Richelieu River to Vermont and New York; they were able to squeeze their way through the Ottawa River and Richelieu canals with as much as 325,000 board feet of lumber on board. Other barges, smaller in size and fewer in number, travelled through the Rideau Canal to Kingston and across Lake Ontario to Oswego, New York; here they entered the Erie Canal, whose cramped confines limited their carrying capacity to 175,000 board feet. In later years, when they were all operated by one company, the barges were colour coded — the larger vessels painted blue and the smaller ones white. Some of the barges were self-propelled, but most were towed, as many as six at a time, by powerful tugboats.[81]

Shipping in the Ottawa Valley hit its peak in the mid-1880s, when six firms, owning 16 tugboats and 133 barges, were reported in service. Most of the vessels were devoted to carrying lumber downriver (on return voyages, they brought back coal to heat the growing cities of Ottawa and Hull). At this time about two-thirds of Valley lumber

Loading lumber onto barges, J.R. Booth sawmill, Ottawa. All the work — stacking lumber in the piling yards and later loading it onto the barges — had to be done by hand, board by board.

exports were being taken out by water; a decade later, about two-thirds were travelling by rail. By the 1890s rail service in the Valley had much improved: track mileage had increased, and spurs were extended right into the piling yards at most large sawmills. Lumbermen who had operated their own tugs and barges sold their fleets to independent carriers. Soon these shipping firms merged into one large provider, the Ottawa Transportation Company, headed by Denis Murphy, who had begun as a steamboat captain on the Ottawa in 1865. Murphy's company had a near monopoly, but the number of vessels fell by nearly half. Railways were now the preferred carrier. J. R. Booth's recently completed Canada Atlantic Railway was the most active line; with terminuses at Georgian Bay and Vermont, it could serve several American markets — Chicago and the midwestern states, as well as New York and the northeast. In 1902 the CAR alone carried 312 million board feet of lumber on its lines, about half the entire output of the Ottawa Valley for that year.[82]

LUMBERING: GROWTH AND DECLINE

Lumbering in the Ottawa Valley reached its peak in the 1880s. Exact output numbers are impossible to find, but reasonably accurate figures are available for some years. These figures show how production in the large, export-driven sawmills rose for several decades before beginning to fall in the late 1880s.[83] A number of changing realities made the downturn inevitable. Most important was an obvious deterioration in the Valley's forest stocks, noticeable by the 1880s. By 1890 some lumbermen, feeling that this deterioration portended a poor future for their industry, began to seek other ways to use the Valley's timber resources. Conditions worsened further in the mid-1890s, when economic depression brought lower lumber prices, driving some producers out of business. Then, in 1900, a disastrous fire destroyed large parts of Ottawa and Hull, with serious consequences to the industry. In the twentieth century, Valley lumbermen had to face competition from new products and new sources of supply, and some of them began moving their money into other ventures, such as pulp and paper and electrical power. Lastly, the Great Depression of the 1930s brought large-scale lumbering in the Ottawa Valley to a virtual end.

Declining forest stocks came as a surprise to some producers because, for many years, they had felt the timberlands of the Ottawa Valley were practically inexhaustible. Still, they should have foreseen the consequences of their work. Timbermen were particularly careless, wasting huge volumes of wood when squaring their timber. As well, both timbermen and lumbermen were guilty of destroying great swaths of young-growth trees when felling the big pines and hauling them out of the bush. Another obvious cause of decline in forest stocks was the ruinous fires that seemed to hit somewhere in the Valley every few years. W. C. Edwards suggested that 20 times more wood was consumed by forest fires than was cut by lumbermen. Though his claim was exaggerated, fire certainly wrought great harm. Edwards maintained that the chief cause of these losses was the settler's habit of burning trees as he cleared his lands (at the same time, of course, Edwards maintained that his own shantymen always followed strict fire-prevention practices). Lumbermen were not blameless, however, for the slash and brush they left in the bush provided the perfect fuel for forest fires. The worst forest fire ever recorded in the province of Ontario occurred in the Ottawa Valley, and it was blamed on both settlers and loggers. This was the horrific blaze that burned much of the land between Englehart and Cobalt in 1922, killing 43 people, destroying several towns and leaving 11,000 people homeless. A great deal of forest was consumed in the fire, though some of the best timberlands had already been cut down for lumber. Earlier (in 1905), the provincial government had delayed issuing mining permits in the silver-rich Cobalt area in order to allow Gillies Brothers to clear a valuable stand of pines, fearing that it might be burned down when hordes of eager prospectors arrived.[84]

Inevitably, lumbermen began to feel the results of ruinous forest fires and their careless logging practices. As early as the 1880s, they could see that the sawlogs arriving at their mills were smaller in size and lower in quality. In 1888 the Gilmour Company reported that, ten years earlier, two-thirds of the sawlogs they cut measured 17 inches or more in diameter, but that now only one-quarter could match this size. Another

Ottawa lumberman estimated that only one-quarter of the lumber sawn in mills at the Chaudière was first-class (lumber that brought the highest profit). In 1884 the Bronsons & Weston Company reported that the proportion of "cull" (lowest-grade) lumber turned out in their mill had risen from 47 percent to 66 percent in only seven years.[85] For decades, Valley lumbermen had had it relatively easy, taking the choicest red and white pines from the most easily accessible timber limits. When most of the high-grade timber was gone, there were two ways they could stay in business. One was to rework their old limits, cutting the less desirable pines that remained (trees of slimmer dimension or not perfectly linear in form) and harvesting more spruce and hemlock. Spruce and hemlock lumber, however, fetched lower prices on the market, while the poorer quality pine logs were less economical to saw. The lumberman's second option was to find and lease yet-untouched timber limits with good stocks of high-quality trees. New timber limits became increasingly expensive to lease, however, and could be found only at greater and greater distances from the major sawmills, thus adding significantly to the costs of producing lumber.

Working timber limits a second time helped ease the supply problem for a while, but, ultimately, there were no more suitable trees left on the old cutting grounds. When this happened in the Mississippi River Valley, it meant the end of large-scale lumbering. The Canada Lumber Company, which owned the last major sawmill in Carleton Place (Peter McLaren's old mill), had to shut down in 1898 when it ran out of wood to saw. With its inland location, the firm was unable to bring in logs from outside the area.[86] Lumbermen located on the Ottawa River, however, could purchase new limits farther up the Valley and float the logs to their mills. By the 1890s most of the large-scale sawmills in the Valley had become more and more dependent on sawlogs cut on limits farther and farther away. The McLachlin Brothers of Arnprior, for example, had timber limits far up the Kipawa River in Quebec and the Montreal River in Ontario, about 300 miles from their mill. The Hawkesbury Lumber Company (formed after the death of John Hamilton in 1888) also had limits in the Kipawa area, and their mill was an additional hundred miles down the Ottawa River. Some lumbermen had limits as far upriver as Lac Expanse (now Lac Simard), about 400 miles beyond Ottawa–Hull, and even on Grand Lac Victoria, nearly five hundred miles away. J. R. Booth operated in this remote area, but he avoided bringing his logs that distance by digging a short canal over to the DuMoine River and driving them down that stream to the Ottawa.[87]

In New Brunswick as well as on the upper Great Lakes and other parts of Canada, sawmilling typically followed the retreating forest frontier. That is, lumbermen usually closed their sawmills when local sources of wood were used up and then rebuilt closer to new, virgin timber limits in the hinterland.[88] This did not happen in the Ottawa Valley. No large-scale sawmills were built north of Pembroke. Ottawa Valley lumbermen would not move; they preferred to stay in place or leave the business altogether. The lumbermen who chose to carry on never seemed to cower at the thought of operating over great distances. Expanded railway service certainly helped mitigate the expense of supplying the ever-more-remote logging shanties. But moving the sawlogs hundreds of miles to the mills was a different matter. In some cases, it took two and even three years to deliver the wood from the stump to the mill. Longer log drives not only meant higher production costs, they also added to the time the lumberman had to wait for a return on his investment. Nevertheless, many of the established lumber kings — Booth, Edwards, the Gilmours, the Maclarens, the McLachlins, the Gillieses — stayed in business for another 40 or more years after it became clear their industry was in decline.

Others, however, chose to leave — for varying reasons. E. B. Eddy was the first to seek better ways to use the Valley's declining forest stocks. In 1889 he withdrew entirely from commercial lumbering to concentrate on manufacturing wood products. He sold off some of his timber limits, logging farms, depots, and piling yards but continued to saw about 15 million board feet of wood in his mill annually. This wood, however, was used solely for Eddy's own purposes — making boxes, pails, tubs, washboards, sashes, and doors, products that brought greater profit than mere lumber. More important, he also erected two pulp mills and soon began manufacturing paper. The next major lumber producers to leave the industry were Messrs. Perley and Pattee. After W. G. Perley died in 1890, his old partner G. B. Pattee seems to have lost confidence in the future of lumbering. Their famous mill ceased sawing wood in 1891 and was sold to J. R. Booth; the firm was dissolved two years later. In the meantime, Pattee turned his interest to hydroelectricity, joining with Erskine Bronson to form the Standard Electric Light Company. Pattee may have congratulated himself on getting out of lumbering, because economic depression struck North America a few years later. Already disadvantaged by sawlogs that were falling in quality and rising in cost, Valley lumbermen now had to cope with lower prices for their products. One major casualty of the depression was the lumber firm William Mason & Son (sawmill in Mechanicsville), which went bankrupt and closed in 1898.[89]

Two years later, on 26 April 1900, came the great fire that caused widespread destruction in Ottawa and Hull, striking another damaging blow to the Valley's lumber industry. The blaze began in a house chimney in Hull and ravaged a large part of that city. With the aid of strong, northerly winds and the highly combustible mills and lumberyards of the Chaudière, it was able to cross the Ottawa River. The fire then burned its way through LeBreton Flats and down Preston and Rochester streets to Dow's Lake, areas filled with both housing and lumberyards. Seven people died in the two cities and 14,000 were left homeless; 3,200 buildings were destroyed, including electrical generating plants, two pulp mills, a paper mill, the Canadian Pacific Railway station, J. R. Booth's personal residence, and two major sawmills — those of the Bronson and Hull lumber companies (the latter mill formerly owned by Robert Hurdman). In addition, more than 100 million board feet of lumber were consumed. Total damage, including housing, lumber, mills, and other buildings, was ultimately reckoned at $6,500,000 (in today's money, more than $110,000,000). The only Chaudière sawmill to escape destruction was Booth's as he had recently installed an advanced sprinkler system, which drenched the entire building with water. His workers stayed on the job to help fight the fire, even as some, who lived nearby, were losing their homes to the blaze. Although he saved his mill, Booth lost all his other buildings and nearly a million dollars worth of lumber.[90]

Surprisingly, the loss of two sawmills at the Chaudière did not reduce total lumber production in the Valley in 1900; indeed, output actually rose slightly over the previous year. No sawlogs had been lost in the fire, only mill capacity and stored lumber, so there was no lack of material with which to work. Within weeks of the fire, the Hull Lumber Company was sawing lumber again, taking over William Mason's vacant mill in Mechanicsville. J. R. Booth had his mill back in operation after a short cleanup period and was able to match his previous year's output. Some Valley mills worked double shifts that summer to help make up the losses. Nevertheless, a lot of the lumber produced was sold "green" (unseasoned); there was no time for air-drying as large parts of Ottawa and Hull had to be rebuilt before winter. The need to fill local requirements did mean, however, that much less wood was sold outside the Valley that year. Increased local sales caused shortages elsewhere, and the wholesale price of lumber in Canada jumped 19 percent in 1900; much of this extraordinary rise can be attributed to the Ottawa-Hull fire.[91] Although it was in decline, the Ottawa Valley lumber industry obviously still played an important role in the national economy.

One longer-term consequence of the fire of 1900 was to heighten fears among the public about the lumber industry's piling grounds. The most efficient place to pile lumber was as close as possible to the mill, the barges, and the railways. But the mills, barges, and railways employed hundreds of people who wanted to live close to their workplace (in those days almost everyone walked to work). The result, in Ottawa, was acres and acres of densely stacked lumber piled along and among thickly populated residential streets. The lumber industry was not blamed for causing the 1900 fire, but piling yards were held responsible for allowing it to spread so widely. For months after the fire, Ottawa's city council debated imposing zoning restrictions on the yards, while lumbermen insisted that such impositions would seriously harm their businesses; in the end, the council made only minor changes to the bylaws. In the meantime, the lumberyards were restocked and houses rebuilt in the burnt-out areas. Three years later, another fire swept through the same neighbourhood, destroying several blocks of new housing and 18 million board feet of lumber. This time the council finally took action, imposing restrictions on the size and location of piling yards. Most lumbermen complied, but J. R. Booth stalled, resisted, and threatened. He eventually moved most of his lumber outside the city limits (to the Merivale Road). But as late as 1909 he was able to get the city council to allow him to keep one lumberyard in a populated area — by threatening to reduce work in his mills.[92] In one thing Booth and his colleagues were right, though, for there is no doubt that dispersing the piling grounds raised the costs of the lumber trade in the Ottawa area.

Another consequence of the great fire was the changes wrought at Chaudière Falls. Here, where the saws of six giant mills had once cut lumber, only two remained — those of J. R. Booth and the Hull Lumber Company, which had rebuilt its premises. The long-term prospects of the Valley's lumber industry were considered poor, and most investors now turned their interests to exploiting the Chaudière's water power for other purposes — electricity and pulp and paper. After losing his sawmill in the conflagration, Erskine Bronson abandoned lumbering, but not the Chaudière. He rebuilt his electrical-generating plant at the Chaudière and led a group that formed Ottawa Electric Company. Later he erected a groundwood pulp mill on his Chaudière hydraulic lot. E.B. Eddy lost his paper mill and one of his pulp mills in the great fire but quickly rebuilt them. Eddy's optimism proved to be infectious — by the beginning of the First World War, two other lumber producers had followed his lead into the pulp-and-paper industry. The Maclaren family opened a pulp mill at Buckingham, while J.R. Booth built two pulp mills and a paper mill at the Chaudière.[93] Both continued to saw lumber for commercial sale, but it was evident that pulp and paper had become the main focus of investors seeking better ways to exploit the forests of the Ottawa Valley.

In the twentieth century, lumbermen also had to cope with new competition in their traditional markets. Structural steel beams, sheet metal, and reinforced concrete came into common use in North America, especially among builders nervous about the flammability of wood as a construction material. Indeed, when W. C. Edwards rebuilt his Rideau Falls sawmill after the 1907 fire, he chose to use reinforced concrete throughout the new building. At the same time, builders who continued to work with wood now had a cheaper source of supply — the Pacific Coast. Lumber from that area was of better quality than the Ottawa Valley could supply, and, sawn from much larger logs, it was cheaper to produce and thus could bear the heavy costs of transport to markets in eastern North America. British Columbia lumber was shipped to Montreal via the Canadian Pacific Railway as early as 1891. It soon became a strong competitor in the Valley's traditional markets, and the opening of the Panama Canal in 1914 gave it an even greater advantage.[94] In the twentieth century, investors could still turn a small profit sawing Ottawa Valley trees into lumber (mainly cheap and second grade), but the industry was no longer the power it once had been.

In the second half of the nineteenth century the Ottawa Valley had been recognized as the leading lumber-producing region in all of Canada. In 1870 an English visitor proclaimed that "the Valley of the Ottawa is at present the principal seat of the lumber trade." Three decades later, the industry's trade journal, the *Canada Lumberman*, noted that "the Ottawa Valley has long been and is yet the most important lumbering centre in Canada." Unfortunately, due to a lack of comparative statistics, one cannot say exactly how much of Canada's total lumber production came from the Valley. In 1888, however, the American consul in Canada supplied figures that showed that pine sawn in the Valley accounted for 55 percent of total Canadian exports to the United States.[95] Nonetheless, it is clear that in the 1890s the Valley's lumber industry entered a shrinking mode and lost its leadership to British Columbia. By the 1930s most of the great sawmills had closed, and lumbering was no longer a significant industry in the Ottawa Valley.

6

PULP AND PAPER

It was fortunate for the people of the Ottawa Valley that, just as lumbering went into decline, a new business — pulp and paper — was born. Pulp-and-paper manufacturing grew quickly to robust manhood and, in the process, reinvigorated the whole forest industry of the Ottawa Valley.

Paper had been manufactured in Canada since the beginning of the nineteenth century, but the industry grew at a slow pace; the Canadian market was small, and the materials used in the manufacturing process, cotton and linen rags, were not abundantly available here. Conditions started to change by the 1880s, though. First, growth in the newspaper industry began to create a strong market for newsprint. At the same time, new technologies were making it possible to manufacture paper using pulped wood, and since wood was much easier to come by than rags, newsprint could now be produced in large quantities and at low cost. Investors in the Ottawa Valley and elsewhere were quick to recognize the potential for profit, and a dynamic, new manufacturing industry was born. Today, while square timbering has long since disappeared from the Valley, and lumbering is only a minor endeavour, the pulp-and-paper industry continues to thrive.

It was the needs of mass-circulation journalism that provided the initial stimulus for large-scale paper-making in Canada. In the 1880s rising literacy levels (thanks to government-supplied programs of free, com-

pulsory education) joined with increasing affluence and a rapid growth
in urban populations to create a lively demand for newspapers. Growing
numbers of readers were hungry for information on local crimes,
national politics, and foreign scandals; at the same time, a burgeoning
retail sector was eager to advertise its wares to consumers.[1] It seemed
that every city with any sense of pride had to have more than one daily
newspaper. By 1900 Canada had 112 dailies (most of them priced at
only one cent each), serving a population of little more than five million. That year the City of Ottawa had three daily newspapers, while the
small villages of Arnprior, Renfrew, and Pembroke had two weeklies
each. Mass-circulation journalism was possible only if there was cheap
newsprint, however, and the Ottawa Valley was eager to supply it.

The Canadian pulp-and-paper industry could not have expanded to
its present-day size, however, without the further stimuli provided by
two political developments early in the twentieth century. First, several
provincial governments banned the export of any unprocessed pulpwood cut on Crown land, thus encouraging the expansion of pulp
milling in Canada. Second, and more important, the industry gained
easier access to the American market. In the early years, American tariffs had made it difficult to sell Canadian pulp or paper across the border, but, in time, the United States began to face shortages of both
products. As result, in 1913 the American government, feeling pressure
from newspaper publishers, removed its import duties on both pulp
and newsprint (though not on other paper products). These two developments made the Canadian pulp-and-paper industry a power in
world markets.

To investors, it was obvious that the Ottawa Valley had all the essen-
tials that the pulp-and-paper industry needed. The Valley's forests held
rich stands of trees that were unwanted for timber or lumber but suitable for wood pulp. The Valley also boasted a labour force with long
experience in harvesting wood and getting it to mills hundreds of miles
away. And the Valley also had ample supplies of water needed in the
manufacture of pulp and paper, as well as cheap hydro energy to power
the industry. As a result, the Ottawa Valley was one of the first areas in
Canada to adopt the new industrial endeavour.

As sawmilling declined, lumbermen who had earlier spent large amounts of money acquiring timber limits in the Ottawa Valley saw pulp and paper as an opportunity to get more out of their investments; in particular, they saw that the new industry would allow them to use wood previously left unused in the bush. For example, logs that were crooked, cracked, or otherwise unsuitable for lumber were accepted at pulp mills, along with logs as small as three inches in diameter or four feet in length. In addition, while earlier generations of Valley timbermen and lumbermen had focused on cutting white spruce and red and white pine, large stocks of other conifers had been little touched and could now be harvested. In particular, black spruce, long spurned by lumbermen, now became a prized asset in the forest; black spruce possessed the best combination of qualities required for the manufacture of wood pulp — low levels of resin and good fibre content. Other species, such as white spruce, balsam, poplar, and jack pine, were also used, though in lesser quantities. The demand for pulpwood allowed some limit-holders to harvest their woodlands for a third time. By cutting pulpwood, it was estimated that investors could add as much as 20 percent to the value of the timber limits they leased. It is easy to see why some of the Valley's leading lumber producers moved to diversify their interests. In fact, most of the capital invested in pulp and paper came from established lumbermen who held extensive timber limits in the Valley: E. B. Eddy, J. R. Booth, Erskine H. Bronson, and the Maclaren family. In addition, other lumbermen were able to benefit from the new industry without investing in it themselves — simply by supplying existing mills with pulpwood cut on their limits. The pulp produced in Valley mills proved to be of a very high quality, considered superior to that of other competing areas, such as Georgian Bay. Most of this pulp was, in turn, fed into local paper mills to make newsprint and other paper products of a high quality.[2]

SEASONAL ROUND: BUSH AND RIVER OPERATIONS

For the pulp-and-paper industry, the seasonal round followed much the same routine as that followed by timber and lumber shantymen. Men spent the winter in the bush cutting pulpwood and the spring moving it down rivers to pulp mills. There was one major difference, though: the work of cutting, hauling, driving, and booming pulpwood was easier than that of timbering and lumbering. Pulpwood was usually smaller and easier to handle and did not require as much care.[3] More attention was given to getting the pulpwood to the mill than in worrying about damaging it en route; quantity was more important than quality. Less skill was required, and men who worked on timbering or lumbering operations one year had no difficulty switching to cutting and driving pulpwood the next season. Still, many older shantymen in the Ottawa Valley were repelled by the thought of taking on this lesser work and refused to switch; as a result, most of the first-generation pulpwood cutters were farmers and not full-time professionals.[4] For a couple of decades (until the last timber raft descended the Ottawa River in 1908), all three forest industries were active at the same time in the Ottawa Valley. In those years, square timber, sawlogs, and pulpwood could all be seen floating down the Ottawa. J. R. Booth was, himself, a major player in all three industries at once.

The acceptance of smaller timber for pulpwood brought about a noticeable change in logging tools. By the 1930s the old double-bit axe, which could weigh up to seven pounds and had a handle 36 inches long, had shrunk to a sleek model weighing as little as two-and-a-half pounds, with a handle as short as 28 inches. The cross-cut saw continued to be used in lumbering operations, but pulpwood cutters quickly switched to the new one-man bucksaw (a saw whose blade is set within an H-shaped frame). With these lighter, modern tools, a logger was expected, by the 1930s, to produce at least two-and-a-half "cords" (the unit of measurement used for pulpwood) per day. Chainsaws did not appear until the mid-1930s.[5]

Another new development of the pulp-and-paper era was the growing use of privately held lands as a source of wood. True, throughout the nineteenth century, Valley timbermen and lumbermen had obtained some of their wood from land patented to agricultural settlers (though most of it was cut on Crown land). With the new demand for pulpwood, however, conditions changed in the twentieth century. Now, some long-established Valley farmers were able to earn good cash

This alligator tug Bonnechere, *1907, possibly owned by McLachlin Bros., is shown winching itself over land on roller logs. Note the taut cable at prow.*

from their woodlots, at least those farmers fortunate to be located near driveable water. (Many had no experience in logging, but, again, pulp manufacturers did not insist on high-quality workmanship.) Wood that these farmers had sold cheaply as firewood in the past now fetched better prices for pulp. In addition, newly arrived settlers clearing their lands for farming in the early years of the twentieth century were able to sell logs to Valley pulp mills; for many settlers, spruce was their first cash crop. In 1903 300 new settlers in the Timiskaming district were reported to have earned an average of nearly $800 each cutting pulp-wood on their own land.[6]

The pulp-and-paper era also saw the adoption of an exciting inno-vation in river-driving: a steam-powered vessel capable of operating on both land and water. Aptly called the "alligator," this amphibious craft was invented at Simcoe, Ontario, and put on the market in 1889 to facilitate river-driving. The new craft helped resolve one of the great problems faced on the river-drive — moving logs on rivers and lakes with little or no current. Tugboats would certainly have helped, but it was too costly to build such vessels in areas far from the Ottawa River.

The alligator, however, was a steam-powered tugboat capable of transporting itself overland into the back country, where it could be used on large, inland stretches of water. It was equipped with a powerful winch and a thick steel cable. When the cable was attached to a tree, it could winch itself out of the water and pull itself across swamps and up small hills, portaging from one navigable body of water to another. After arriving in the back country, it served as a tugboat, pulling large booms of sawlogs or pulpwood along the still waters of interior lakes such as Kamaniskeg in Ontario and Baskatong in Quebec. In the autumn alligators also saw service towing scows carrying three or four tons of freight (and even horses) up inland rivers to supply the shanties. This versatile new craft brought great savings to forest industries in both Canada and the United States, reducing manpower needs by shortening the time spent on river-drives. The alligator arrived in the Ottawa Valley just as lumbering was beginning to decline and as pulp and paper was emerging as the new centre of interest. Both industries quickly recognized its value. McLachlin Brothers were using alligators by 1892 and J. R. Booth by 1895, and they saw service for another 50 years or so.[7]

MANUFACTURING PULP AND PAPER

Two methods were employed to convert the cellulose fibres of wood into the pulp needed by papermakers. "Ground pulp" (also called "mechanical pulp" because it was mechanically processed) was produced by pressing wood against rapidly revolving grindstones. This method yielded cheap pulp suitable for wallboard and for use in papers where colour, strength, and durability were not important. In the early decades of the industry, ground pulp always accounted for more than half of Canada's output. The second method employed chemicals to turn wood into pulp. "Chemical pulp" could cost twice as much or more to prepare, but it yielded finer, stronger, and longer-lasting paper. In this process, chipping machines sliced pulpwood into small particles which were conveyed to large digesters, where the wood was steamed, and then cooked in a water-and-chemical solution. Several chemicals can be used for this process, but bisulphite lime predominated in the early years. After cooking for several hours, the pulp was washed, screened, dried, and then shaped into bales or rolls for delivery to a paper mill. Pulp made from both processes could be combined at the mill; indeed, newsprint was made from a mixture of three or four parts ground pulp and one part sulphite.[8]

After the wood pulp arrived at the paper mill, water was added, and it underwent further processing, beating, and refining. In the next stage, new materials such as clay, talc, bleaches, and dye might be added, the quantities depending on the kind of paper desired. Finally, the liquid pulp was allowed to flow onto the wire screens of a paper-making machine and then pressed into sheets and heat-dried by rollers. Some mills turned out a wide variety of paper products, but newsprint has been the most important ever since the industry grew into maturity around 1890. In 1922, for example, newsprint represented fully 79 percent of Canada's total output. Board materials accounted for another 8 percent of national production; these products included cardboard (both corrugated and layered, for use in packaging) and wallboard (ground pulp that had been pressed and baked into panels of varying thicknesses, for use in construction). The remaining 13 percent of Canada's 1922 output consisted of wrapping paper, book and writing paper, tissue paper, wallpaper, and paper bags.[9] Ottawa Valley mills participated in the manufacture of all these products.

OTTAWA VALLEY PULP-AND-PAPER MILLS

Ezra Butler Eddy was the prescient pioneer of pulp and paper in the Ottawa Valley. He had both the foresight to abandon lumbering, a declining though still profitable industry, and the nerve to jump into a new endeavour about which few people knew anything. In 1889 Eddy erected two mills on the site of the old Wright, Batson & Currier sawmill: one to make ground pulp and the other to make sulphite pulp (the latter would have resembled the sulphite mill he erected in 1902, whose ruins can be seen today beside the Canadian Museum of Civilization). Eddy was just as bold in entering paper manufacturing. Starting in 1890 by making tissue paper, within three years he had installed machinery to turn out newsprint, book paper, cardboard, and paper bags. It was said at the time that no one else in the industry in North America had accomplished so much so quickly. A few years earlier, Eddy had incorporated his enterprises as a joint-stock company with three partners; there was no doubt, though, that Eddy was the entrepreneurial force of the company. By 1899 the E. B. Eddy Co. had become, along with the Canada Paper Co. of Windsor Mills, Quebec, the leading manufacturer of paper in Canada. The next year, however, came the great Ottawa-Hull fire that destroyed his ground pulp mill and his papermaking plant. His losses totalled about $3,000,000, of which only about 5 percent is thought to have been covered by insurance. Still, with his early successes, Eddy remained confident in the new industry, and though he was now 73 years old, he was able to persuade his bankers to lend his firm the money to rebuild. Within a year he had replaced his losses with new pulp and paper mills that were nearly twice as large. After his death in 1906, his old partners continued to operate the business, retaining the Eddy name. In 1913 the firm completed an ambitious expansion of its pulp- and papermaking capacity and added a large new hydroelectric power plant.[10]

E. B. Eddy's confidence in the future of pulp-and-paper manufacturing in the Ottawa Valley was contagious for other investors soon followed his lead. J. R. Booth quickly made his presence felt in the new industry: in just six years (1904 to 1910), he completed two large pulp mills (one ground, one sulphite), a major papermaking plant, and a cardboard factory. The James Maclaren Company (operated by the children of the lumber king) opened a pulp mill at Buckingham, on the Lièvre River, in 1901 (they added a paper mill at Masson, farther downriver, in 1929). Erskine H. Bronson abandoned lumbering altogether after losing his Chaudière sawmill in the great fire of 1900, replacing it with a ground-pulp mill on his old hydraulic lot. And Charles Riordon, who had pulp and paper mills at Merritton, Ontario, erected a large sulphite pulp mill at Hawkesbury in 1898 and opened another at Temiskaming, Quebec, in 1919. After Riordon went bankrupt, these installations were taken over (in 1925) by the Canadian International Paper Company. This multinational firm went on to build a huge pulp-

and-paper manufacturing complex at Gatineau Point and diversified the Temiskaming mill to produce rayon cellulose (at one time, it supplied nearly half the world's output of this textile fibre). Except for Riordon and CIP, the pulp-and-paper industry in the Ottawa Valley was built by people with a long history in the local lumber trade. And until the arrival of CIP, the industry was totally controlled by Canadians; in this respect, the Ottawa Valley's experience in pulp and paper differed from that elsewhere in Canada, where the industry was dominated by American and British investors from the outset. The industry here was also noticeably different in another respect: in other parts of the country, pulp and paper mills were usually located in remote areas close to sources of pulpwood; in the Valley, however, investors chose to bring their pulpwood long distances and build their mills at the old sawmilling sites. Again, it was the wonderful water-power resources of the Ottawa, Gatineau, and Lièvre rivers that decided where mills would be located.[11]

When pulp-and-paper manufacturing began in the Ottawa Valley, direct-drive water power was still the chief source of energy used in sawmills; understandably, the new industry chose, whenever possible, to stick with the proven technology of channelling water down penstocks and over turbines. Water turbines proved to be particularly suitable to manufacturing ground pulp and all paper products. Most Valley mills relied on water power until the 1920s, though some were equipped with auxiliary supplies of steam and electrical power for use in emergencies, such as low water levels or thick ice on the rivers. Sulphite pulp mills were the exception. Since steam was an essential element in the cooking process, owners of these mills chose to go with the same source of power throughout the plant. Eddy and Booth relied largely on sawdust and mill scraps to fuel their steam boilers, but Riordon imported coal for his Hawkesbury sulphite mill. It was not until the 1920s that the Valley's existing pulp and paper mills were converted to electrical power. Electricity offered more efficiency, more reliability, lower maintenance costs, and wider flexibility in the arrangement of machinery. The new mills built at Temiskaming, Gatineau Point, and Masson were designed for electrical power from the outset,

and all three projects involved the construction of huge hydro-generat-
ing complexes. Ottawa Valley pulp-and-paper manufacturers did not
rely on public utilities for their electrical power. Despite the high costs
of building large dams and elaborate generating plants, they preferred
to produce their own hydroelectricity.[12]

Before 1913, despite high American tariffs, more than half of
Canadian wood pulp was exported to the United States. The Ottawa
Valley was an exception, however, as little pulp seems to have been
shipped out of the region. Most of the pulp produced in the Valley's
mills before 1930 was consumed locally, perhaps because here the
pulp-and-paper industry was highly integrated. For example, nearly
half the pulp that E. B. Eddy and J. R. Booth used in their paper mills
was supplied by their own, contiguous pulp mills. Their remaining
pulp requirements were filled largely by purchases from the nearby
Maclaren, Riordon, and Bronson mills. When the American tariffs were
removed in 1913 the Canadian pulp-and-paper industry expanded rapidly. In the Ottawa Valley investors responded to the new opportunities by integrating the industry even more: the new paper mills built at
Gatineau Point and Masson were financed by companies that already
had active pulp mills in the Valley. E. B. Eddy and J. R. Booth responded by expanding their already integrated businesses. As a result, while
newsprint exports to the United States surged, most of the Valley's pulp
production continued to be used locally.[13]

Ottawa Valley pulp and paper mills were never numerous, but they
were among the largest in Canada. In 1908, for example, the E. B. Eddy
and J. R. Booth paper mills ranked as the second and third largest in the
country.[14] Unfortunately, we do not know how much pulp and paper was
manufactured in Valley mills. However, in the early years of the industry,
figures showing the rated capacity (the tonnage that each mill was capable of producing) of all pulp-and-paper manufacturers in Canada were
periodically published. These figures[15] show that Ottawa Valley mills
increased their capacity to produce pulp and paper prodigiously in the
first 30 years of industrial operations. However, the industry was growing
rapidly in other areas of Canada at this time too, and the figures show
that the Valley was only a moderate performer on the national stage.

Pulp-and-paper manufacturing in the Ottawa Valley did not achieve the premier status that timbering and lumbering had gained in earlier years, but the new industry proved of great value nonetheless. It had a strong, revitalizing impact on the economy and people of the Valley. Just as lumbering went into decline, pulp and paper arrived to provide a new outlet for the Valley's rich forest endowment, saving thousands of bush jobs in the process. And for those who got work in the pulp and paper mills, the new industry offered more lucrative employment opportunities than did sawmills: manufacturing pulp and paper required higher skills than sawing lumber, so wage levels were higher. Moreover, unlike lumbering, the pulp-and-paper industry could operate in any season, thus bringing more stability to the labour force. That industry is still healthy today, and continues to be a significant employer in many parts of the Ottawa Valley. The Valley's long tradition of going into the bush to harvest timber remains alive today because of the demand of paper mills for pulpwood.

7

SHANTYMEN

"The men are off to the shanties again." These words were heard every fall up and down the Ottawa Valley, and the men referred to were known everywhere as shantymen. Shantymen were the workers of the forest industry, and they did many different jobs in it. The word shantyman was generic and included those who felled the big pines and those who hewed them into marketable timbers; it included the teamsters who hauled the sawlogs to driveable streams, as well as the blacksmiths who shod their horses; it included the river drivers who moved the wood down the Valley's tributaries and the raftsmen who took the square-timber cribs down the Ottawa and St. Lawrence rivers to Quebec. A shantyman's work could take three seasons: a winter cutting and hauling in the bush, spring on the river-drive, and a summer of rafting. Some men worked all three seasons, others one or two, but even if they did not live in shanties in spring or summer, they were all shantymen nonetheless. These men formed a small, but well known, subculture in the nineteenth century. From the earliest years of the forest industry, the Canadian public held strong feelings about shantymen, feelings that evolved over the years. Indeed, the public image of shantymen passed through three stages that can be summed up as the bad, the pitiful, and the good.

For many in the public, shantymen were seen only as dirty, dishevelled, drunken, depraved, improvident, reckless, dangerous, thieving, brawling, blaspheming vagabonds (not many insults were spared). Few in the wider population knew anything about the long months the men spent toiling peacefully and productively in their isolated shanties. What the public saw and heard about was men coming out of the bush in springtime, looking for a drink and a fight (and sometimes a woman); they were men who would throw away their whole winter's pay in a short, hectic spree. The shantymen who returned directly and peacefully to their homes were not noticed. It was the river drivers and raftsmen who were taking the winter's harvest downriver who attracted public attention as they drank, caroused, and fought all the way down the Ottawa River to Montreal and Quebec. Usually they simply scandalized communities along the way by beating one another up; sometimes, however, they were accused of vandalism and petty theft as they passed through.

The shantyman's bad reputation was established quite early. A fur trader heading up the Ottawa bound for the North-West in 1829 wrote that local communities were

> kept in continued bodily fear from those villainous raftmen or shantymen who on their way to Quebec commit every species of cruelty and injustice on the peaceable settler. The poor farmer thinks himself happy if he can escape the depredations of these unprincipled lords at the expense perhaps of his only hen or goose or perhaps one of his two sheep. . . . [Shantymen] are the most depraved and dissipated set of villains on earth.[1]

Three years earlier a group of raftsmen, refused credit in the taverns of Bytown, plundered several establishments and beat up the proprietors.[2] The shantyman's public image hit its lowest point in the 1830s, when residents of Bytown witnessed Irish newcomers, known as "Shiners" (see below), fighting savagely to get jobs in the timber trade. As decades passed, however, laws were more effectively enforced and local populations felt less threatened. Nevertheless, the Valley's shantymen were branded with a reputation for disorderly conduct through much of the nineteenth century, especially as local newspapers seemed to take delight in reporting incidents of scandalous behaviour.[3]

At the same time, however, some people began to feel that shanty-men were more to be pitied than maligned; that they were, in truth, more victims than villains; that they were victims of misunderstanding or unwarranted slander. Some pointed out that these men were victims of predatory sharks, who took advantage of their vulnerability when they came out of the bush in the spring and fleeced them of all their earnings. Some began to see valid reasons for the shantyman's unre-fined conduct: it was perfectly understandable for men who had spent seven or eight months doing hard, unpleasant work, far from the delights of society, to indulge in a spree on their return. Moreover, the work they did was dangerous to life, limb, and health: some died on the job and more were maimed. Equally important, people began to acknowledge that the work shantymen did was of great value to the national economy. And if they led vagabond, rootless lives, maybe it was because they could not find steady work in their home communi-ties.[4] To one observer, John MacTaggart (an engineer working on the construction of the Rideau Canal), the shantyman's bad public image was the result of the sneers of an effete, hypocritical, urban bourgeoisie. MacTaggart allowed that the Ottawa Valley shantyman was known to drink and fight and throw away his money, but, as he noted,

these things being perfectly natural to the shantyman, he could hardly endure life without them. In the conceited towns he is held in abhorrence by the clerk and counter-jumper, who know no more of the laws of Nature, or the elements of human life, than a parcel of magpies. They fancy that the wood-cutter from the wilderness should be made up of nods and smiles, starch and ruffles, like their dear affected selves, never thinking that he is a creature by himself, like the sailor, bred amid dangers and difficulties, and made somewhat rogu-ish by the sharking rogues of the cities. . . . The lumberman, [another name sometimes used for the shantyman] with all his roughness of manner, is the person who does good to the

country. He brings an article to market with much risk. He . . .
is the means of bringing the greater portion of cash to Canada.
. . . To get a lumberman in debt is the drift of the storekeeper,
as there he keeps his victim, feeds, clothes, kicks, and tanta-
lizes him to madness, making him a character far worse than
he otherwise would be. . . . The lumberman has a rough beard,
a wild countenance, is in the habit of using uncouth language,
and performing many ugly actions, certainly. . . . [Still] the
poor lumbermen and shantymen are not properly represented; we have the tales of the cities respecting them, and these
are false. To know them . . . we must live with them for a time,
and partake of all their joys and sorrows; we must run the
rapids with them, and get well wet with spray and sweat alter-
nately, then begin to judge of their character.[5]

Around the end of the nineteenth century, the public's image of shantymen began to change from the bad or the pitiful to one of romantic
admiration; these tough workers now became paragons of gallantry
and manliness. (This turnabout was also seen in other all-male sub-
cultures, such as those of voyageurs, sailors, and cowboys, whose
images also evolved from defamation to romanticization.) Shantymen
were now seen as men who lived close to nature, blithely facing danger every day. They were seen as athletes who could fell a tree in two or
three swings of an axe and who could dance on logs as they rode down
white-water rivers.[6] They were still known as fighters, but more now as
righteous defenders of the underdog. In Quebec, nationalist writers
embellished the fighting exploits of a real-life Valley raftsman, Joe
Montferrand (1802-1864), and made him a legend. Portraying him as
the champion of his people, they told tales of him thrashing the tough-
est, meanest English, Irish, and Scottish bullies along the Ottawa River,
often taking on many foes at a time. The Joe Montferrand of popular
legend was depicted as a giant of a man who embodied the ideals of
French Canadian character — strength, bravery, generosity, politeness,
perseverance, religious fidelity. The fighting raftsman became a national hero in Quebec. He was later adopted in English Canada as Joe

Mufferaw, a giant who performed mighty deeds in the wilderness. He may also have been the model for the American folk hero Paul Bunyan.[7]

In English Canada, evolving attitudes towards shantymen were highlighted by two events at the turn of the century. In 1901 the Duke of York (the future King George V) paid a royal visit to Canada, and, understandably, one of his most important stops was in the nation's capital. In Ottawa the formal welcoming ceremonies focussed on the Valley's timber and lumber trades, especially the romantic aspects. After running the Chaudière timber slide with Prime Minister Laurier, the duke and his duchess were taken to Rockcliffe Park, where shantymen showed off their skills in tree-felling and log-rolling. The royal party was then treated to a meal of pork and beans in an "authentic" shanty specially built for the occasion. Reporters covering the royal tour for British, American, and Canadian newspapers paid a good deal of attention in their stories to the brawny, colourfully attired shantymen. The result was that the exciting and exotic lives led by Ottawa Valley bushmen and rivermen were widely publicized and became part of Canada's mythic treasury.[8]

Later the same year, the publication of the novel *The Man from Glengarry: A Tale of the Ottawa*, by Ralph Connor (the pen name of Rev. Charles W. Gordon), changed public opinion further. In this book, set in the 1850s, two young blueblood ladies go down to the Quebec City waterfront to ogle the dashing shantymen arriving on their timber rafts. They succeed in meeting one of the men, a young Scottish Canadian from Glengarry County, who is known to one of the ladies. Invited to join their social circle, the shy man from the wilderness is contrasted with a foppish, worldly, English military officer serving in the Quebec City garrison. From the outset, it is obvious that Connor has found a new subject to fill the role of a wholly Canadian, romantic hero — the unpretentious shantyman, unpolished but considerate, pious and modest, athletic and strong, a formidable fighter — but only in a defensive role. Connor's book was a bestseller in its day and is still in print more than a hundred years later; it was made into a movie in the 1920s. The shantyman's new, improved image became standard in the twentieth century, and manliness was the central point of that image.[9] In later years, his manly exploits were taken to an affectionate level of cartoonishness and spoofery in the animated film *The Log Drivers' Waltz*,[10] and the Stompin' Tom Connors song "Big Joe Mufferaw."

Shantymen were not unique to the Ottawa Valley. Men who did this kind of work were an important part of the economy in the St. John and Miramichi valleys of New Brunswick, in the Saguenay and St. Maurice regions of Quebec, in the Trent River valley and the Great Lakes hinterlands of Ontario, and even in Michigan. They all lived similar lives, but it was the Ottawa Valley shantyman who was best known to Canadians. After all, the Valley was the leading producer of timber and lumber in Canada for a good part of the nineteenth century. As well, these men, with their colourful clothing and high-spirited carousing, were highly conspicuous on the streets of cities such as Ottawa, Hull, Montreal, and Quebec. The public image of shantymen across Canada, whether good, bad, or pitiful, was essentially formed in the Ottawa Valley.

WORKING IN THE BUSH

Every autumn, for more than a century, battalions of men volunteered to perform manly toil, living in shanties in remote reaches of the Ottawa Valley. There they dwelled in a totally masculine world (no women are known to have worked in the Valley's shanties, though some lived with their husbands at logging farms).[11] It is difficult to say precisely how many men went to work each year in the shanties, though it is clear that the numbers fluctuated annually as timber and lumber prices went up and down. However, an informed estimate made during the peak years of production in the Valley (the 1880s) put the figure at more than 8,000 men.[12]

The word "shantyman" may have had its origin in the Ottawa Valley. The word "shanty" itself comes from the French *chantier*, meaning a workplace. In nineteenth-century North America, shanty had two meanings. In a general sense, it denoted a crudely built wooden dwelling, often the first erected by settlers as they cleared their land;

today, the word is used to designate a low-quality tenement. In a more specific form, shanty referred to the rough, temporary, multi-purpose structures built in the bush for use in harvesting timber; today, it would be called a "logging camp." The earliest known use of the word "shantyman" dates from 1821. In a letter to a government official, an Ottawa Valley settler, Hamnet Pinhey, complained about the "Shanty Men . . . employed in falling, squaring and rafting the pines" of his area, describing them as "habituated to a roving and . . . dissolute life."[13] The first known appearance of the word in a published form can be seen in an 1829 travel book written by the engineer, John MacTaggart. He explained to his readers that shantymen were those who "cut down the pine trees . . . [and] live in huts in the woods . . . [that] are called shanties, . . . hence, shantymen."[14] The word "shantyman" remained in common use well into the twentieth century in Canada and parts of the United States, but today it has been replaced by "logger" or "lumberjack."

The men who populated the Valley's shanties came from a variety of backgrounds. Occasionally, a small operator would scrape together enough money to finance a season's work in the bush, hire a few friends and relatives, and spend the winter timbering with them in a shanty. In these cases, the timberman (who invested the money) lived as a shantyman, sharing the work equally with his workers. However, as the business became more complex over the years, it became rare to find a timberman actually doing the work in the bush; he usually found he had only enough time for occasional visits to his shanties.

By the second half of the nineteenth century, the shanty labour force was generally made up of two classes of workers: part-timers, who followed other occupations in the off-season, and men who considered themselves full-time professionals. The part-timers included both farmers, who left the shanties as soon as the cutting and hauling tasks ended and hurried home for spring planting, as well as men who left at the same time to work in the big lumber mills when sawing operations resumed in the spring. Professionals, on the other hand, generally stayed on the employer's payroll to work as river drivers and raftsmen; when finished, these men usually spent the rest of the summer resting, either in the Ottawa-Hull area or in their home regions. Shantymen hired as teamsters usually came from the nearest settled townships, while the rest came from every township in the Valley and even far beyond. For example, the 1861 census shows that shanties in the remote Timiskaming area were drawing men from as far as Grenville and Glengarry counties in Ontario and St-Hyacinthe, Trois-Rivières, and Quebec City in Quebec. By the turn of the twentieth century, men were coming from the Gaspé, 500 miles away, to work in the Valley's shanties. Shanty populations included men of English, Irish, and Scottish Canadian descent, but French Canadians predominated, especially among the professionals (one estimate reckoned that French Canadians made up 70 percent of the Valley workforce). Some Aboriginals are also known to have been employed in the shanties and, by the turn of the twentieth century, Polish immigrants (recently settled in Renfrew County) were brought into the mix. Some shanties were restricted to men of the same ethnic background, but most were mixed, housing men of two, three, or four nationalities. Despite differences in work arrangements, place of residence, ethnicity, language, and religion, these men shared a number of important qualities: strong backs, a willingness to endure the hardships and dangers of shanty life, and a pride in the work they did.[15]

In the Ottawa Valley, the most important shanty building was commonly called a "camboose shanty," from the French *cambuse* (referring to the large, open fireplace used for both cooking and heating). The camboose shanty became the central feature of the shantyman's life as it was used for many functions at once: cooking, eating, and sleeping; laundry and ablutions; recreation; and even storage of equipment and provisions. Intended to last for only a few years, the walls of the shanty were roughly constructed of green logs chinked with mud, moss, and bits of wood; the side walls seldom rose higher than six feet, the gable ends only ten feet to the peak. The building was roofed by "scoops" (logs hollowed out like troughs) placed side by side; by alternating the convex and concave surfaces and resting the edge of one scoop on another, every other scoop formed a channel to carry off rain and melting snow. The roof featured a large opening in the centre, with a short,

Camboose shanty, Blanche River, Quebec, 1875. All of these men lived in this low-roofed shanty.

wooden chimney rising above it; the opening allowed the smoke of the camboose to escape and, at the same time, let air and light in (early shanties had no windows and only one small door). The floor was formed of roughly hewn timbers. The only material employed to build the camboose shanty was wood cut from trees felled on site (few nails or spikes were used); the only construction tools needed were axes, saws, cant hooks, and augers. The advance party of shantymen, sent ahead of the main gang in September, could usually complete the job in a week or so.

The interior of the shanty was dominated by the camboose, which sat in the centre of the building. It consisted of a square frame of hardwood timber (six to 12 feet square), holding a foot or so of sand or gravel on which a fire was kept burning day and night. Posts stood at each corner of the camboose to hold cooking implements, including the sturdy, adjustable crane that swung heavy pots and kettles out over the fire. Three walls of the shanty were lined with double-tiered bunks in which the men slept with their feet to the fire. Sometimes two men had to share a bunk, sleeping together on a mattress of balsam boughs or hay and covering themselves with heavy woollen blankets. A wooden bench

The interior of a camboose shanty. Note the crane holding the heavy cooking pot over the fire and the men lying in bunks in the rear.

sat at the end of each bunk on which the men would sit and eat for there were no chairs and only the cook had a table. The rest of the shanty interior was cluttered with piles of firewood, barrels of water, crates of food supplies, a desk for the foreman or clerk, and grindstones for sharpening axes.[16]

As the timber and lumber trades grew over the decades, so did the number of men and shanty buildings. Small timbering ventures with fewer than ten men were common in the early years, and some persisted until the end of the nineteenth century. Generally, however, shanties grew larger, with some accommodating up to 70 men. In addition to the camboose shanty, every operation, small or large, had to have at least two other buildings — stables and privies. Over time, the number of buildings increased as employers tried to provide for more specialized needs. Among the first additions were blacksmith's workshops and separate storehouses to hold feed for the animals and food for the men. By the end of the century, larger outfits were providing

A post-camboose shanty. A stove has replaced the bulky camboose oven freeing up more interior space. The addition of windows allows better lighting.

individual buildings to serve as cookeries, dining halls, laundries, bunkhouses, and the foreman's quarters. The new-style shanty buildings combined both traditional and modern materials: logs for the walls, but tarpaper and boards for the gable ends and roofs. By this time, box stoves and cooking ranges had come into common use in the settled parts of Canada; now they came to the shanties. In 1901 the Ontario government stepped into the picture, passing legislation that mandated a separate cookhouse building and imposed minimum standards for shanty ventilation (300 cubic feet of air space per man), as well as for latrines and garbage disposal. Despite these improvements, however, the traditional, multi-purpose camboose shanties did not totally disappear from the Ottawa Valley; they continued to be used in some parts into the twentieth century, years after they had been abandoned elsewhere in Canada. The employers who stuck with the old ways claimed that their workers found the camboose shanty more cheerful and healthful, but perhaps they were simply trying to avoid the extra costs that improvements would bring.[17]

Everyone who lived in the traditional camboose shanties of the Ottawa Valley was treated equally (except for wages). Everyone, including foremen, ate the same food, drank from the same water dipper, slept on the same kind of bedding, and worked the same hours. But, as in any other workplace, there was a hierarchy of duties to be followed, a hierarchy that was evident in the payrolls. At the bottom of the shanty wage scale were the "general hands," unskilled labourers who did such work as cutting and maintaining the hauling trails and skid roads; this sort of work was usually reserved for newcomers to shanty life. In the middle range were the fellers, scorers, liners, and teamsters, who spent the winter cutting and hauling the wood. Next came the indispensable cooks and highly skilled hewers. And, at the top of the scale, was the foreman. The range in pay from bottom to top was not unusually wide, so wage differentials do not seem to have caused any discord in Valley shanties. At the beginning of the twentieth century, general hands were being paid $18 to $25 per month (including board); middle-range shantymen were earning $25 to $40; cooks were getting $40 to $45; while hewers took in $45 to $60. Foremen at this time could make between $50 and $75 a month, a wage that reflected the heavy responsibilities they were expected to bear.[18]

The foreman was the personal representative of the timbermen and lumbermen who paid the bills; he had to have their full trust for it was he who made the crucial day-to-day decisions that made the difference between profit and loss. It was the foreman who chose the site for the shanty and supervised its construction. It was he who decided what trees should be cut and how the wood should be taken out of the bush. And it was the foreman who was responsible for getting the most out of the workforce. Keeping the men busy at work for months at a time could be difficult, for life in the bush was far from pleasant: after a long, hard day of toil, the men had to spend most of their non-working hours in the cramped confines of a smoky, smelly camboose shanty. Because it took so long to replace men in these remote areas, desertion was the most serious problem a foreman faced. For a long time, it seems that the Ottawa Valley foreman's idea of human-resource management was the iron fist. On several occasions, foremen are reported to have beaten shantymen to keep them on the job. By the 1880s, however, a veteran shantyman noted that "the old, bullying brute force principle of governing [the shanties] is now about entirely done away with."[19]

Besides relying on the fists of their foremen, employers had other ways of deterring desertion. By the 1850s most Ottawa Valley shantymen were required to sign contracts (many of them marked with a simple X) when hired to work in the bush. One example of such a document, dated 21 September 1877, can be seen in the Ontario Archives. In this contract, Louis Fiset agrees "to labor for and faithfully serve Gillies Bros. or any of their foremen as a chainer or general hand . . . at the rate of ten Dollars per month, with the usual shanty board." He further agrees "to forfeit all wages if I leave the employ before the expiration of my agreement [no termination date was given], without just cause, or the consent of my employer or foreman."[20] These legal documents not only allowed employers to refuse to pay a deserter for any work done before he left but also allowed prosecution for breach of contract. In 1854, for example, John Egan had 25 men arrested in Ottawa for leaving his shanties without permission. The *Bytown Gazette* reported that the men told the court they had quit because "the pork with which they were supplied in the shanty was unsound, and unfit for use; so much so, that they could not eat it, and had lived for several days on nothing but bread and tea." The magistrates of Bytown decided that the Master and Servant Law did not allow them to consider the men's reasons for leaving. They were found guilty of breaking their contracts and given the choice of paying a fine of one shilling or spending a week in jail. Another tactic timbermen and lumbermen could use to deter desertion was to post the names of runaways in newspapers and threaten anyone hiring them with prosecution (a form of blacklisting). Historian Ian Radforth has surveyed the *Bytown Gazette* over long periods, looking for reports of employers using either of these tactics, and found surprisingly few incidents; as a result, he has concluded that the desertion rate was remarkably low, especially considering the thousands of men who worked in Valley shanties over these years.[21] Bullying foremen, threats of prosecution, blacklists, and the prospect of forfeiting their wages undoubtedly discouraged some shantymen from leaving work before their contracts expired. Nevertheless, shantymen willingly returned year after year to toil under conditions they knew could be unpleasant.

Work in the bush could also be arduous and dangerous. Shantymen spent their days felling mighty pines and hauling heavy timbers and thus were subject to back injuries and hernias. Still, many continued to work while injured, knowing that not only would they not be paid for time missed, but they would have the costs of room and board deducted from their wages. In addition, their job entailed working with sharp, heavy tools, in frigid temperatures, in deep snow, on uneven terrain; this kind of work inevitably led to serious accidents, and in the remote shanties, there was no hope of getting quick medical treatment. There were many ways to die doing bush work. Some men were killed by falling trees that landed unpredictably or that recoiled unexpectedly at the stump. Some bled to death after gashing themselves badly with their axes. Still others were crushed to death by logs that slipped while being piled on wagons or roll-ways.[22]

The men worked from dawn to dark in the bush, but as it was winter, their days were usually no longer than ten hours. This meant, then, that they spent more than half their time in the shanty, with its lack of privacy, poor hygiene, and other discomforts. Shanties were warm enough but dark and gloomy as the only light came from the camboose fire and a few candles. Lamps improved conditions when they arrived late in the nineteenth century, but the coal oil that fuelled them also added to the odours emanating from unwashed bodies and unlaundered clothing. An English traveller visiting the Ottawa Valley in 1861 was appalled by the uncleanliness he found in the shanties. He noted, for example, that

By the side [of the camboose] was a small wooden trough, which from the presence of a piece of soap beside it, and of a towel hanging close by, I concluded to be the contrivance for

washing. From the colour of the towel, I guessed it to be a public one, which I afterwards found to be indeed the fact. . . . The
colour of the [men's] blankets was beyond description, a kind
of smoky brown, verging upon dingy black. . . . [Even worse]
the all-pervading grease and smoke sickened me.[23]

Shanty owners provided little in the way of washing facilities, and
water was in short supply, but the men were not noticeably concerned.
More than one Valley shantyman has reported that his fellow workers
removed only their footwear when going to sleep. One recalls that
"quite a number would never change their under-clothes or shirts until
the clothes wore out, and as to washing their feet, such a thing never
came to their minds."[24] Inattention to laundering often resulted in
infestations of lice, but the men remained stoical, some even insisting
that unwashed clothing kept them warmer. Despite the poor hygiene,
however, shanties were not known as unhealthy places. Occasionally
influenza was reported, and in 1883 most of the shanties on the
Bonnechere were hit by an outbreak of diarrhea, causing many men to
leave. Contagious diseases such as these would certainly spread quickly in the congested confines of a shanty, but, generally, shantymen were
a surprisingly healthy bunch. Indeed, some spent their whole working
lives in the bush. Crawford Corbett of Nepean Township spent 53 winters toiling in the Valley's shanties before dying in a train accident.[25]

Doing hard labour in cold weather requires heavy inputs of calories
to fuel the body. Shanty owners seldom stinted on quantity, but the
food they provided was plain and monotonous because it was expensive to add piquancy and variety to diets in remote areas. In the early
years the men lived on little more than salt pork, hardtack (sea bis-
cuits), molasses, dried fish, and tea. Around the middle of the nineteenth century, owners made a few dietary improvements: bread, baked
in the sand of the camboose, displaced hardtack; beans supplemented
the pork ration; and rice and raisin puddings added a dessert to daily
meals. Finally, late in the century, newly constructed railways made
heavy, bulky, and perishable foods more available to shanties in the
Madawaska, Timiskaming, and Gatineau areas. Beef, for example,

could now be brought in on the hoof, adding fresh meat to shanty fare. Other additions included butter, sugar, potatoes for stews, peas for soups, and even canned goods. Shantymen savoured the change in diet, but some owners grumbled that it caused a decline in their health (but, again, the owners may have been simply lamenting the extra costs they had to bear).[26] Everything considered, shanty cuisine may have lacked many of the ingredients that nutritionists today consider essential, but it was probably better than the flimsy fare that labourers in urban areas were eating at the time, and there is no evidence that shantymen suffered from dietary insufficiencies.

Two staples — tea and salt pork — dominated shanty menus in the Ottawa Valley for more than a century. Visitors to the shanties of the Ottawa Valley never failed to comment on the quantity and strength of the tea consumed. One traveller reported that shantymen insisted on a potable "strong enough . . . to float an axe in." Another described the tea he found in the shanties as

> not the effeminate trash which we drink [in the cities]. It is, like patent medicines, a double distilled, highly concentrated, compact extract of the Chinese shrub. It is, in fact, a tea soup. . . . The taste of this tea is alkaline, and it has a decided coppery flavor. . . . On the Ottawa there are thousands of men who drink their pound of tea per week, and some double this quantity.[27]

The men drank tea several times a day, with sugar, no milk. Tea was probably the men's main source of vitamin C, saving them from the ravages of scurvy. Also, since they usually had lunch in the bush, the tea they drank there was important in maintaining both body fluids and heat in cold weather. Tea was the only beverage available to the men after alcohol was banned from the shanties. In the early years, timbermen provided their men with liberal helpings of rum and whisky, but the trouble these spirits caused among men living in the crowded confines of a shanty eventually led to a ban on all alcohol products. Not all timbermen agreed at first and indeed, the Wright family was split on the policy in the 1830s. By the next decade, however, everyone could see that prohibition brought improvements in efficiency, order, and safety. The prohibition of alcohol from Ottawa Valley shanties was never enshrined in statute; it was a practice that owners voluntarily followed and universally applied. They had, however, to guarantee munificent supplies of tea to substitute for rum and whisky.[28]

The second staple — barrelled pork preserved in brine — provided the shantyman's main source of protein. The pork was either boiled and served directly from the pot or cooked in stews. However, in the years before beans were introduced, little more was added to the stews than flour and pork grease. The men preferred their pork fried, but shanty owners considered this method wasteful in a food that was so hard to deliver to remote areas. In 1857 a number of Ottawa Valley timbermen joined together to declare that they would no longer allow pork to be fried in their shanties; however, the prohibition provoked strong opposition among shantymen, and the policy was relaxed for a while. Nevertheless, the question of frying pork remained a source of dispute for the rest of the century. Some owners even included a stipulation in the men's contracts that they must not expect fried pork in their shanty diet (the "usual shanty board" seen in Louis Fiset's contract of 1877). In practice, though, owners did not always enforce their own rule, so sometimes Valley shantymen were treated to fried pork on Sundays.[29]

Saturday night and Sunday were the times to do the things there was no time for during the work week. Few shanties in the Valley were located close enough to settled areas to allow men to get home for a day, so they had to make the best of their time off. Saturday night was the time to party: the men stayed up much later, playing cards and other games, telling stories, singing, and dancing. Every shanty seemed to have at least one fiddler, and one veteran shantyman recalled his amazement at "how proficient some of those log-rollers were with the violin when they couldn't read a note of music." He says they provided the music for both clog and square dancing, with "half the men wearing hats to represent the opposite sex."[30]

Sundays were quieter, most men getting extra sleep. Some attended to personal chores, such as mending or laundering their clothing and cutting new boughs to freshen their bedding. Few men were able to read, but this would have been difficult anyhow due to poor lighting in the shanties. Sunday was also the day the men could replenish their personal supplies from the "van," described as "an immense chest, made of the strongest wood, ribbed with iron bands, and secured by a mighty padlock," which only a foreman could open.[31] The van held a selection of goods the men could buy, particularly shirts, trousers, jackets, mitts, socks, boots, moccasins, and soap, as well as lotions (for sore bodies) and "pain killers" (which may have contained alcohol and even narcotics). The most common purchase was tobacco, for both chewing and smoking (most of the men smoked pipes day and night, with obvious effects on the shanty's air quality). Shantymen often complained that employers took advantage of them as a captive clientele, charging exorbitant prices for goods sold from the van. Employers, in turn, always denied making more profit on these sales than merchants in town, claiming the prices simply reflected the high costs of transportation to remote shanties.[32]

As the nineteenth century progressed, Canadian churches became increasingly concerned about the plight of the men who spent half the year in the shanties, isolated from society. The churches were particularly troubled by the apparent ungodliness of shanty life, fearing it would lead the men to moral degeneracy. The Roman Catholic Church worried about shantymen living so many months without benefit of sacraments and religious instruction, and it was the first to take action. In the winter of 1845, it sent two Oblate priests up the Gatineau River to preach the gospel, hear confession (important for men who faced death daily), and celebrate mass in the shanties. Within a few years it had established an extensive missionary program in the Ottawa Valley, and most shanties could count on receiving at least one visit every winter from a priest carrying a portable altar and holy vessels. Later in the century some shanties were also served by itinerant Methodist preachers and other Protestant missionaries.[33]

At the end of the century, Rev. Alfred Fitzpatrick of the Presbyterian Church took another approach to improving life in the shanties (as well as in mining camps and railway work sites). In 1899 he founded the Canadian Reading Camp Association (renamed Frontier College in 1919), seeking to spread the social gospel of the Presbyterian Church, especially the belief that education was the key to social reform. Fitzpatrick wrote that

> The isolation and consequent moral degradation of these [shanty]men, led us to the belief that they ought to be surrounded with home-like influences and innocent pastimes; that they ought to be kept in touch with the outside world, and led to sympathize with its problems by the beautiful in art and literature. It was felt, in short, that they should be given the privilege of an education.[34]

The first step in the educational program was to bring basic literacy to shantymen. In 1902 Fitzpatrick wrote to the *Ottawa Citizen*, indicating he had begun operations in the Ottawa Valley. He now challenged unemployed "school teachers or college graduates" to join his group and work alongside the men in the bush by day and conduct reading and writing classes in the shanties at night; his association would give the volunteers a $10 or $20 monthly bonus beyond the regular shanty pay. He noted that "candidates who speak French are preferred." Fitzpatrick needed cooperation from owners, of course, but two years later he reported that only one Valley lumberman, J. R. Booth, had given him any support.[35] The movement does not seem to have found much success in the Ottawa Valley. The local lumber industry was in decline by this time anyway, and the association turned its attention to other parts of the frontier.

THE RIVER-DRIVE

At the end of March, as the snows of winter melted away and the air smelt of spring, shantymen began to dream of getting out of the bush. Many would do so as river drivers, accompanying the winter's harvest down the tributaries to the Ottawa River, where the square timber would be assembled into rafts and the sawlogs and pulpwood put into booms. The spring drive marked the second season in the shantyman's life. Not all who had spent the winter in the shanties were needed for the drive, so this is when the part-timers left and headed home. Those who stayed on for the drive were the professional shantymen, men who were well aware that river work was both miserable and dangerous. Still, they also saw benefits in it. Work on the drive paid better than work in the shanties, it lasted only two to eight weeks (except on the Gatineau River, the longest tributary, where it could go on for three or four months), and the men were closer to home when it ended. The drive also offered some excitement after months of monotony and confinement in the shanties. In later years, however, opportunities for employment in the big lumber mills, which typically began sawing in April, proved more enticing than the river-drive. The growth of rail service also made it easier for shantymen to get out of remote areas.

Eventually, with fewer shantymen agreeing to stay on for the drive, lumbermen had to hire extra men each spring and send them up-country to reinforce their drive crews, so they could be sure their winter's cut of sawlogs was brought downriver. By the beginning of the twentieth century it was estimated that less than half the men working on the drive in the Ottawa Valley had spent the winter in the shanties. (Unfortunately, there are no exact figures that show the total number of river-drivers employed each season in the Valley, but one can make a rough estimate that, at the beginning of the twentieth century, about 3,500 were engaged in this work; in fact, 350 drivers were employed on the Gatineau River alone.)[36] It is ironic that, just as shantymen were finally gaining a more favourable public image, the men themselves were losing enthusiasm for the work.

Almost any kind of work would have been easier than the spring river-drive. The job was to move the winter's cut along small, up-country streams and then down larger tributaries to the Ottawa River while those waters were swollen with the spring runoff. It was imperative that the men, using pike poles and peaveys, keep the wood moving constantly downstream. The need to keep going often meant seven-day work weeks. The Lord's Day Act, passed in Ontario in 1906, prohibited work on Sundays and did not exempt the river-drive; everyone knew, though, that its provisions would be almost unenforceable in remote areas.[37] Some of the drives, such as that on the Gatineau River, were over a hundred miles in length. Depending on the amount of winter snowfall and the extent of April showers, the drive was usually over by the end of May. There were years, however, when water levels dropped quickly, and wood was left stranded until the next year's drive. Every river flowing out of the Canadian Shield was cursed by narrow, twisting gorges, where log-jams could be regularly expected. Over time, many of these hazards were made passable by single-stick slides, but not all. Some drivers were posted at these unimproved gorges to steer logs individually through the tricky channel. Most drivers, however, spent their time moving down the river looking for logs that had been caught on shallow or shoal and "sweeping"(pushing) them back into the mainstream. If they were lucky, the men were able to work from the riverbank or from the relative comfort of a pointer boat. Sometimes, though, they had to wade hip-deep in the icy water to do the job. Other times they worked while standing on a log, "birling" (rolling) it to remain upright. Log-rolling was the special skill of river drivers; it allowed them to dance from log to log and even to ride logs down foaming rapids, earning them a wide reputation for poise and agility. Despite their athleticism, however, slips and dunkings were inevitable. Working on the drive, then, meant the men were often wet for days at a time.

The men found little solace when they camped for the night. The only shelter was a lean-to or tent pitched beside the stream. If it did not rain, the drivers could maintain a warming fire, but even then their clothes were not always dry in the morning. A few lines from the Ottawa Valley folk song, "A Shantyman's Life" shows the men's misgivings about an upcoming drive:

When the spring comes in, double hardships begin
For the water is piercing cold.
Dripping wet will be our clothes and our limbs half froze,
And our pike poles we scarce can hold.[38]

The only comfort the river driver could count on to alleviate his misery was the assurance of plentiful nourishment. The cook's role on the

A log jam on the Montréal River. Breaking up log jams such as this posed a serious hazard for river drivers.

drive was even more important than it was in the shanty. He had to make sure the men got four feedings a day: full meals in the morning and evening, in addition to two lunches to sustain them during the day. As well, the chilling working conditions sometimes led the foreman to relax the shanty ban on alcohol and provide the drivers with whisky to warm their bodies. In reality, relaxing the prohibition was a proactive move to prevent drunkenness and desertion, for as the drive progressed downriver, access to saloons became easier. It would have been difficult to keep the cold and thirsty drivers away from the saloon-keepers who clamoured to serve them. On many drives, however, the strategy of providing whisky at the camp failed to stifle the appeal of the saloon, and bingeing sprees could not be avoided. Desertion on the drive was easy when the men got into areas with road and rail service, but some runaway drivers were caught and prosecuted by their employers. In 1888, for instance, two men were convicted in Hull of breaking their contracts and fined three dollars each or a month in jail.[39]

Working conditions on the drive were certainly miserable, but it was

the danger of the job that drew the most public attention. Accidents
were common and death was not rare; newspapers carried frequent
reports of drownings and other fatalities (especially those resulting
from collapsing log-jams). Most drownings occurred when drivers
slipped off logs or rocks and could not be rescued. There were also
cases of men drowning when their canoes, full of camp supplies (the
drive camp had to be moved almost every day to keep up with the
logs), capsized as they tried to run rapids. T. C. Keefer, a government
engineer, reported that 80 men drowned in the Valley in the spring of
1845.[40] This figure is hard to believe, but 1845 was an unusual year,
the first year of a huge surge in square-timber production; the death
toll was, no doubt, magnified by the greater number of inexperienced
men hired to get the wood out of the bush. As the century progressed,
the number of drownings declined. The installation of timber slides
and other river improvements certainly lessened hazards on the drive,
as did the replacement of canoes by the more stable pointer boat. Later
on, the introduction of caulked boots, their soles studded with quar-
ter-inch spikes, gave drivers surer footing when walking on logs. Of
course, life jackets, flotation vests, and safety helmets were not used
until well into the twentieth century. Moreover, few drivers could
swim; it was certainly not a requirement of the job. In any case, even a
good swimmer had little chance of surviving in the icy, fast-moving
waters of the spring runoff. Drownings were part of life on the drive
and were remembered in Valley songs; one, for example, commemo-
rated a driver who slipped from a log and

> As he could not swim, to the bottom sank
> On the cold Black River stream.[41]

The deaths that generated the most publicity were those that occurred
when drivers were called on to break up log-jams. In 1885, seven men
were reported to have died trying to dislodge a jam on the Mattawa
River.[42] When timbers, sawlogs, and pulpwood jammed in a river
gorge, they acted as a dam, blocking the whole channel. The drive foreman (usually the man who had supervised the winter's work in the

shanty) had to act quickly as water levels rose behind the barrier and the jam grew into a mountain of tangled sticks. First, he inspected the entanglement to locate the "key-logs," which, if dislodged, would release the jam (he hoped). Then he called for a few volunteers who would venture into the quivering mass of wood and remove the offending logs. It was an unwritten rule that no one could be compelled to take the risk, but shantymen valued bravery highly, and peer approval usually moved them to volunteer.

The foreman had a few options: he could have the drivers chop the key-logs out by axe or pry them loose with peaveys; on rivers closer to settled areas, he might be able to bring in a windlass, tie a rope to the key-logs, and yank them out. Using a windlass was a little less dangerous, but all methods required a volunteer to climb deep into the core of the jam and deal with the critical logs. This act (of bravery or foolhardiness) entailed undoubted mortal risk for the men never knew when the jam might give way. At the first sign of movement, the men had to scramble for their lives, jumping from one lurching timber to another until they reached the safety of shore. This is when drivers had to call on all their gifts of agility, speed, and sure-footedness. If they did not make it to shore they would be swept away by the surging water or crushed under tons of timber cascading down the channel. The only precaution taken was to fasten a rope around the men's waists, but this tactic was often of little use against such a mighty force, and many died. Most deaths on the drive happened in remote areas, and although the foreman allowed the men time to recover the bodies, the need to keep the logs moving usually meant the dead were buried quickly on the riverbank. Sometimes the fatalities were reported in newspapers, but certainly no inquests were held, nor any formal burial rites observed. Usually, the drivers erected crosses at the gravesites, lonely markers that wilderness travellers would come across many years later.[43]

Death under the weight of a collapsing log-jam is without doubt a dramatic event. At least three incidents of men dying in this manner in the Ottawa Valley were immortalized in song, becoming cherished pieces of Canadian folklore.[44] The ballad "Jimmy Judge" tells the story of "as fine a young man as ever the sun shone on," who died in 1864 when a jam on the Bonnechere River broke up and tumbled down on him. It gives particular attention to the intense grief his death brought to his parents and "the lass that loved him." Jimmy may have been an atypical shantyman for the *Ottawa Citizen* reported that he was the son of a prominent Aylmer physician. Another song, "The Jam on Gerry's Rocks," became popular in logging camps all over North America. It tells of tragedy at another jam on the Bonnechere River (the year not known). One Sunday morning, the drive foreman asked for help in removing a jam of logs that was quickly growing to great proportions. Most of the men were reluctant to work on the Sabbath, "but six Canadian shantyboys did volunteer and go," the song says. Shortly after, they were all dead, as well as their foreman, "young Monroe." Understandably, this ballad celebrates the "six young shantyboys, so manly and so brave" who died that day, but it celebrates the foreman who died too. He is not blamed for tempting fate by asking the men to undertake such a risky task on a Sunday. Indeed, a good deal of the lyrics focuses on how Monroe's crew were full of "sad grief and woe" on finding his mangled body. It also makes a point of noting that the remaining drivers took up a collection for the disconsolate belle he left behind. A third song, "Jimmy Whelan," tells of a log-jam on the Mississippi River in the 1870s. Three drivers answered the foreman's call for volunteers and were all swept away when the jam collapsed without warning. In this case, two men were saved (we are not told how), but the "noble-hearted Whelan . . . met with a watery grave." The song carries on to warn drivers to "shun all danger" and think of the grief their parents would suffer if they were to meet an early death. It is intriguing to see that in none of these songs do the river drivers ever complain about the work they are expected to do. They seem to accept the discomforts and dangers of the drive with equanimity and good humour.

By the end of May the high water levels on the tributaries of the Ottawa River usually subsided, bringing the spring drive to an end. By this time the men were pining to get back to the comforts of "civilization"; after six to eight months of exile, toil, and hardship, it was time to take their pay and go enjoy themselves. The drivers were paid off at the mouths of the tributaries, but paydays here could be turbulent affairs: sometimes hundreds of men, from shanties all over the adjacent hinterland, were paid at once. Naturally, these occasions were ideal for predatory saloon-keepers eager to supply whisky (usually of the lowest grade) to the thirsty throngs with cash in their pockets. Often the result was mass drunkenness and widespread fighting. Eventually, however, the shantymen would recover and begin to head south — by foot, steamboat, or rail. Sometimes they would stop in towns along the way to pick up more booze, and this could precipitate more fighting and occasionally petty theft (such as chicken-coop raids). When the shantymen reached larger commercial centres such as Hull and Ottawa, they knew they could get whisky any time; now was the hour to satisfy other neglected needs — edible treats, personal services, new clothing, and other adornments. In 1890, the weekly *Arnprior Chronicle* published a list of expenditures that one shantyman is said to have incurred on a three-day spree in Ottawa. He toured the shops buying earrings, dressy boots, a new suit, a pipe, a watch, and a ring. He visited a barber and had his hair cut, shampooed, and dyed. He had his photograph taken, paying for 24 copies. He cruised the saloons of Lower Town and indulged himself with three servings of oysters for breakfast. He lost two dollars when he bet another shantyman he could beat him wrestling, and had to pay a dollar for stitches to sew up a cut he suffered in another fight. Before heading home, he went through $96 of the $150 he had been paid.[45] True, such a spree was not uncommon among men celebrating the end of the spring drive, but the newspaper account was full of condescension. Stories such as this confirmed the shantyman's reputation for drunkenness and improvidence and allowed mainstream society to be suitably scandalized.

RAFTING ON THE OTTAWA

Not all shantymen went home at the end of May; there was still work to be done. When the river drivers reached the mouths of the tributary rivers, the sawlogs (and in later years the pulpwood) that they had brought downstream were turned over to the Upper Ottawa Improvement Co.; this outfit then took on the responsibility of delivering the wood to mills farther down the Ottawa River. However, the winter's output of square timber, which had also been driven down the tributaries, still lay in the water and had to be dealt with. Men were needed to assemble the timber into cribs and rafts to be floated hundreds of miles down the Ottawa and St. Lawrence rivers to Quebec City. More important, men were also needed to work as crew (some rafts carried as many as 80) for the two to three-month journey; these were the "raftsmen" of fame and infamy. Some shantymen had signed contracts the previous autumn to serve on the rafts the following summer, but others had to be convinced to stay on for a third season of work to fill out the crew. Although rafting could be dangerous, the job offered some attractions. For many shantymen, especially those living along the St. Lawrence River, rafting was a convenient way to get home (and, of course, they were being paid as they travelled). In addition, there was always excitement on the trip.

For the timberman who owned the rafts, choosing a pilot was crucial. The pilot's responsibilities were heavy for he was entrusted with getting the payload all the way to Quebec; a single raft could be worth as much as $100,000 (well over a million dollars today). The pilot had to make critical decisions along the route, balancing the safety of the cargo and the welfare of his crew with the need to minimize the owner's expenses. He was expected to know all the quirks of navigation on the Ottawa and St. Lawrence, conditions that could change from week to week. Without a good pilot, the timberman could lose a whole year's investment. Pilots, therefore, were paid at least double the wages of other raftsmen. Some pilots worked only on the rafts, but most were men who had spent the winter serving as foremen in the shanties. Most of the pilots and their crews were francophones from Quebec for they had built a reputation for skill and dependability. Raftsmen of English, Irish, and Scottish ancestry were employed in the early years of the timber trade, but they became rarer as the nineteenth century progressed.[46]

In these later years, however, timbermen turned to a new source of raftsmen — Indians, mainly Mohawks from Kahnawake. While a few

Aboriginals did work winters in the shanties, more were hired as raftsmen. Again, as in the case of the river-drive, it became harder in later
years to get shantymen to stay on for an additional season of work; timbermen had to hire extras in Montreal and send them upriver to make
sure they had enough men to crew their rafts. Mohawks were highly
regarded as raftsmen and were often hired as reinforcements. There
were even cases in which most of a raft's crew was Indian, including the
pilot.[47]

As on the river-drive, the potential for accidental death and drowning was always present on the rafts. On the open river, raftsmen were
vulnerable to lightning strikes (two died in one 1896 storm), and men
were thrown off lurching timber cribs or fell through spaces between
cribs (filled as they were with bark and other debris, the gaps often
appeared solid). The greatest danger, however, was found at the turbulent rapids and steep waterfalls that interrupted navigation along the
Ottawa River. At some, such as the Deux-Rivières and Allumettes
rapids, the pilots had no choice but to run the cribs through the white
water. The worst rapids and falls, though, were provided with timber
slides to carry cribs safely around the hazards. Still, timbermen expected their pilots to save time and money whenever possible, and, as a
result, pilots often decided to spurn the slide and run the cribs through
the rapids. Using this option, the pilot could avoid the expense of
slideage tolls and save time by not having to completely disassemble
and reassemble his raft (as has been seen, only one crib could pass
through a slide, but cribs were often able to run rapids in "bands" of
two to six). Water levels were the pilot's prime consideration in deciding whether to take the chance: at most rapids, low levels were the danger, but at some, high waters were feared. Each crib or band of cribs was
manned by at least two raftsmen, who used pike poles and oars to steer
their way through the white water, trying to dodge the immense boulders that blocked their way. Sometimes the pilot miscalculated the
risks, and cribs capsized or were smashed to pieces on the rocks. After
a crib broke up, the pilot was usually able to find and salvage most of
the scattered timber. The men on the cribs, however, did not always
survive. In the nineteenth century numerous graves could be seen

below the rapids at such places as Calumet and Portage-du-Fort. In 1889 six men were lost from a single raft (four at Rocher Capitaine and one each at Calumet and Des-Joachims) when the pilot chose to run the rapids rather than use the slides.[48] One wonders if these deaths were due to a reckless pilot or a timberman who pushed him to take undue risks. Today, much safer inflatable rafts treat tourists to a white-water experience at some of the same rapids on the Ottawa River.

Using a timber slide to bypass rapids and waterfalls did not always guarantee safe passage, however. Cribs would occasionally hit the water too abruptly at the bottom of a slide, throwing raftsmen into the river. A more serious problem, however, was the raftsmen's accuracy in getting the crib to the entrance of the slide. The men on board used oars and pike poles to negotiate their approach to the entrance, but sometimes contrary winds and currents foiled their manoeuvres. If the crib missed the entrance, there was no second chance; it was swept on by the swift current. Few raftsmen survived plunging over the steep waterfalls of the Chats or the Chaudière, where ten men were reported killed in 1835.[49] Still, there were a few remarkable escapes. In August 1854, for instance, a crib carrying eight raftsmen missed the Chaudière slide

The rescue of raftsmen at Chaudière Falls aroused considerable local excitement and this drawing was published within a year.

but miraculously got stuck on the brink of the falls, in part due to the low water levels in late summer. A wide chasm separated the men from safety on the Hull shore. Fortunately for the men, a large crowd soon gathered and effected an ingenious rescue. First, they threw a light cord across the gap, to which was attached a strong rope and, finally, a thick cable. The raftsmen fastened their end of the cable to the crib, while the townspeople built a tripod on shore to secure the other end. Then a ring was slipped onto the cable and sent across the gap with a second rope. Finally, the men tied themselves to the ring and were pulled individually along the cable to safety. The dramatic rescue caused a great sensation in Bytown and Hull.[50]

Rafting was dangerous at times and the work could be hectic, but it also included spells of peaceful quietude and opportunities for rowdy revelry. On busy days there was a variety of jobs to do. The men might, for example, spend their time taking the timber cribs through rapids or slides and then reassembling them into rafts. They might spend days recovering timbers that had broken loose from cribs while running through white water. On wide, slow-moving stretches of the Ottawa, such as lakes Timiskaming, Chats, and Deschênes, they might have to use long oars to row the huge islands of timber downriver. On other days, however, there was little for the men to do but relax in the sun as the raft drifted serenely with the current or was towed by steamboats. There were also times when contrary winds forced rafts to anchor along shore for days at a stretch, but then, when the weather changed, the raftsmen often had to row long hours (even through the night) to take advantage of the favourable winds. Still, the raft was not only a workplace, it was also the men's residence for the duration of the journey. Shelter on board was primitive. On some rafts each man built his own, tiny personal quarters from wood scraps; one observer described them as "a little hut, no larger than a dog-kennel, with just a hole in front by which to creep in on hands and knees."[51] On other rafts the men were sheltered together in larger, makeshift cabins built of rough boards.

Every raft had one crib set aside to carry a cookery with a sand oven similar to the camboose found in the shanties. And, just as in the shanties, there was always plenty of food. At the beginning of the voyage, when the rafts left their remote point of origin up the Ottawa, meals usually had no more variety than the customary shanty fare of pork, hardtack, molasses, and tea. But as the raft floated past more settled areas along the river, the pilot was able to buy fresh food, such as eggs, fish, and vegetables, to relieve the dietary monotony everyone had endured through a long winter and spring. More pressing, however, was the raftsmen's urge to relieve the powerful thirst they had developed after many months of teetotalling. They were not surprised to discover that many of the stopping places along the Ottawa River were well equipped with saloons ready to indulge their cravings. Some of the most nefarious examples were found near timber slides and rapids. Here, after running a crib through a slide or rapids, the men would have to pass numerous grog vendors as they walked back upriver to board another crib. A traveller passing the Calumet slide only a few years after it opened was appalled to see whisky vendors harassing raftsmen to risk taking a drink as they worked. He said they were "beset at every point by these harpies; and perhaps the sober raftsman, who in the morning ran the rapids with safety, before night loses his caution and his life."[52] Rafting accidents were often attributed to crews impaired by visits to riverside saloons. Alcohol also brought losses to the raft owner. In 1821, for example, a traveller reported seeing several cribs floating loose in the Ottawa River at Pointe-Fortune, having broken away from the main raft while the crew was drinking in a saloon. On other occasions, when bad weather might keep a raft snubbed to shore for several days, the men would venture into nearby towns and villages, where they would succumb to the enticements of eager saloon-keepers. Drunkenness and fighting ensued, and the townspeople would be scandalized. Whisky was prohibited on the rafts, and although pilots were fairly successful in maintaining the ban, it was hard to keep the men out of the saloons they encountered along the river.[53]

After the raftsmen completed their voyage to Quebec and were paid off, their revelling became even rowdier. The novelist Ralph Connor neither approved of nor condemned their behaviour in the port city. In his book, Connor explained to his readers that the raftsmen's drinking,

fighting, and improvidence were quite understandable: after all, their
sprees marked the end of many months of isolation, deprivation, and
toil. He told of the "hardship and danger" of their work and the "wild
surroundings" they worked in, adding that it was "small wonder that
often the shanty-men were wild and reckless." Connor went on to
show how local schemers took advantage of the men as they celebrated. He deplored how so many "a poor fellow in a wild carouse in
Quebec, or more frequently in some river town, would fling into the
hands of sharks and harlots and tavern-keepers . . . the earnings of his
long winter's work, and would wake to find himself sick and penni-
less."[54] After recovering from the celebrations, some shantymen went
to home to their families in the countryside, but, as years passed, more
and more made Quebec, Montreal, Hull, and Ottawa their summer residence. Wherever they went, though, shantymen carried with them a
reputation for drinking and fighting.

A REPUTATION FOR VIOLENCE

The worst violence ever seen in the Ottawa Valley came in the early
years of the timber trade (1835-1837), when gangs of "Shiners" terror-
ized the streets of Bytown and the waters of the Ottawa. A number of
possible origins have been suggested for the name "Shiner," but it was
most likely a corruption of the French word *chêneur*, oak-cutter, a difficult job often given to newcomers to the shanties (as the Irish were).
Irish immigrants were certainly used to hard work. A large number of
the men who laboured on the construction of the Rideau Canal were
Irish, but when the project was completed in 1832, they were left without employment. They had no money to buy land and lacked the skills
and contacts to get work in the timber shanties, where French
Canadians held most of the jobs. In their desperation, these Irish
immigrants were induced by a few unscrupulous timbermen, led by
Peter Aylen, to drive the French out and take their place. The result was
two years of dispiriting lawlessness in the Valley.

In the 1830s some Valley timbermen paid little heed to the government's system of granting licences to cut timber on Crown lands. These
scofflaws would brazenly begin cutting wherever they chose, even if it

were on private land or on a timber limit already granted to another operator. If challenged, they would simply have their shantymen impose their will by brute force. One of the leading offenders was Peter Aylen, an ambitious timberman of Irish background. Aylen saw opportunity in mustering tough, destitute Irishmen to help him improve his competitive position. Aylen (and others such as Andrew Leamy of Hull and Walter Beckwith of Westmeath) began hiring only Irishmen to work in his shanties on the Gatineau and other tributaries, even though they had yet to learn the arts of the timber trade. Grateful for the jobs, the greenhorns gave Aylen their loyalty. In effect, they gave him a private army, which he used to attack and chase away the (mostly French) shanty crews of his rivals and destroy their rafts and booms. The Shiners gave Aylen a decided edge in the timber trade.

After some success in the bush and on the river, Aylen turned his attention to Bytown, where he seems to have tried to take political and economic control of the community. Aylen and his army (estimated at about 200 men) launched a reign of terror in the town, highlighted by beatings, arson, jail-breaking, extortion, intimidation of magistrates, and political interference. Aylen fuelled Shiner fervour with lavish offerings of food and whisky (though the men were, no doubt, the willing agents of his bullying tactics). He proclaimed himself the champion of Irish rights, but this was only a ploy to forward his personal goals of wealth, power, and prestige. For a time, near-anarchy prevailed in Bytown and surrounding area. Raftsmen were assaulted at the Chaudière and citizens harassed in town. Some families left town, fearing for their lives. Ultimately, the town's establishment was able to restore law and order, and Aylen gave up his scheming. In the end, he still achieved his goals, though not in Bytown. In 1837 he sold most of his assets and moved across the river to Aylmer. He was now a wealthy man, and as such became a leader in his new community, a successful lumberman, a pillar of respectability.[55]

Peace came to the Valley surprisingly quickly, especially as the government began at last to pay more attention to this remote part of the province. For example, the justice system had long suffered because the only place accused criminals could be locked up and tried was in Perth,

50 miles up the Rideau waterway. In 1842, however, Bytown, the centre with the largest population in the Valley, finally got its own jail,
courthouse, and sheriff. And, in 1847, public security improved further
when the provincial government incorporated Bytown as a municipal-
ity, allowing the community to hire its first full-time police force. For a
while in the 1840s, violence periodically flared up in the bush: these
incidents were usually over disputed timber-limit boundaries, with one
shanty gang called on to fight another. Gradually, however, limit-holders learned the advantages of peaceful cooperation over aggressive
competition; the success of river-drive cooperatives had a calming
effect on all ends of the timber trade. The Irish learned too. In a short
time they managed to learn the skills of the timber trade, and within a
few years employers felt comfortable enough to mix Irish and French
in the same shanty. In Bytown itself, an Irish Canadian and a French
Canadian were elected mayors in consecutive years (1852 and1853).[56]

Still, the violence of what some called the "Shiners' War" gave the
Valley a reputation for lawlessness, a characterization that outsiders
persisted in holding for a long time. In 1849, a Montreal newspaper
sneered about Bytown's "base, ruffianly, rowdy population from the
Rafts and Shanties" and claimed that racial and religious conflict continued to torment the Valley. The Bytown Packet retorted with an angry
editorial, claiming that peace prevailed both in the town and in the
shanties. Valley people became quite defensive about the Shiner lega-
cy, even minimizing the violence of the past. In 1882, for example, an
old-timer recalling the past claimed that stories of terrible Shiner
excesses were nothing but "marvelous tales which had little or no foun-
dation." Shiners had committed assaults, he admitted, but these men
were a relatively harmless bunch, whose misdeeds had been much
exaggerated; he maintained that "no startling atrocities can be laid to
the charge of the Shiners."[57]

The two years of Shiner violence was one of the few times that shantymen could be accused of directly harming ordinary citizens of the
Valley; they usually fought only among themselves. Although violence
among shantymen declined after 1850, there continued to be occasional incidents on the rivers and streams of the Valley as well as the

streets and saloons of Ottawa's Lower Town.

One place that violence could break out was on the lesser tributaries of the Valley, where timbermen had not got around to establishing river-drive cooperatives. On these rivers, fighting was almost inevitable if more than one gang of shantymen tried to drive timber or sawlogs downstream at the same time. Everyone wanted to move the winter's cut along and get home as quickly as possible, so it was not hard for foremen to get their men to fight for priority on the river. Trouble often arose at bottlenecks in the river where men had to work from shore. Ralph Connor, in his novel, tells of how two drive gangs came to blows over which had first claim on moving its timber past such a constriction (this was on the Castor River in the 1850s). Haste was also important in rafting, and sometimes resulted in violence on the Ottawa River when rival crews wanted to use the same timber slide at the same time. One such incident occurred at the Chaudière slide one summer day in 1876. In this case, ethnicity added to the competitive fervour as one crew was French and the other Indian. Each vied to run more cribs down the slide than the other before the facility closed for the day; tensions rose, and, in the evening, fighting broke out. Ottawa police were called in and several raftsmen were arrested. The *Ottawa Citizen* claimed the French crew had been drinking and blamed them for provoking the disturbance.[58]

In Ottawa, police became quite familiar with shantymen over the years, especially in the city's Lower Town, which had become the centre of life for these men. As early as the 1840s, Lower Town started to serve as the main hiring point for the forest industries of the whole Valley. More and more shantymen began to spend their summers in the area's hotels and boarding houses, and timber and lumber firms would call there to hire them for the upcoming winter. Some hotel and boarding-house keepers were accused of inducing shantymen to run up large tabs at their establishments by offering the men credit to gamble and buy whisky. Sometimes employers had to pay off the men's inflated bills before they left for the shanties; as a result, some men spent their first month or two in the bush working to pay off debts now owed to their employer. Saloons did good business with the shantymen, too. In 1851 Bytown had 70 licensed taverns, in addition to an unknowable number of illegal grog-houses. Since there were only 7,700 residents in the town, most of these outlets were undoubtedly intended to serve the passing shantyman.[59]

In September the shantymen who had summered in Ottawa were joined by battalions more seeking jobs for the coming year. For a month or more, the sidewalks of Lower Town teemed with shantymen, many of them decked out in their distinctive, colourful costume: blanket coat, bright red flannel shirt, *habitant* toque and sash, corduroy trousers tucked into the boots. In this uniform, the shantymen could be taken for an invading army, and some citizens dreaded their yearly appearance. Merchants, brothel-keepers, and tavern owners welcomed them, however. Inevitably, there was fighting in the taverns and brawling in the streets; some free-for-alls were said to involve a hundred or more combatants. Although shantymen usually kept the violence to themselves, the police were often called on to restore order. Newspapers carried sensational and disapproving accounts of their misdeeds. The mayhem witnessed on, and reported from, the streets of the nation's capital only confirmed the shantyman's poor public image. The annual gatherings of the shantymen lasted until the end of the nineteenth century; by this time, as the timber trade was fading away, public attitudes were changing. In 1891 the proportion of drunk and disorderly charges laid in Ottawa was among the highest in Ontario, but the city's police chief did not single out shantymen as the troublemakers. In 1898 the *Ottawa Journal* turned nostalgic with a feature on "The Passing of the Shantyman"; the newspaper now regretted the imminent disappearance of these "picturesque French Canadian people" and, at the same time, recognized how their spending had done so much for local businesses in the past. There was no mention of drinking or fighting.[60]

PRIDE OF VOCATION

Most shantymen would have agreed that their life was one of toil, isolation, deprivation, poor pay, bullying foremen, monotonous diet, cramped and smelly shanties, and the danger and discomforts of river-driving. Surprisingly, however, they seldom showed any discontent. For example, there is no record of any collective action, such as work stoppages, ever occurring in Ottawa Valley shanties. True, few shantymen left memoirs of their life in the bush or on the river, so it is difficult to ascertain their private feelings. Still, the only hint of discontent found in the public record is an occasional reference to men deserting their shanties and periodic grumblings about low pay.[61] One place where the shantymen's private feelings can be found is in their folk songs; here again, though, the men show no bitterness about their lives. Many of the songs, for example, tell of terrible accidents, but neither foremen nor owners are ever blamed.[62]

Was anyone responsible for the high rate of injury and death among shantymen or was it simply an unavoidable consequence of the work they did? Everyone recognized the bravery shantymen showed while carrying out their tasks in the face of possible injury and death. But perhaps bosses, hoping to save time and money, may have been a little cavalier about the risks they expected the men to take. While this explanation is possible, there is no hard evidence to back it, and the Bronsons & Weston Lumber Co. records contain letters in which bosses urge their foremen to take precautions and put the safety of workers first.[63] (At the same time, there are no known examples of owners paying compensation to injured men or bereaved families, but this may be more of a twenty-first-century expectation.) Some observers have placed some of the responsibility for accidents on shantymen themselves, suggesting that they may have taken unnecessary risks in their work, that they may occasionally have strayed beyond bravery into recklessness. Contemporary newspapers opined that foolhardy behaviour may have contributed to a high rate of accidents.[64] Bravado was certainly not unknown among shantymen, and it could lead to recklessness. Stories are told of river drivers, for example, who showed off their bravery by accepting dares to ride logs through white water.[65] As well, some shanty songs carried warnings about the price of overconfidence. One, for example, told of "Johnny Stiles," who was killed dislodging a log-jam; Johnny was praised as a good man, "but he always seemed careless and wild." Ian Radforth contends that, in shanty songs, "accidents were more often attributed to chance, but carelessness could also play a role."[66] Still, though they knew that it could lead to recklessness, bravery remained a deep source of pride for shantymen.

Even though shantymen were well aware of the dangerous and disagreeable conditions they could expect, thousands of them still showed up in Ottawa's Lower Town every September ready to sign on for another year's work. Why would these men put up with such conditions? Some had no other option. For example, part-timers (sawmill hands and struggling farmers) needed shanty work to earn urgently needed cash in the off-season. And many full-timers (those coming from areas where farming and other job prospects were poor) were also drawn to the shanties by a need for cash. For others, however, pay was not the only inducement. For these men, going to the shanties may have been a means of escaping the social restraints of their home parishes, a way to enjoy the freedom of the frontier and its all-male culture.[67] Other men may have been attracted by the prospect of adventure in the wilderness and a life of physical challenges. In earlier generations, the fur trade had provided similar opportunities, creating a corps of *voyageurs* who headed to the north country every year. But after the Montreal-based North West Company was taken over by the Hudson's Bay Company of London, England, in 1821, fewer *voyageurs* were hired in Upper and Lower Canada. Life in the shanties offered a new outlet for men of independent spirit.

Those who chose a shanty life developed a strong feeling of pride in their vocation, a pride that helped them endure the seemingly intolerable conditions of their work. Shantymen had many reasons for this pride. First of all, they could point to their overall achievements; they could remind themselves and others that their labours brought considerable wealth to the country. More important, however, they took pride in the noble, manly qualities their vocation demanded. Bravery, physical strength, and endurance obviously counted high among these qualities. Yet another was cheerfulness in the face of adversity. After all, it would not be manly to complain about working and living conditions. In their own eyes, these qualities made shantymen a special breed of men. In later years their self-esteem must have been reinforced by their changing image in the public's eyes: mainstream society, which for decades had focussed on the shantymen's improvidence, drinking, and fighting, came to acknowledge their nobler qualities. The work that shantymen did could only have been accomplished by men with a strong pride of vocation.

8

TIMBER BARONS AND LUMBER KINGS

The timbermen and lumbermen who dominated the economy of the Ottawa Valley were accustomed to having the public, especially the media, attach noble honorifics to their names. Like many other industrial and financial tycoons of the time, they were routinely dubbed "barons" and "kings" and their investment holdings were called "empires," over which they were deemed to reign. In the public's eye, the measure of nobility was the degree of power and influence these men commanded, and that power and influence came from the size of their empires — the number of people they employed, the extent of the timber limits they controlled, the amount of money they circulated buying supplies for their operations. Those recognized as noble had to be "big men," large-scale operators with good staying power. A "timber baron" might be one who was able to send significant volumes of square timber (say a half-dozen rafts) to market every year for a number of years. Similarly, a "lumber king" might be one who was able to maintain high levels of lumber production (say ten million board feet) at his sawmill year after year. In the years that passed between Philemon Wright's 1806 rafting trip down the Ottawa River and the end of large-scale lumbering in the 1920s, hundreds of venture capitalists went into the bush to seek their fortunes. Many aspired to nobility, but few attained the rank. Only 50 or so succeeded in building their forest operations to a scale where they could be considered barons or kings.

The barons and kings, of course, were all male. There were no timber baronesses. The first time a woman is known to have possessed any degree of authority in an Ottawa Valley lumber firm was in 1921, when J. R. Booth incorporated his business and appointed his daughter, Helen Gertrude Fleck, to the board of directors. It is not known how much influence she exercised on the board.

Booth, like many in the Valley, was both a baron and a king. Most of these double- achievers (men such as Bronson, Perley, Pattee, Young, McLachlin, and the Gillies brothers) started in lumber and then found that good profits could still be gained in the old, established square-timber trade. In contrast, few of those who began life as timbermen expanded into sawing lumber for export (only Allan Gilmour and Robert Hurdman come to mind). Timbermen were markedly conservative. Even those who had amassed enough money to invest in large-scale lumbering preferred to stick with their first interest. For example, one well-known timber baron was Alexander Fraser, who sent rafts down the Ottawa River every year for nearly 50 years; despite his success in timber (he left an estate of three to four million dollars), he never ventured into lumbering (though his sons did, on a minor scale).[1]

The largest number among the barons and kings who ruled the Valley's forests were Canadian-born (Fraser was born in Goulbourn Township). Only one of this group, Joseph Aumond, was French Canadian (they may have found it more difficult to raise capital). Natives of England and Ireland were few, but Scots and Americans were amply represented. Americans were particularly noticeable in Ottawa–Hull, where seven of them (A. H. Baldwin, Henry Bronson, J.M. Currier, E. B. Eddy, G. B. Pattee, W.G. Perley, and Levi Young) gave birth to the sawmilling industry. Although the public continued to regard them as American for years after their arrival, most of them soon became British subjects. They quickly involved themselves in the community, joining local churches and supporting an array of charities. Six of them entered active politics: Bronson, Pattee, and Baldwin served as aldermen on the Ottawa city council; Eddy was elected both mayor of Hull and member of the Quebec legislative assembly; Currier and Perley represented Ottawa federally in the House of Commons.

GETTING STARTED IN THE BUSINESS

There were several ways to get started in the forest industry, and these can be seen in the lives of those who made it as timber barons or lumber kings. Some had the good fortune to be able to enter the industry at the top: these were men blessed with enough capital to begin operating on a large scale almost immediately. George Hamilton, for example, was able to build his Hawkesbury lumber business quickly with the help of his family's marketing and financial connections in England. Similarly, Allan Gilmour's early success was based on the wealth and commercial influence of his extended family in Britain. Men such as Bronson and Perley arrived in Bytown with sufficient money to build and equip large sawmills from the outset. The Gillies brothers were set up in lumbering by their father, who sold most of the assets he had acquired and gave the proceeds to his sons as an advance on their inheritance. Many families such as the Gillies, of course, also had sons who grew up in the business, but, in reality, only a few of the second generation were able to maintain their fathers' ranks in the forest elite. Some, such as the lumber king A.H. Baldwin, ultimately went bankrupt and had nothing to leave their sons; W.H. Baldwin tried to make it on his own and, though experienced in the business, failed to become a major producer like his father.[2] Others, like H. F. Bronson's son Erskine, chose to get out of lumbering altogether and invest in pulp manufacturing and hydroelectric power. E. B. Eddy had no sons and left only a small portion of his estate to his only grandson. Still, several sons did manage to carry on as second-generation Ottawa Valley nobility — men such as John Hamilton, Ruggles Wright, Robert Hurdman, Albert Maclaren, the Brysons, the Gillieses, and the McLachlins. For these men, the forest nobility proved to be hereditary.

Compared to these few who were able to enter the industry at the top, however, most timber barons and lumber kings had to take slower and more difficult paths to positions in the forest nobility. Some began their careers in the bush or on the river, learning the business from the bottom up. John Egan, who became the Valley's leading timber producer in the 1850s, began as a depot clerk, purchasing and distributing shanty supplies for an early timberman. William Mackey, active in timbering for over 50 years, got his first knowledge of the business while working on the construction of government timber slides on the Ottawa River and then worked as a shantyman for James Skead. Others arrived in the Valley with useful woodworking skills that gave them an entree into the industry. J. R. Booth, for example, worked as a carpenter on heavy construction projects before arriving in Ottawa. E. B. Eddy's first business venture was manufacturing phosphorous matches from wood splints, a skill he had learned before coming to Hull.[3] While probably none of the Valley's barons or kings came from truly indigent backgrounds, the paths they took to the top came close to the exalted "rags-to-riches" archetype; certainly, many entered the forest industry with little money.

Timbermen and lumbermen starting with little capital had few options open to them. In the early years, timbermen needing money to pay for the wages and supplies required for the next season's bush operations depended largely on advances from the Quebec merchants to whom they sold their products. Later, if they survived in the trade long enough, a few were able to pay their own way, using accumulated profits. For lumbermen, entering the business was even more difficult: they had to bear not only the costs of bush operations but also the costs of erecting large mills and equipping them with expensive machinery. A few of the lumbermen who started small and rose to the top (men such as Currier and Young) relied on silent partners to help cover these expenses. Private investors were hard to find, however, so most impecunious lumbermen had to rely on banks for capital.

The spectacular growth in sawmilling in the Ottawa Valley after 1850 could not have been accomplished without bank loans. The Canadian banking system matured at precisely the right time for lumbermen aspiring to operate on a large scale. In 1850, Bytown (population 7,000) had only three banks, but by 1878 the City of Ottawa (population 25,000), had nine. The experiences of J.R. Booth and E.B. Eddy illustrate the importance of banks in their emergence as lumber kings. For Booth, the single most important step on his path to becoming the greatest of all lumber kings was taken in 1867, when he acquired the rich and extensive timber limits belonging to the estate of the late John Egan. The limits cost

$45,000, and Booth could not have obtained them without a loan from the Ottawa branch of the Bank of North America. These timberlands, lying along the Madawaska River, ultimately proved to be the most productive in the Ottawa Valley, and the foundation of Booth's success. In 1882, E. B. Eddy had been sawing lumber on a large scale for only about a dozen years when a terrible fire destroyed his sawmill, planing mill, machine shop, and other wood-manufacturing facilities; insurance covered only half the losses. On the edge of bankruptcy, Eddy managed to convince the Bank of Montreal to grant him a loan to carry on (though he had to allow the local manager to supervise his financial affairs for a while). With the bank's assistance, he was able to rebuild his mills on a larger scale and with more up-to-date equipment — and, what's more, he managed to have the construction work completed and the whole complex back in full operation within six months.[4] Eddy's persuasive words at the bank allowed him to solidify his standing as a lumber king.

In 1874, four Valley timber barons and lumber kings (Alex Fraser, Allan Gilmour, George Bryson, and James Maclaren) joined some local merchants to organize their own bank, the Bank of Ottawa. In those days, if they could get a government bank charter, people could literally print their own money; Maclaren, who contributed nearly a third of the initial capital and served as president until his death in 1892, had his photograph featured on the bills the bank issued. His son succeeded him as president, and two other lumbermen's sons followed their fathers onto the board of directors. The "B of O" was widely known as "the lumberman's bank" and its emblem was the shantyman's broadaxe. Within a few years, most towns in the Valley had a branch, allowing the savings of the local population to be put to use in the expansion of the lumber industry (and in the making of lumber kings). The Bank of Ottawa grew and flourished for decades, establishing branches in six provinces. In 1919, however, it was absorbed by the Bank of Nova Scotia, as part of a movement of financial restructuring after the First World War. Its name disappeared, and the Valley lost its only homegrown bank; even so, descendants of the Maclaren family sat on the Bank of Nova Scotia's board of directors into the 1970s.[5]

For most of the nineteenth century, the Ottawa Valley timber and lumber trade was controlled by families or small partnerships. While many of the businesses were incorporated late in the century, they all remained privately owned. Whether partnership or corporation, usually one man made all the important decisions; he imprinted his personality on the firm, thus gaining recognition as a timber baron or lumber king. The St. Anthony Lumber Company would be the only exception among large-scale producers; its president was an employee, not an owner.

SUCCEEDING IN THE BUSINESS: QUESTIONABLE METHODS?

In the nineteenth century, the monikers "lumber king" and "timber baron" were a part of everyone's vocabulary in the Ottawa Valley. The words recognized the power these men could command and usually carried no hint of irony or ill will. The expression "robber baron," however, was different and certainly defamatory. This epithet came into common use in the United States around the turn of the twentieth century to describe the ruthless capitalists who were accused of causing grievous harm to American society. Shocking stories of big-business scandals south of the border were widely circulated in Canadian newspapers and magazines. These stories told of great fortunes being amassed through large-scale fraud; they told of businessmen bribing governments to gain lucrative favours; they told of insidious cartels engaging in price fixing to minimize market competition; they told of absentee owners who sucked the wealth out of one region and spent the proceeds lavishly in far-off places; they told of uncaring investors who got rich while their employees were maimed or killed on the job; and they told of employers hiring armed thugs to beat up union organizers and strikers, replacing them with more docile (often immigrant) workers. The robber-baron epithet could be applied to businessmen in Canada, too (Robert Dunsmuir, the Vancouver Island coal-mining magnate, for instance). However, although the timber and lumber tycoons of the Ottawa Valley were undoubtedly wealthy and powerful, their public image remained largely untarnished.

Still, there is no doubt that their behaviour was not beyond reproach. It is clear, for instance, that Ottawa Valley timbermen and lumbermen blithely defrauded the government of timber duties owed for cutting trees on Crown land (examples of such malfeasance by George Hamilton, Ruggles Wright, John Egan, and E. B. Eddy were seen in Chapter 2).[6] For these men, duty evasion seems to have been viewed simply as part of the general routine of doing business. No Valley baron or king was ever convicted of fraud, but, at the same time, none seems to have felt any embarrassment in breaking the law. These men probably would have pleaded that they were already making heavy contributions to the public treasury as it was.

When it came to facing the prospect of organized labour, the Valley's lumber kings were no different than any other industrialists of the time: they were hostile, and they succeeded in restricting union activity in their sawmills to a fairly minor scale. In the 1880s the Knights of Labor, Canada's leading workers' organization, tried but failed to establish unions in Ottawa–Hull mills (the seasonal nature of sawmill work made organizing difficult). Brief strikes were reported periodically over the years, but little came of them — until 1891. In September-October of that year, one walkout succeeded in halting the saws of all mills at the Chaudière: 2,400 mill hands walked off the job in Ottawa and Hull, severely limiting lumber production for four and a half weeks. The strike may, indeed, have been the largest industrial shutdown seen in Canada up to that time. In 1891 the average daily pay of an Ottawa–Hull mill hand was $1.06 for an 11-hour day (usually for a five- or six-day week). Lumber prices had fallen recently, and local mill owners (men such as Booth, Bronson, Perley, Mason, and Hurdman) acted as they always had in the past: they cut wages. This time, however, the workers walked off the job and within four days closed down eight mills. Remarkably, this collective action seems to have been taken spontaneously, without the involvement of any labour union. Still, like most industrialists, the lumber kings feared the prospect of unions; the notion of sharing decision-making authority with workers' committees was loathsome, and they were determined to keep organized labour out of their mills. During the strike, the mill owners succeeded in maintaining a fairly united front, though one or two offered to concede a ten-hour work-day (albeit at the reduced wage level). Some

owners managed to recruit a few strikebreakers to move lumber out of
their mills and got police squads to protect them. Militiamen were
called in to guard the mills (largely Ottawa public servants, these men
were surprised when their employer docked pay for their absence). In
the end, the owners outlasted the workers. There were no direct negotiations between the two parties and, after 31 days, the men drifted
back to work, with the lumber kings rescinding the wage cuts but
maintaining the old working hours.[7]

In 1891 the cities of Ottawa and Hull remained relatively peaceful,
but in 1906, a similar dispute in Buckingham at the James Maclaren &
Company sawmill ended in violence and death. In this case, Albert
Maclaren, head of the family business, locked his employees out of the
sawmill when they asked for more pay and shorter workdays. The mill
hands joined together to form a rudimentary union and confronted
management when it tried to move some lumber out of the mill. In the
ensuing melee, two workers were killed by gunshots fired by security
men, employees of a strikebreaking agency brought in by the company. Later, one of the agents also died from injuries suffered in the clash.
The local militia was called in to restore order in the town. Charges
were laid against Albert Maclaren, his brother, and some of the agents,
but they were eventually dropped, probably as a result of political
interference. Six workers, however, were convicted of participating in a
riot and sentenced to two months in prison. After revoking the lockout,
the Maclarens drew up a blacklist of over 250 men who were barred for
life from working in the sawmill. With this action, the family succeeded in keeping unions out of their business for another 40 years.[8]

Apart from the turbulent events of 1891 and 1906, labour-manage-
ment relations remained fairly calm in Valley sawmills during the age
of the lumber kings. Some Ottawa–Hull mill hands joined other workers to form a Knights of Labor local, which helped negotiate disputes
in the years after 1891. Still, no lumber king ever seems to have recognized a union as a bargaining unit at an Ottawa Valley sawmill. A few
walkouts were reported after 1891 (as at Hawkesbury in 1903), but the
Valley's lumber kings made some efforts to mollify their workers (and
keep unions out of their mills). A ten-hour workday became standard

at the Chaudière by 1895, and a few years later, some mills were offering accident insurance on a payroll-deduction basis.[9]

In 1910 a railway strike forced J. R. Booth to close his sawmill, rendering a thousand hands idle for a week; Booth, however, chose to pay them their wages regardless. When he accepted their thanks, the old lumber king made it clear that it had not been easy for him to make this gesture for he claimed that, in addition to the $12,000 (over $200,000 in today's money) he had paid out in unearned wages, the strike had cost him as much or more in lost business. Still, he said, "I felt I could stand the loss better than you could."[10] Business historian Michael Bliss has cited Booth's gesture as "an example of classic paternalism" and "benevolent feudalism." It is possible that Booth may have been motivated by the notion that "happy workers are better workers," but Bliss indicates that paternalistic acts such as this were typical of employers hoping to keep organized labour out of their mills and factories.[11] Regardless of intent, however, the workers could still enjoy the results. It would be churlish, for example, to disparage the McLachlin Brothers of Arnprior for their paternalism: in the 1890s they would close their sawmills one day a year and take their employees and families to Ottawa by train to attend the Central Canada Exhibition; all expenses were paid, including the day's wages. In 1899, 1275 people took part.[12]

In another form of paternalism, some Valley lumbermen ran varying versions of "company towns." A few (for example, Gilmour at Chelsea and Hamilton at Hawkesbury) provided housing for their mill hands. At Rockland, W.C. Edwards went farther: he not only provided housing, he instituted a system of "truck pay," whereby workers were paid in "scrip" (similar to Canadian Tire Money), which could be redeemed only at the Edwards Company store. The St. Anthony Lumber Company, at Whitney, Ontario, went the farthest. This town, in the wilderness of the upper Madawaska, was intended to be a fully controlled community from the outset. The company (Edward C. Whitney, president) owned all property in the town, and non-workers were denied residence. The sale of whiskey was prohibited, and drunkenness could bring instant dismissal. Single men were accommodated in com-

pany boarding houses; married men were provided with cottages and
large garden plots that they were strongly encouraged to cultivate. It is
not known how closely the rules were enforced, but the owners were
clearly hoping to maintain a reliable workforce at their big sawmill.[13]

While lumber kings sometimes showed benevolent concern towards
their community, they were not reluctant to use their economic clout
to get their way in local affairs. A good example are the tactics J.R.
Booth employed in the face of Ottawa city council's wishes that he
move his highly flammable lumberyards out of the city. For years after
the great fire of 1900, Booth resisted, protested, stalled, and threatened, gaining exemptions, postponements, and extensions to dead-
lines. The old lumber king knew he was arguing from a position of
strength for, as he pointed out more than once, he was the city's largest
taxpayer.[14]

J. R. Booth preferred to exercise his influence outside politics, giving
his support to candidates whom he hoped would look after his interests. Many other barons and kings, however, chose to enter active politics, beginning with Philemon Wright, who was elected to a term
(1830-34) in the Lower Canada assembly. Some of Booth's peers
served as reeves or mayors in their communities, and many sought and
gained public office at higher levels — in the provincial assemblies, in
the House of Commons, and in the Senate. In 1900 political urges
became so strong among lumber kings that two of them faced off
against one another in Russell County; here, George Perley, the
Conservative, challenged the incumbent Liberal Member of
Parliament, W. C. Edwards. Perley lost but later found success in
Argenteuil, where he won seven terms in parliament. As large employers of local labour, lumber kings were able to mobilize great numbers
of people to support politicians they favoured — or themselves, if they
chose to run personally. David Gillies, for instance, had enough influence in the Pontiac (where he and his brother did much of their logging) that he was able to win four elections to represent the county in
the Quebec assembly, even though both his residence and sawmill
were in Ontario.

In the early years, when voting was done in public (the secret ballot

did not arrive in Canada until 1874), the Ottawa Valley had a reputation for political thuggery and skullduggery, and lumbermen were
often complicit in the mischief. Late in life, one veteran political organ-
izer, P. J. Loughrin, recalled his role in the 1872 federal election in the
Pontiac, one in which both contestants were supported by lumber
firms. "My job, in that election, was to distribute about a hundred river
drivers we had brought down out of the bush around the different
polling stations to prevent anybody voting who didn't vote the right
way." As he said, "whichever candidate had possession of the polls got
all the votes at that poll." The day before the election, both parties sent
horses and wagons into the bush to pick up all the river drivers working for lumbermen who supported their candidate. In all, 350 men
were mustered, divided into gangs and sent out to the polling stations.
At Chapeau, Loughrin found that the opponent's gang was just as big
as his, so everyone there was able to vote freely. However, at three other
polls, he said, "we were supreme. Little fighting was needed. If our gang
outnumbered the enemy, the enemy withdrew. Such fights as there
were were real manly lumbermen's stuff – knock him down and kick
his head off, all fair and square." He claimed that only the gangs
fought, that voters were never harmed. As one approached the polling
station, "a good, firm sample of a man walked up to you and asked you
how you intended to vote. If you gave the wrong answer, you were
politely informed that it was no use trying. So kindly go about your
business. If you persisted, the gang removed you to a distance by gentle force." When the polls closed, the gangs were rewarded with ample
gin and whiskey and then returned to the bush. Most of the river drivers had no vote to cast as they were transient workers far from their
homes. Loughrin ended his account chuckling about how dead men
voted in those times. That day, he said he wore "four different suits of
clothes and four different hats, so as to vote for four men who had
passed away during the past four years. Both sides did this. It was one
of the little customs of the day."[15]

Businessmen have always been eager to influence government activities, both to protect and to further their interests. Most usually find
they cannot spare the time to enter active politics and choose, instead,

to help elect candidates who they feel will look after them. As seen in the 1872 Pontiac election, some lumbermen found it convenient to exert influence from the sidelines. However, the number of lumbermen who chose to get into active politics in the Ottawa Valley was surprisingly high. More than 20 served as MPs or MLAs before the First World War, though none left an appreciable mark on Canadian history. Only two gained a cabinet post, and they were minor. Erskine Bronson served for eight years as a Liberal minister-without-portfolio in the Ontario governments of Oliver Mowat and Arthur Hardy; he had no formal responsibilities but was considered the representative of the lumber industry. Later, Sir George Perley served as minister-without-portfolio federally in Sir Robert Borden's Conservative government.

It is difficult to say what benefits Bronson and other lumbermen-politicians gained from their politicking. Bronson was able to convince Mowat to grant a construction subsidy for J.R. Booth's railway to Georgian Bay, a project that benefited all timber limit-holders in the Madawaska Valley. He was unable, however, to persuade the Ontario government not to raise timber-limit fees.[16] On the federal stage, several issues concerned lumbermen. They complained, for example, about Sir John A. Macdonald's National Policy, which instituted protective tariffs and meant higher costs for the sawmill machinery and other imports they needed. Nevertheless, Macdonald managed to recruit Peter White, the Pembroke lumber king, to the Conservative Party; White was able to win four successive terms in parliament, though the tariffs remained in force. Another issue was navigation on the Ottawa River. Many lumbermen dreamed of the day when canals would be built to carry shipping up the Ottawa, Mattawa, and French rivers to Georgian Bay and the Great Lakes. Lumbermen failed to convince politicians to support the idea, however. For decades governments refused to even consider the project, and when Sir Robert Borden finally established a commission to enquire into its feasibility, it was rejected as impossibly expensive. Although it is difficult to point to any particular benefits gained by lumbermen-politicians, there is no doubt that all governments were sympathetic to their interests. After all, lumbermen were granted virtually unrestricted rights to cut timber on Crown land for relatively low fees; they were not required to purchase the timberlands they exploited, nor were they asked to reforest them after stripping them of trees. Governments helped these men build empires and fortunes.

As the empires and fortunes grew, the timber and lumber trades fell into fewer hands. Not grievously fewer hands, though, for, despite the strength of the barons and kings, there always seemed to be room for newcomers and small dealers. For example, in the middle years of the nineteenth century, John Egan was unquestionably the paramount timber baron in the Valley — in 1854 he owned one-fifth of all rafts sent down the Ottawa. Nonetheless, 80 other men turned out at least one raft of square timber that year. By 1881 the number of timbermen operating in the Valley had fallen by half, but the leading producer, J. R. Booth, accounted for only 8 percent of the total. Eight years later, Booth had fallen to fourth place in output, and indeed only two of the top five names were the same; the new leader, Robert Klock of Aylmer, contributed 13 percent of the total.[17] In all these years, there were always a few timbermen who managed to survive despite sending only one raft to market; economy of scale, it seems, was not absolutely essential.

Concentration of ownership was not an overly serious problem in the lumber industry either. While a number of lumber kings left the trade over the years, a few important new producers (such as St. Anthony's, W. C. Edwards, and Robert Hurdman) were able to join their ranks. Between 1880 and 1915, there were always from 12 to 18 large-scale sawmills turning out lumber in the Ottawa Valley. Over this 35-year period, the top five producers generally accounted for around half the Valley's total output. J. R. Booth led his rivals through most of that time, but his share of the total was usually only about 15 percent.[18] The output figures include only large-scale producers, however; they do not take into account the small sawmills that could be found in nearly every village in the Valley. Small lumbermen were able to survive because manufacturers had succeeded in designing small-capacity, portable, yet fully integrated, sawmill kits, which were both efficient and inexpensive. The 1901 census shows more than a hundred mills sawing lumber on a small scale in the Ottawa Valley.[19]

Although their numbers did not dwindle down to a precious few (at least not until the 1920s), the Valley's timber barons and lumber kings were never an ardently competitive bunch; they preferred cooperation. To be sure, in the early years their gangs had sometimes fought it out in the bush and on the river-drive. The Valley's most violent period was the "Shiners' War" of the 1830s; it was at this low point that many of the leading timbermen got together to form an association to find ways to resolve disputes and raise the timber trade to what they termed a more "respectable footing."[20] The association helped bring peace to the trade and led to further cooperative efforts. As was seen earlier, one of the first was the Madawaska River Improvement Company. This joint-stock company, chartered in 1853, built and maintained slides, dams, booms, and other improvements to facilitate the drive on the upper Madawaska; over the decades many of the Valley's forest nobility served on its board of directors. These men could see that drive facilities were an obvious target for joint action as it was hopelessly inefficient for each investor to try to provide his own. Success on the Madawaska led to further cooperative endeavours as joint-stock companies were organized to build and maintain improvements on several more rivers in the Valley. The best known is, of course, the Upper Ottawa Improvement Company, established in 1868 by the top seven lumber kings working in the Valley at the time. Another obvious example of cooperation was the Bank of Ottawa, the "lumberman's bank." Yet another area where lumbermen advanced their common interests was in railways. Good rail service was essential to every lumber king's success, but, again, no one tried to gain an advantage over others by building a line for his own exclusive use. Valley lumber kings such as Booth, Currier, Perley, and McLachlin worked together, planning and investing in new rail projects; others gave political support. Lastly, one further example of cooperation was in shipping: in this case, men such as W. G. Perley, H. F. Bronson, and James Skead collaborated to provide a reliable steamboat service on the upper Ottawa River for everyone's use.

Surprisingly, although the Ottawa Valley forest elite was not large, there was little intermarriage among the families. Nevertheless, the timber barons and lumber kings all knew one another and had many opportunities and forums where they could get together and discuss how to further their shared interests. The best examples were the lobbying groups they organized over the decades — the Ottawa Association of Lumber Manufacturers, the Quebec Limitholders Association, the Ontario Lumberman's Association. There is, however, no indication that discussion ever led to collusion; there is no hint they ever plotted to fix prices to their common benefit (this was made a criminal offence in 1900). Indeed, they showed early on that they were incapable of agreeing on even a common system of lumber grading, an expedient more easily accomplished (and perfectly legal). Still, while there is no evidence of price-fixing, it is certain there was little competition in lumber pricing because producers usually found it easier to simply follow J. R. Booth's lead. In 1908, for example, some Ottawa lumbermen announced small reductions, but, a little later, when Booth announced that his rates would remain firm, the others quickly raised their prices to his levels.[21]

In building their fortunes, there is no doubt that the timber barons and lumber kings of the Ottawa Valley often overstepped the lines of propriety and the law. However, the public did not liken their behaviour to that shown by the infamous robber barons of their era. Valley barons were not averse to defrauding the government of timber-duty payments. They disliked labour unions, but, with the exception of Albert Maclaren, they did not resort to strong-arm tactics to destroy them. They were not reluctant to use rough tactics in election campaigns, but there is no evidence that they ever tried to bribe governments to gain political favours. They did not always compete vigorously in the marketplace, but they never stooped to price-fixing. The indifference they showed to the dangers their employees faced on the job appears shocking today, but in the nineteenth century, these workers, especially shantymen, seem to have accepted the dangers with little objection. Nor could anyone complain about absentee owners siphoning away the wealth of the region; the lords of the forest chose to live their lives in the Valley, and their money remained where it was made (though, it is true, a few firms had foreign-based partners who earned profits from lumber, and a few invested in Pacific Coast lumber ventures in later years). Questionable business practices played only a small part in the making of timber barons and lumber kings. In reality, the Valley's nobility found success largely through following legitimate, conventional business practices of the day — especially vertical integration and diversification.

SUCCEEDING IN THE BUSINESS: LEGITIMATE AND CONVENTIONAL METHODS

For Ottawa Valley timbermen and lumbermen, vertical integration seemed a natural route to success; they hoped that controlling as many parts of the business as possible would bring them a measure of security and stability in an industry full of unpredictables. Cutting their own trees in the bush and driving their timber and sawlogs down the Ottawa River was an obvious first step in integrating their businesses, but there were other factors that could be controlled. Many of them, for instance, established logging farms to grow fodder for their animals and food for their shantymen. As well, some lumbermen built, operated, and maintained their own fleets of barges and tugs to deliver their products to market. Some built or helped finance railways to service their timber limits, their sawmills, and their markets. Controlling their transportation needs relieved some of their worries about having enough sawlogs on hand at their mill or getting their lumber to market on time. Doing their own marketing abroad, however, remained largely unattainable. Sales to Britain were made through export brokers, except for Allan Gilmour and the Hamiltons, who had family connections there. For sales in the United States, a number of lumbermen went to the trouble of opening sales offices across the border, but these still dealt only with wholesalers. Though most sold lumber directly to customers in local markets, no Valley lumberman seems to have ever retailed his products outside the country. Integration brought some security and stability to their businesses, but lumbermen found that diversifying their interests by making better use of waste material also helped.

Sawing logs into precisely measured boards produced a great deal of waste wood, which was often just burned as fuel or dumped into rivers.

It made sense for lumbermen to seek effective ways to use refuse slabs, edgings, butt ends, and the like from their mills to create additional products. Diversifying their production brought them new sources of profit and provided a cushion when lumber prices fell. One commodity that could be easily made from mill refuse was laths, wooden strips that served as a backing for plaster walls and ceilings. Many Ottawa Valley lumbermen chose this way to diversify their businesses, building separate lath mills alongside their lumber mills. They installed conveyor chains to take their lumber refuse to the lath mill next door, where a special set of saws cut it into the desired dimensions. The nineteenth-century construction boom in North America created a strong market for laths, and they proved to be a valuable by-product for Valley lumbermen. A large proportion of the output was exported, selling in New England, Pennsylvania, and Ohio. Another product that could easily be manufactured from mill waste was wooden shingles. Most of the Valley's lumber kings took up shingle-making, and it proved to be a profitable sideline, especially as shingles had a limited lifespan and had to be replaced every ten years or so. Shingles, too, found good markets in the United States.

It was an outsider, not a lumberman, who found a third way to create a profitable commodity from mill waste. Early in the twentieth century, Chester Pickering came to Ottawa from Boston with a plan to use sawdust — the most abundant refuse in a lumber mill — as a cleaning agent, particularly as a means to remove household dust. For decades, the only use that could be found for sawdust was as a fuel in steam mills or as an insulator in the storage of ice for iceboxes. Pickering added oil to absorb household dust, green dye for better visibility, and nitrobenzol to add a pleasing aroma. He called the new product Dustbane, and soon people all across Canada were sweeping their floors with it. With river-pollution regulations now being more strictly enforced (see Chapter 9), Ottawa's lumber kings were happy to sell their piles of sawdust to Pickering, and he made the city the headquarters of his company. In 1941 he used his fortune to build the Lord Elgin Hotel.[22]

One of the great success stories of the Ottawa Valley was E.B. Eddy's

match factory. Shortly after arriving in Hull in 1854, Eddy launched his
match-making career, his first commercial venture. Recent chemical
advances had led to the development of a match that could be reliably
ignited by friction, and Eddy had learned the basics of the trade in the
United States. He rented a shed from Ruggles Wright and began making matches by hand, dipping wood splints into solutions of sulphur
and phosphorus. His wife taught local women and children how to
package them at home. Within ten years he moved from making small
batches of matches manually to large-scale production in a mechanized factory driven by water power. He started by using waste wood
from sawmills already established at the Chaudière, but by 1870 he
had entered lumbering there himself and could use refuse from his
own mill. Progressively adding more and better machinery, Eddy
expanded his output steadily. In 1865 he was turning out 72,000
matches per day; by 1873, daily output had risen to 115,000; in 1891,
to 22,000,000; and by the time he died in 1906, production had
reached 52,000,000 a day! No one else seems to have tried making
matches in the Ottawa Valley until the Canadian Match Company
established a factory at Pembroke in the 1920s (later taken over by the
E. B. Eddy Company); periodically, however, small mills were built to
produce match splints.

In the early years, Eddy himself travelled extensively to market his
matches. His market was largely confined to Canada, however, for
American tariffs made it difficult to compete in the United States. In
1880 he tried to meet the challenge by opening a factory at
Ogdensburg, N.Y., and, at first, enjoyed some success. At this time,
however, most of the large American producers were merging to form
a gigantic combine, the Diamond Match Company, which soon controlled over 85 percent of the American market. Eddy was forced to
retreat to Canada, but Diamond soon opened factories north of the
border. Nevertheless, E. B. Eddy remained one of the leading producers at home. The census of 1891 shows that he was the second-largest
manufacturer of matches in Canada, with one-third of total Canadian
output.[23] Unlike other lumber kings, Eddy began his career using
sawmill waste to make a lucrative commodity; he used profits from

match-making to diversify into lumber and pulp and paper. Matches allowed him to survive economic slumps and gain renown as a lumber king and a pulp-and-paper pioneer.

Diversification and integration — these were the conventional business practices of the day, these were the strategies that lumber kings (and, to a lesser degree, timber barons) had to follow if they were to survive and grow for they were working in a high-risk industry. There were so many unpredictables. Forest fires sometimes wiped out the timber on the limits for which they had paid so much. Sawmill fires destroyed the heavy machinery into which they had put so much money. Too much snow could delay sleighs taking supplies to the shanties; too little snow could hamper hauling operations in the bush. Low river levels could cause timber and sawlogs to be stranded on the drive; high river levels could swamp the sawmills, suspending all work. As for the products that timbermen and lumbermen turned out, they were prone to wide and unforeseeable price fluctuations. And since the major markets were outside the country, news of price shifts was slow to reach the Ottawa Valley. Lastly, interest charges on the money they borrowed were hard to control for it could take from six to 24 months (depending on the weather) before their timber or lumber arrived at market and accounts could be settled.

Timber and lumber were classic boom-and-bust industries, with many bankruptcies and near-bankruptcies over the decades. Small or large, no one was immune to failure. In his memoirs, Sir Richard Scott, long-time unofficial representative of forest industries in the Senate, made a point of noting the high number of Valley men who had invested much but "died poor." Among the well-known timber barons and lumber kings who went bankrupt were John Egan, James Skead, J. M. Currier, A.H. Baldwin, and William Mason. On the other hand, many others did very well. On his death in 1902, the timberman William Mackey left an estate of $1,200,000. E. B. Eddy left more than two-and-a-half million dollars, and James Maclaren about $5,000,000 (perhaps $90,000,000 in today's money).[24]

LIFE AS A BARON OR KING

The forest nobility of the Ottawa Valley preferred to stay close to their businesses. Many came from afar, but they all made their homes where they made their money. Not one timber baron or lumber king born outside the Valley tried to run his business from back home. And not one moved out to seek the excitement of life in a big city; no one was seduced by the cultural attractions and better shopping of Montreal, Quebec City, New York, or London (Toronto in the nineteenth century had little to offer). Nor did they show any wish to mingle in wider, grander social circles than could be found in the Valley; they were content to act on a smaller stage at home.

Even on the smaller social stage of the Ottawa Valley, however, a timberman's economic power did not, at first, make him part of the elite. In the first half of the nineteenth century, when timber dominated the economy, the Valley's tiny upper crust was largely made up of gentlemen farmers, members of the learned professions, and half-pay British officers. The early timber barons were not accepted as social leaders; some, like the Wrights, were considered too uncouth; others, like Peter Aylen, too violent. The second half of the century, the age of lumber, was different, however, as lumber kings were increasingly accepted into the highest social circles. In the Ottawa Valley, the undisputed social leader after Confederation was the governor general. For those who cared about their place in society, the main goal was to attend the various fancy-dress balls and other gatherings that His Excellency hosted throughout the year at Rideau Hall. The invitees usually included politicians, professionals, judges, military officers, government officials, and lumber kings. The social historian Sandra Gwyn ranks lumber kings the lowest among those given entree to Rideau Hall, however. For some like J. R. Booth, wealth did not overcome their reputation for rustic manners and the rough nature of their business (he and others such as Robert Hurdman continued to visit their shanties regularly, even in old age). For those (such as the McLachlins and Gillies families) living outside Ottawa or Hull, distance may have made it too difficult to participate frequently in high-society events.[25]

Whether or not they had any aspirations to social rank, the Valley's barons and kings made a point of building houses that proclaimed their economic rank. The residences they erected were both opulent, and physically imposing. When W.G. Perley's new residence on Wellington Street was completed in 1875, the *Ottawa Citizen* described it as "palatial" and "perhaps one of the most costly and magnificently fitted up private dwellings in the Dominion. In the construction of this building, economy was never dreamt of, much less practised." The new Perley home rose three storeys above a two-storey basement. "The style of architecture is French, the brickwork being relieved by handsome sandstone dressings." Inside, the building featured a "ballroom with a domed and panelled ceiling, and an ornamental gallery in rear for the orchestra. The interior trimmings of the building are all made of black walnut." It also included substantial stables and a bowling alley. The cost was estimated at about $75,000 (about $1,300,000 in today's money).[26] Other lumber kings had equally impressive residences. For instance, Allan Gilmour's on Vittoria Street, near where the Supreme Court building now stands, included a conservatory and an art gallery. Another example was the majestic mansion built by J. M. Currier at 24 Sussex Drive, later bought by another lumber king, W.C. Edwards; today it serves as the official residence of the prime minister. In early Ottawa, the homes of lumber kings were certainly imposing, but they were not unique; there were other, equally grand residences evident around town, mainly belonging to merchants. However, in the small mill towns of the Valley, the splendour of the local lumberman's house was usually unmatched by any other in the area (the Maclarens in Buckingham and the Hamiltons in Hawkesbury would be good examples). To be sure, when lumber kings were building new, upscale residences, they were seeking to provide a more comfortable home life for their families; there is no doubt, however, that they were also employing architectural grandeur to make a visual statement of their importance in the community.

Understandably, the kingly homes the lumbermen built were usually erected after they made their fortunes. Most of these men, however, had begun their careers living in modest homes close to their sawmills (the big exception was Allan Gilmour, who had wealthy kin). Indeed, for many years after beginning their careers in lumber, all six owners of large-scale sawmills at Chaudière Falls lived, with their families, within a block or two of their mill. Their immediate neighbours included the men who worked for them in the sawmills.[27] It was a convenient situation for everyone, as both owners and workers preferred to walk to work. Even after they had made their fortunes and moved to more grandiose residences, the six still chose to live within sight of their mills. Similarly, in the smaller communities, the town's lumber king usually lived close by his mill.

Curiously, the mansions the timber barons and lumber kings erected were almost exclusively constructed of brick or stone, and, in declining to use wood in their personal monuments, they may have been snubbing the very source of their wealth. Most of these men had risen from humble beginnings and hoped that moving to a more imposing residence would mark their change in status. For them, brick and stone were more majestic and enduring — and these were important considerations when erecting a monument. This thinking can be seen in Fort Coulonge, Quebec, where four houses erected by the town's lumber nobility still stand today. In 1854 George Bryson built a wood farmhouse just outside of town, using lumber sawn in his own mill. Within two decades his timber and lumber operations had grown and prospered and two sons had joined him in the business. A wooden dwelling, however, was not suitable for the second generation, no matter how elegant. John Bryson was unmarried and only 22 years old in 1872 when he built a splendid stone house in town. His younger brother, George, Jr., was only 24 and recently married in 1876 when he built an equally handsome stone residence next door. When their father reached his retirement years in the 1890s, he too chose to build a stone house nearby. Surprisingly, the wood house he had erected years earlier was in no way a humble habitation but rather a large, striking, delightfully exotic structure, and though built of wood, it has also proved itself thoroughly enduring, lasting 150 years. Nevertheless, it was not good enough for George Bryson; even in his eighties, he felt it was not too late to upgrade his living standards.[28]

It is remarkable that only one Ottawa Valley lumber king ever built a personal residence designed to showcase the beauty, strength, and utility of pine as a construction material. It is true that some barons and kings took care to highlight these qualities in the interior wood-work of their homes (J. R. Booth's house, still standing at 252 Metcalfe Street in Ottawa, is a good example). But only David Gillies, a third-generation director of his family's lumber firm, saw any need to demonstrate the merits of Ottawa Valley lumber in house-building. In 1937 he erected a large, Colonial Revival house in Arnprior, in which he took pains to feature white pine that had been cut on his timber limits up the Ottawa River; all the wood used, inside and out, was sawn and planed at his Braeside mill. The unusually wide (ten-inch) clap-board cladding he used gave the exterior an especially graceful appear-ance.[29] David Gillies's house was perhaps the last grand residence built in the Valley by an active lumber king. His worthy effort came too late, however, for high-grade pine was now hard to find in the Valley, and lumbering, as a major industry, was essentially finished.

ALLAN GILMOUR AND J. R. BOOTH

Two men in particular, Allan Gilmour and J. R. Booth, show the range of personalities found in the Valley's forest nobility. The two enjoyed the dual status of both timber baron and lumber king and amassed great fortunes in their lifetimes. But they lived far different lives. Booth embodied the public's image of the rugged lumber king — a man who enjoyed visiting his shanties and sawmills, where he could oversee his men at work. Gilmour was the exception to the archetypical lumber king — a man more comfortable in a salon than a shanty or sawmill. More of the Valley's forest nobility resembled Booth than Gilmour, though many of the second generation enjoyed more exalted and refined lives than their fathers.

Allan Gilmour was born in Lanarkshire, Scotland, in 1816. His father was a farmer, but he got an early boost in life from his uncle, who headed a large multi-national timber and shipbuilding business centred in Glasgow. The business recruited family members to run sub-sidiary companies abroad, including New Brunswick, Quebec, Montreal, and the United States. At the age of 16, Gilmour was sent out with a cousin to work for the Montreal subsidiary that supplied provisions to Ottawa Valley timbermen and bought their products for export to Britain. In 1840 the two cousins took over direction of the Montreal firm, changing its name to Gilmour & Company. Allan Gilmour was the driving force, however, and he would lead it through two complete makeovers before he retired. In the 1840s he opened an office in Bytown and moved the firm directly into timber production. Since he was (with his family's help) already shipping square timber to Britain and selling it there, his move into active production made his business the only fully integrated operation in the Ottawa Valley. More changes came in the 1850s. At the beginning of the decade, Gilmour was the second-largest timber producer in the Valley, but within a few years he left the trade to focus on lumbering. Seeing the growing potential of an export-driven lumber industry in the Valley, he acquired a small sawmill at Chelsea Falls on the Gatineau River in 1853 and rebuilt it for large-scale production. The same year he took up residence in Bytown and made it the firm's headquarters. Within a few years, Gilmour & Company was one of the Valley's leading exporters of lumber. By 1873 his Chelsea mill was sawing about 35 million board feet

of deals, boards, and planks for export to both Britain and the United States. That year Gilmour retired and turned the company over to four nephews. One of them, John, moved to Ottawa and took charge.

Although Gilmour was only 57, he had been in the forest industry for 40 years. It had made him rich, but he had had enough of it now, particularly the rough conditions that were a necessary part of the business. In the early years he

Allan Gilmour, 1816-1895

had to go into the bush to inspect his operations personally, but he did not enjoy mingling with rowdy shantymen, river-drivers, and raftsmen. Later he had to keep a regular check on his sawmills, but these visits were not pleasant for him. An old employee remembered him as bad-tempered when things went wrong in the mill and one who avoided all contact with his workmen. At his death, an obituarist wrote that he was a "shy man, not prone to easy familiarity."[30] Retirement freed him of his business demands and allowed him to follow the dreams he had long put off. Now he had time for curling, fowl shooting, salmon fishing, and yachting. Now he was free to explore the library he had collected and to go abroad to see the things he had read about. Gilmour had not been born into wealth or cultivation; he developed his artistic sensibilities on his own. In his retirement he travelled extensively through England, Scotland, Italy, France, Germany, and Austria; he also took a long trip to the Middle East, where he viewed the pyramids, sailed on the Nile, and toured the Holy Land.

Still, despite the infinite cultural attractions he found abroad, Ottawa remained Gilmour's home. In this small city he moved in the highest social circles, hobnobbing with prime ministers, governors general, and Supreme Court justices. He curled with Prime Minister Alexander Mackenzie. He took Lord Dufferin (Governor General, 1872-78) and his wife to his private angling grounds on the north shore of the St. Lawrence for a week of salmon fishing. He worked with Lord Lorne, the next Governor General (1878-83), promoting the arts in Canada. Gilmour was himself a patron of the arts. In his elegant home overlooking the Ottawa River, he maintained a large collection of paintings (including a few Krieghoffs) to which he granted private viewings. In 1879 he helped organize the Art Association of Ottawa, which promoted the notion of a national art gallery. Within a year Lord Lorne brought together a number of supporters, including Gilmour, to found the Royal Canadian Academy of Arts, from which grew today's National Gallery of Canada. Next to the governor general, Gilmour gave the academy the largest cash donation and before his death, donated at least one of his paintings to the Gallery.[31] When Gilmour died, unmarried, in Ottawa, at age 78, he cannot have regretted leaving the world of lumber before he was too old to enjoy the fortune he had built.

John Rudolphus Booth was born in Shefford County, Quebec, near the village of Waterloo, in 1827. Growing up on a farm, he did not enjoy a lengthy education. In his early youth, Booth worked as a carpenter on bridge projects with the Central Vermont Railroad. By 1854, he was living in Ottawa with his wife and daughter and learning the lumber business. He began by managing a small sawmill in Hull for Andrew Leamy and then went into business for himself, making shingles and then sawing boards in a mill leased from Alonzo Wright. Booth showed an audacious spirit from the outset: without a proven reputation, he bid for and won a contract to supply lumber for the construction of the new parliament buildings. With profits from this venture he was able to buy his own mill, and his lumber career took off. More bold decisions followed: purchasing the Egan timber limits on the Madawaska in the 1860s and buying up further timberlands from lumbermen who lost faith in the industry during the depression of the 1870s. He was always looking for opportunities to expand, even if it meant going deeply into debt. His audacity paid off, and by the 1890s he was the leading lumber producer in the world. Booth always thought big; he was no conservative in business matters. No other lumber king had the nerve to build a 427-mile railway linking his timber limits to his sawmill to his markets. He was always open to new initiatives: acquiring more timber limits, investing in the latest mill technology, or entering new business ventures (he was 78 years old when he built his first paper mill). The only change he was not open to was delegating decision-making to others. Booth had absolute confidence in his own business instincts (perhaps with good reason); he believed in micro-management, hands-on personal leadership. His two sons held high positions in his enterprises for decades, but he remained the boss. It was well known that Booth discouraged initiative or independent action by those he hired to manage his railways and mills; he always insisted that his orders be carried out exactly as issued.

J. R. Booth was a timber baron, lumber king, and pulp-and-paper magnate, a rare triple-hitter. Though he undoubtedly relished his

success, it was not so much
for the social or economic
status that it brought as for
the freedom it gave him to
exercise his business talents.
Business was his life. It is
understandable, then, that
he kept control of his business as long into old age as
possible. Happily for him,
his energies did not flag
with the years. At 86 he suffered a compound fracture
of a leg when a beam fell on
him as he supervised the
demolition of an old store-
house. The accident did not
slow him down, however.

John Rudolphus Booth, 1827-1925

Within months he was seen walking along the log sorting booms on
the Ottawa River, and he continued to visit his Madawaska timber
limits and Chaudière mills almost until his death at 98. (He never
owned an automobile, preferring to travel by horse-drawn cutter or
buggy.) It was only at age 93 that he felt compelled to relinquish
some control: to avert estate difficulties after his death, he incorporated his firm, sharing authority with a board of directors (his
lawyer, his daughter, and two sons joined him on the board). Booth
could not retire; apart from flower gardening, he had few other interests in life beyond business.

Booth's wife died in 1886, and he lived 40 years a widower. He lived
simply and frugally, regularly dressing in the garb of a working man. In
the 1920s he was described as routinely wearing "much the same suit
of clothes today that he did in the old days when he was struggling to
make good." The suit, usually worn and rumpled, was typically made
of navy-blue serge and accompanied by a gaudy red necktie. Elegant
dress was not important (though his portrait shows him attentively

attired), and, in any case, he was not active in society at any level. He
prized privacy and shunned refinements. Unlike other lumber kings,
he did not seek invitations to dine with the governor general. He did,
however, choose to proclaim his high economic status in the residences
he erected. Both the Wellington Street House, destroyed in the fire of
1900, and the Metcalfe Street house (still standing) that replaced it
matched any other in Ottawa for grandeur (except Rideau Hall, of
course). Booth lived quietly at 252 Metcalfe Street until his death in
December 1925.[32]

EMPIRES AND PUBLIC IMAGE

The Valley's timber barons and lumber kings reigned over large populations and vast empires. Some of the empires were of truly aristocrat-
ic proportions: at times Gilmour and Booth each held about 3,000
square miles in timber limits,[33] an area larger than Prince Edward
Island and three times the size of the Duchy of Luxembourg. As
Michael Bliss has said, these men "were as important to their communities, and seemed at times almost as powerful, as the feudal barons of
old England."[34] The power this aristocracy wielded touched the lives of
tens of thousands of people in the Valley. The supplies they needed for
their bush operations provided a useful market for local farmers. The
sawmills they built gave birth to towns and cities. The work they
offered in the shanties and mills gave employment to armies of men.
For this, they were quietly esteemed as celebrities in their communities.
Their public image was benign. They lived steady lives, without scan-
dal or lavish socializing. They were not considered grasping profiteers,
nor did wealth condemn them. Indeed, the monumental residences
these men built were often a source of pride to local people. It also
helped, of course, that they supported the appropriate charities: the
Ladies' College, the orphanage, the hospital, and the church. The only
bad press they got was for polluting rivers and piling lumber in residential areas. These complaints were minor, however, and did not tar-
nish their names appreciably. The timber barons and lumber kings of
the Ottawa Valley were never likened to the "robber barons" of mythic
infamy.

9

WAS IT WORTHWHILE CUTTING DOWN ALL THOSE TREES?

For a long time the forest industry enjoyed a good public image in Canada. Lumbermen's associations across the country made sure that the people and their governments knew the value of the industry — the wealth it brought to Canada, the jobs it provided, the stimulus it gave to commerce, the revenue it supplied to government treasuries. Governments, for their part, were not hard to convince and gladly helped out with timber slides, canals, and cheap timber-limit licences. By the 1930s, however, most of the easily accessible timberlands of New Brunswick, Quebec, and Ontario had been logged out. The lumber industry remained strong in British Columbia, but the once-bustling sawmills of eastern Canada were falling into decrepitude. It was in these years that some observers began to question what Canadians had received in return for allowing lumbermen to cut down all those trees (the trees, after all, belonged to all Canadians since most of them grew on Crown land). Where praise of the forest industry had once been nearly universal, now faults were found. Some critics, for example, felt that, in many parts of Canada, the industry had not helped the growth of agriculture but had actually retarded it. Some were disappointed that the forest industry had failed to generate many jobs in the high-paying manufacturing sector. Others criticized it for wastefulness, for not getting the most out of the timber resources it was licensed to cut. Still others pointed out the downsides of the industry:

polluted rivers and abandoned sawmill towns. The Ottawa Valley was not exempt from censure. Each of these criticisms could certainly be applied to the Valley, though not all with equal degrees of severity.

LINKS TO AGRICULTURE

Most observers had no doubts that lumbering was generally good for agriculture, that it stimulated and facilitated farming in nearby areas. After all, agricultural settlers in Canada usually followed close behind the men who felled the forests. As a result, some pioneer farmers were pleased to find that lumbermen had already cleared their land of those "nuisance" stands of timber, making it easier for them to get started ploughing and planting. Some also found that lumbermen had endowed their areas with roads they had opened for logging purposes. Once established, farmers were able to enjoy a ready market in the shanties for the crops they grew; sales to lumber outfits helped move them out of subsistence farming into the cash-based economy of the outside world. Also, in wintertime, when they and their horses were underemployed, farmers could take cash-paying jobs in the shanties. In the twentieth century, some were able to earn extra money selling pulp-wood they cut on their own woodlots. The additional sources of income allowed them to buy better farm equipment and upgrade their breeds of livestock, thus improving their productivity. The benefits of lumbering seem manifold.

The critics, however, noted that lumbering could also have a nega-tive impact on agriculture. They pointed out, for example, the sad results of pioneers who tried to farm poor land close to logging oper-ations, planning to profit from their proximity by selling provisions to the shanties. For too many of them, the plan proved ruinous. Other critics argued that taking work in the shanties stymied progress in agri-culture; they maintained that while cash from shanty work could help farmers in the short term, the jobs were often harmful in the long term. Winter employment in the bush, they claimed, deterred farmers from developing a serious vocation for agriculture, that farming never became a priority for those who took work in the shanties. Too many men, they felt, preferred the relative freedom of life in the bush to the

responsibilities of tilling and sowing their land; for many, the isolation of a farm compared poorly with the comradeship of the shanty.
The chance to get away to the bush led them to leave home early in
the fall, before preparing their fields, and if they stayed on for the
river-drive in the spring, they were usually late returning for planting.
The result was not only poor crops but also a debilitating indifference
to improving their farming practices.[1]

In the Ottawa Valley, however, the story was quite different. Here, as
in other parts of Canada, farmers hoped to benefit from links to forest
industries, and many succeeded. To be sure, there were exceptions.
Philemon Wright, for example, tried to strengthen his family's farming
prospects by earning supplementary income in the timber trade;
instead, he found that, in the end, farming became supplementary to
the family's timber business. The turnabout was a great disappointment for Wright as it dashed his dreams of living a bucolic life of agrarian independence. Later in the nineteenth century, many Ottawa Valley
pioneers suffered when they made the mistake of trying to farm the
rocky timberlands of the Canadian Shield. In many cases the land was
totally unsuited to cultivation, and the settlers spent years of misery
before ultimately abandoning their holdings. The unhappy results of
these attempts can still be seen today in forlorn clearings up and down
the Madawaska and Gatineau valleys.

Still, on balance, it is clear that in the Ottawa Valley forest industries
had a more positive impact on agriculture than elsewhere in Canada.
Farmers fortunate to have land in the fertile parts of the Valley often
prospered by getting involved with lumbering. In Prescott County, for
example, one historian has concluded that agriculture would not have
been possible at all without the cash that farmers earned supplying
provisions to the shanties and taking winter jobs there. In Nepean
Township, another historian has found little agricultural neglect and
considerable benefit among farmers who had links to forest industries.[2] Even Arthur Lower, an historian and harsh critic of lumbering in
general, felt the Ottawa Valley was an exception to his view of the
industry's impact in other parts of the country. Lower concluded that,
in the Valley, lumbering and farming "harmonized perfectly."[3]

The reason why the forest industry in the Ottawa Valley had a more positive impact on agriculture may have been its remote location. Transport costs made it difficult for farmers in outside areas to supply high-bulk products to Valley lumbermen; local farmers thus enjoyed a near-monopoly in items such as hay, oats, and livestock, products in which they wisely chose to specialize.[4] Farming in Prescott, Nepean, and other areas put down healthy roots and was able to survive long after the links to lumbering weakened. That weakening came about late in the nineteenth century, when lumbering went into decline and local farmers lost their captive market. At the same time, railways were built connecting the Valley to the outside world, and local farmers lost their locational advantage. Agriculture was well established by this time, however, and farmers were able to adapt successfully by switching to dairy products; they took advantage of the new rail connections to sell to the growing populations of Montreal, Ottawa, and Hull.[5] Favourable links between agriculture and forest industries are another sign of the Ottawa Valley's distinctiveness.

LINKS TO MANUFACTURING

Canada was founded, in large part, by people hoping to gain a living by exploiting its natural resources, its staple products. Beginning with codfish and furs, the newcomers were able to find a long series of other staples to sell outside the country — timber, lumber, wheat, minerals, oil, and gas, for example. Historians and economists have long stewed over whether Canadians got the most they could from exploiting these resources, especially whether staple-exporting businesses generated growth in other sectors of the economy.[6] As has been seen, they agreed that forest industries were useful in encouraging the development of agriculture, at least in the Ottawa Valley. A good test of whether it was truly worthwhile cutting down all those trees would be if forest industries stimulated growth in manufacturing. Jobs in manufacturing were more highly prized than jobs in staples production for they usually paid higher wages and were more likely to provide work in all seasons of the year.

Felling the pine, moving it downriver, sawing it into lumber, and sending it to market all required heavy expenditures in machinery, tools, and other specialized articles. Unfortunately, almost none of the heavy machinery used in Ottawa Valley sawmills was manufactured locally; it all came from the outside, from Montreal, western Ontario, and the United States. Several entrepreneurs, however, saw an opportunity in manufacturing some of the lumber industry's other needs locally, and there were a few modest success stories. One, of course, was the Cockburn family's famous pointer boats, made at Pembroke. Another was James W. Woods of Ottawa, who made shantymen's clothing and tents and sold them across Canada. There was the Farmer family of Arnprior, who operated a thriving boot-making factory, specializing in caulked boots for river drivers. Thomas Pink turned out a range of logging tools — peavies, skidding tongs, cant hooks, etc. — at his Pembroke iron works. The Ottawa Saw Works Company produced many forms of mill saws at its Chaudière plant. Two Valley axe manufacturers did well, too. The Walters family of Hull made axes that were well known across Canada and the United States. The timberman, Nathaniel Blasdell, began making axes in the 1840s and, in the 1860s, diversified into general metalworking; his Victoria Foundry at the Chaudière turned out an array of iron castings, small machinery, boilers, and steam engines. The steam engines were built mainly for use in the large fleet of motorized barges and tugs that carried the Valley's lumber output to market. And most of that fleet was built in the shipyards of Hull.[7]

These early manufacturing successes may seem impressive, and, indeed, they did help diversify the local economy and provide well-paying, all-season jobs for some people. However, these businesses remained stubbornly tied to lumbering, even after that industry went into obvious decline in the twentieth century. Unlike farmers, none of them adapted well to the changing times. One business with good growth potential, for example, might have been tool manufacturing. But investors who had done well making tools for lumbermen failed to build on their reputation and expertise to develop a wider range of products for the new economy. As a result, these outfits remained small and tool manufacturing in the Valley never grew into anything substantial.

And what about the hundreds of millions of board feet that were sawn in Valley lumber mills every year? Unfortunately, most of the lumber was shipped out of the Valley without further value being added. Little use was made of the Valley's prodigious lumber output (and abundant hydro power) to manufacture consumer products, to develop a local woodworking industry that would create more wealth than lumbering. True, some lumbermen made a few wood products as a sideline for local sale, but only two — James Davidson and E.B. Eddy — succeeded in manufacturing on a large scale. Davidson specialized in making doors, windows, and sashes, and at one time claimed to be the largest manufacturer in Canada. By 1906 his factory in Ottawa was able to turn out one door every minute — 600 a day.[8] Eddy, for his part, focused on making pails and washtubs, commodities increasingly in demand in Canada's growing urban centres. His container factory in Hull was mechanized at an early date and, by 1872, was housed in its own building, where all components were sawn, planed, assembled, and painted; here he was able turn out 600,000 pails and 45,000 wash tubs a year. By 1891 the factory accounted for 99 percent of all pail and tub manufacturing in Canada.[9] Sales declined in the twentieth century, however, as metal tubs and pails took over the market.

Apart from these minor successes, Ottawa Valley investors seemed unable to make further use of locally sawn wood. One product that might have found a ready market was office furniture and shelving, especially given the growing federal bureaucracy in Ottawa. However, hardwoods were preferred in furniture, and transport difficulties made it impossible for Valley lumbermen to supply enough maple, oak, or ash (they would not float very far) to make large-scale production possible. Pine tables, chairs, beds, etc. were made in the Valley but only by small, scattered producers; the products were considered rustic and failed to generate even a moderate-sized furniture industry.

Pulp and paper, it is true, became a major manufacturing industry in the Ottawa Valley, an industry that brought good jobs to many people. Its emergence, however, was not linked to the inputs or outputs of timbering or lumbering; it simply represented a third stage in the exploitation of the Valley's forest resources. The pulp-and-paper industry grew from the need of lumbermen to find a new use for the poorer-quality timber remaining on the timber limits they leased combined with the opportunity to profit from a burgeoning new market for paper products.

DEPLETED FORESTS

For nearly a century Ottawa Valley timbermen and lumbermen felt that the forests they exploited were nearly inexhaustible. By the 1880s, however, they began to realize that every year the logs they were work-ing with were getting smaller in size and lower in quality; moreover, they had to go farther to get them, adding to production costs. At the same time, they also began to realize that their own carelessness was at least partly to blame for these problems. They acknowledged, for exam-ple, that in making square timber, they left unpardonable quantities of wood behind unused in the bush. They also knew that their logging practices often destroyed great swaths of new-growth trees, the forests of the future. Even worse, these bad habits produced huge amounts of slash and brush, the perfect fuel for the forest fires that regularly attacked the Valley's timberlands. The time had come to take action, and Valley lumbermen (especially George Bryson, E. H. Bronson, Thomas White, and W.C. Edwards) took the lead in promoting a national conservation movement to protect the country's remaining forest stock. They knew they first had to start by taking better care in managing their own timber limits, but they also sought government support. In 1882 George Bryson, a member of the Quebec legislative council, prepared a report that recommended several ways in which government and industry could work together to conserve the coun-try's forests. Within a few years, both Quebec and Ontario implement-ed some of the recommendations, most notably those relating to for-est fires. Each province created a corps of forest rangers, who were to patrol the timberlands, pointing out fire hazards and fighting fires when they broke out. In Quebec limit-holders bore all the costs, while in Ontario they paid half.[10] Valley lumbermen showed they were pre-pared to pay for measures that would help protect the timber resources they were licensed to cut.

Although lumbermen accepted some of the blame for forest fires, they claimed that settlers were a greater threat: the fires they set to clear their lands sometimes broke loose and burned wide expanses of nearby timberlands (settlers were also accused of illegal cutting on licensed timber limits). Bryson and others urged the provinces to create forest reserves, where settlement would not be allowed. In 1893 the Ontario government responded to their wishes by setting aside 18 townships in the Madawaska Highlands to create Algonquin Park, the first provincial park in Canada. The new park was expected to serve several purposes: a forest reserve, a fish and game preserve, a wilderness recreation area for public enjoyment. Farming, hunting, trapping, and mining were all prohibited, but logging was not. E. H. Bronson, who was a minister in the Ontario cabinet, played an important role in establishing the park. He had extensive timber limits in the area, along with J.R. Booth, the McLachlin Brothers, and the St. Anthony's Lumber Company. and they were all allowed to continue cutting in the park (albeit in areas out of public view). Indeed, the Madawaska forests were more intensively (and extensively) logged after the park was created than before. This came about because Booth's Ottawa, Arnprior & Parry Sound Railway was completed through the park three years after its creation, making the forests much easier to harvest. In Algonquin Park, "forest reserve" did not mean preserving timberlands in a state of nature. Rather, it meant keeping them healthy for the use of lumbermen. Besides cutting trees in the park, lumbermen were also allowed to build rail spurs to get their logs out, erect dams to aid their riverdrives, and maintain "logging farms" to service their shanties; a few small sawmills were even permitted to operate within park limits. These lumbering operations, of course, often conflicted with the notion of preserving wildlife and providing visitors with a wilderness experience, but Booth and the others usually got their way; indeed, logging is still carried on in the park today.[11] Clearly, Ottawa Valley lumbermen benefited nicely from the creation of Algonquin Park.

POLLUTED RIVERS
One offence that certainly threatened the lumber industry's public image was the callousness it showed in dumping sawmill waste into

the nation's rivers. No river in Canada suffered more from this pernicious practice than the Ottawa, especially the stretch directly below
Chaudière Falls, with its high concentration of mills. As early as 1860,
only five years after sawmilling began on a large scale at the Chaudière,
engineers reported that sawdust and other mill refuse was beginning to
block the entrance locks to the Rideau Canal, nearly a mile downstream.[12] The federal government, which was responsible for protect-
ing fisheries and inland shipping, always professed to be concerned
about these matters. Still, though reports were issued by the federal
government (at least four in a fifteen-year period)[13] and legislation was
passed, conditions on the Ottawa River went from poor to dismal. The
lumber kings of Ottawa and Hull were able to delay serious anti-pollution regulations for decades by diligent political lobbying. They
made it clear that if tough restrictions were imposed on them, they
would simply close their mills and move to more congenial locations.[14] They even commissioned their own engineering study by
Sandford Fleming, the inventor of Standard Time. Not surprisingly,
Fleming found that discharging sawmill waste into the Ottawa had little effect on navigation; he also pointed out that people living along
the river depended on the sawmill refuse they scavenged from the river
for their winter's firewood.[15] Members of Parliament could see the pollution from their office windows, but it was not until the end of the
nineteenth century that the government forced lumbermen to clean up
their habits, and by that time Ottawa River mills were sawing much less
lumber anyhow.

In the 1880s seven large mills were sawing half a billion board feet of
lumber every year in the Ottawa–Hull area. Although many advances
had been made in mill technology, it was estimated that 10 percent of
the wood sawn in these lumber mills (as much as 92,500 cubic yards a
year) went to waste. The waste included sawdust, as well as butt ends,
bark, edgings, and slabs, for which little use could be found; the one
steam-powered mill in the area took some of the refuse to fuel its boilers, but most of it ended up in the Ottawa River. Some of the refuse floated on the surface, forming a thick crust that drifted with the wind from
one side of the river to the other. Most of it, however, sank to the river

bottom, where it built up dense shoals of vegetation that were slow to decay. In bays where the water moved slowly, drilling tests found some shoals to be 40 feet deep. The result was an unsightly mess that offended the senses, fouled fish-spawning grounds, and deterred recreational boating. For the government, a bigger worry was the harm to navigation. For example, "deadheads" (slabs stuck upright in the refuse shoals) sometimes broke steamboat propellers. At other times, shallower waters made it more difficult for raftsmen to reassemble their cribs after descending the Chaudière timber slide. More serious was the fact that steamboats and barges sometimes got stuck on the shoals as they approached the entrance to the Rideau Canal or the Queen's Wharf (public docks on the Ottawa side of the river); at these times, the government was expected to clear away the obstructions with dredges.[16]

Then there were the sawdust explosions. On these occasions, pockets of methane gas, which had accumulated in the shoals as the refuse decomposed, exploded, sometimes with surprising force. Every few years, citizens of Ottawa and Hull told of narrow escapes from these eruptions. In 1889 two men claimed that their skiff was nearly swamped by a gusher of "water and sawdust [that] shot at least forty feet into the air." In another case, a government engineer reported seeing a barge "thrown clear up on top of the water" by exploding methane. The eruptions were strong enough to shatter thick winter ice. One incident was reported by J. St. Denis Lemoine, sergeant-at-arms of the Senate. He said that, one Saturday night in February, he and a party of snowshoers were crossing the Ottawa River when he was hurled into the air by sawdust exploding under the ice. Although he fell onto broken ice and got a little wet, he escaped injury. Less fortunate was John Kemp, a Montebello-area farmer. In 1897 he was crossing the river with another man when their boat was upset by a sawdust explosion. The two managed to catch hold of the boat but were rocked by a second eruption. Kemp lost his grip and drowned. The Ottawa River was more than a disgraceful mess; it was dangerous.[17]

In 1873 parliament passed an "Act for the better protection of navigable streams and rivers."[18] The act prohibited dumping any form of sawmill waste in rivers across the country but allowed for exemptions if it could be shown that "the public interest would not be injuriously affected thereby." Ottawa–Hull mill owners applied for and received an exemption that allowed them to discharge sawdust within a two-mile stretch of the Ottawa River below Chaudière Falls. The prohibition against dumping larger pieces of refuse remained in force, however, and lumbermen did take serious measures to comply. Most of them installed "hogging machines" to chip the slabs, butt ends, etc. into pieces measuring about half-an-inch by six inches, which were then thrown into the river (along with the sawdust). Unfortunately, government engineers soon found that this tactic only worsened matters for the chips mixed with the sawdust to make harder-packed shoals that dredges found more difficult to remove.[19] Conditions continued to deteriorate, while governments protected the lumber interests: in 1885 the Province of Ontario passed an act compelling judges to "take into consideration the importance of the lumber trade" if anti-pollution injunctions were ever brought against Ottawa River mill owners.[20]

By the 1890s, however, local citizens were becoming less indulgent towards the lumber industry, perhaps because production was now in obvious decline. Senator Francis Clemow of Ottawa led a campaign to clean up the river, and the federal government finally agreed that something had to be done. This time it amended the Fisheries Act to attack the problem. Lumbermen were told that the exemption allowing sawdust dumping would be terminated but were given until May 1895 to make alternative arrangements. When the time arrived, however, the officials backed down, and the question was again set aside until the new government of Sir Wilfrid Laurier established an amended deadline of June 1898. One by one the owners began to comply, arranging for their waste to be used in pulp mills or installing incinerators to burn it (they had long pleaded that burning mill waste would make fire-insurance premiums prohibitively high). Only J. R. Booth held out, managing to stall for another three years. It was not until September 1901 that the government took action, fining Booth twice ($20 and costs) for violating the Fisheries Act. Now, faced with further prosecution, he gave in and promised to install an incinerator over the winter.[21] Although Booth and other mill owners in Ottawa and Hull had threatened to move their mills if tough anti-pollution measures were imposed, they stayed put. It would be a long time before conditions in the Ottawa River improved much. In fact, even in the 1960s, engineers sounding the river bottom for the construction of the Macdonald–Cartier Interprovincial Bridge found that sawmill waste deposits still measured more than ten feet deep in places.[22]

In 1882 Oscar Wilde, visiting Ottawa on the lecture circuit, professed to be outraged by the unsightly pollution he beheld in the Ottawa River. Ottawa newspapers were, in turn, equally outraged at Wilde's insolence: it was a pity the river was sullied, they retorted, but the lumber industry could not survive without dumping its waste, and it would be tragic if the mills moved away.[23] A few years later the *Canada Lumberman*, the voice of the forest industry, noted that the Ottawa was the only river in Canada that was exempt from legislation banning sawdust dumping. It went on, however, to point out that "there is no other river which has such enormous lumber interests on its banks and the government has . . . permitted the sawdust nuisance out of deference to the great interests concerned."[24] Still later, the Ottawa Board of Trade implored the government not to prosecute the mill owners, whose investments meant so much to the local economy.[25] For decades the lumber kings of Ottawa and Hull succeeded in getting their message across: the public should know that a polluted Ottawa River was a small price to pay for a viable lumber industry, and surely it was obvious that the benefits that lumbering brought to the Valley far outweighed any harm done to the waterway.

OTHER DOWNSIDES

There were other downsides to the forest industry. Arthur Lower complained that most of the profits made in cutting down all those trees across the country went to foreigners — the British and Americans who, quite naturally, spent their fortunes where they lived. The result, Lower claimed, was that while these "forest buccaneers" stripped Canada of its forest wealth, local people got only a few crumbs from the rich man's table.[26] This was Lower's view of the forest industry across Canada. The Ottawa Valley experience, however, was an exception. As was seen in

Chapter 8, there were no absentee mill owners here. Not one of the timber barons or lumber kings who made their fortunes in the local forests resided outside the Valley. Their profits, for the most part, remained at home.[27]

Lower and others[28] have also pointed out that lumbering was a notoriously transient industry; when forests were logged out, mill owners would close down their operations and quickly move on to greener timberlands, leaving behind only ghost towns and broken dreams. This sad experience certainly occurred in many parts of Canada, but the Ottawa Valley was again an exception (one which Lower acknowledged). Most of the Valley's large-scale sawmills lasted two generations or more, allowing the towns where they operated to develop a wider economic base. All the big lumber mills ultimately closed when log supplies ran out, but no towns were abandoned. Mill closures were a great shock to towns like Arnprior, but they survived. The loss of the sawmill in a one-industry hamlet was, of course, a more serious matter. Still, while many of the small sawmills that once dotted the Valley eventually shut down, few communities disappeared totally. Herron's Mills (north of Lanark) and Balaclava (west of Renfrew) in Ontario, along with North Nation Mills (north of Papineauville) in Quebec, are among the few sawmill ghost towns known in the Valley.[29]

WEALTH FOR SOME, A LIVING FOR MANY

All in all, Canadians did well by the forest industry of the Ottawa Valley. Perhaps timbermen and lumbermen did not always get the most out of all the trees they cut down. And maybe polluting the Ottawa River was an unpleasant price to pay. The benefits, however, were undeniable. Without the forest industry, much of the Valley would not have been settled: the industry encouraged growth in farming, gave birth to towns and villages, and supplied everyone with cheap materials to build their homes, barns, bridges, and businesses. The industry provided jobs and fostered commerce. It stocked government treasuries with the funds needed to pay for the public works and services on which people depended. The forest products sold abroad helped keep Canada's import-export accounts in balance. The industry attracted foreign capital to exploit the forests, yet most of the profits stayed at home. In short, cutting down all those trees brought wealth to some and a living to many more.

10

ENDINGS AND REMAINDERS

On 10 December 1925, huge throngs turned out in Ottawa to mark the funeral of John Rudolphus Booth, who had died two days earlier at the age of 98. The previous day hundreds of people had filed past the lumber king's casket as he lay in state at his Metcalfe Street residence. Though Booth had long shunned public appearances, he was nonetheless a celebrity. The funeral service at St. Andrew's Presbyterian church at Wellington and Kent streets was kept simple, just as the unpretentious tycoon had wanted. An extraordinary array of notables filled the pews, including three prime ministers (Mackenzie King, Sir Robert Borden, and Arthur Meighen), members of parliament, senior military officers, city councillors, union leaders, corporate executives, and a few of his fellow lumber kings (Daniel McLachlin II, David Gillies, John S. Gillies, and Sir George Perley). More than 150 automobiles followed the hearse to Beechwood Cemetery. Watching the funeral procession in miserable weather were more than a thousand workers from the Booth pulp, paper, and lumber mills, as well as many ordinary citizens. After all, the man had touched the lives of countless people, in one way or another, in the 70 years he had lived in Ottawa. His funeral was the largest the city had ever seen.[1]

It was evident to everyone that the death of J.R. Booth symbolized the end of an era. Through most of its history, the forest industry had dominated life in Bytown and Ottawa. In recent decades, though, it had fallen in importance. Now, in the public's mind, the death of the greatest lumber king of all brought the great age of lumbering to a close. Lumbering was no longer the main engine of the local economy and would never again carry the weight it once had. Indeed, for some time now a new industry — government — had prevailed in Ottawa. The 1921 census shows more than 12,000 public servants residing in Ottawa compared to only 574 shantymen, sawmill hands, and pulp–and-paper workers. The city was no longer a "lumber town," it was a "government town."[2]

The 1920s brought major changes to all of the Ottawa Valley. Within ten years most of the remaining large-scale lumber mills closed down: St. Anthony's at Whitney and the W.C. Edwards mill at Rideau Falls in 1922; Edwards's other mill at Rockland, 1926; three more in 1929 — Hawkesbury Lumber Company, the Gilmour–Hughson steam-powered mill in Hull and McLachlin Brothers of Arnprior, and, lastly, the Maclaren mill at Buckingham in 1932. J. R. Booth's son, Jackson, continued to saw lumber at their Chaudière Falls mill until about 1946 before closing it and opening a new facility at Tee Lake in Témiscamingue County in Quebec. Obviously, it was cheaper for the Booths to saw their lumber close to their Kipawa timber limits than to drive their sawlogs hundreds of miles down the Ottawa River. The long distances from stump to saw had made large-scale lumbering uneconomic in the Ottawa Valley.[3] Surprisingly, the Booths were the only Valley lumbermen to move their milling operations; the others simply chose to leave lumbering altogether. Only one company — Gillies Brothers — managed to carry on sawing at its original location, and for a remarkably long time; their mill at Braeside (sold to Consolidated Paper Company in 1963) did not close until 1992.

While the lumber kings and their big sawmills had largely disappeared by the middle of the twentieth century, lumbering, however, did not die out in the Ottawa Valley. The lumbering tradition lived on with dozens of smaller mills operating in towns, villages, and rural areas; they could be found in most parts of the Valley but never far from their timber sources. At the same time, further advances in technology brought major changes to the industry. Most notably, as improved electrical and internal-combustion engines became available, they were adapted to sawmills, allowing them to end their dependence on water-power or steam-power sites. Rather than taking the trees to the saw, now the saw could be taken to the trees: lumber could be sawn almost anywhere, even deep in the bush if desired. Small sawmills were still important to local communities, but the lumber industry came to play a lesser and lesser role in the economy of the Valley as a whole.

Men still felled trees in the bush, moved logs to riversides, and drove them downstream to mills. More and more, though, the logs were intended for pulp mills, not lumber mills. As lumbering stagnated, the pulp-and-paper industry flourished and grew in the Valley. Work in the bush and on the rivers was also much affected by new technology. In the bush, bucksaws gave way to motorized chainsaws, while horses yielded to all-terrain vehicles. On the rivers, diesel-powered tugs replaced steamers, and when the traditional river-drives were abandoned, the tugs were, in their turn, replaced by trucks. Today, the workers are better protected — safety boots, hard hats, and life preservers are mandatory. The last surviving drive on the Ottawa River, the drive bringing sawlogs from the historic Gillies timber limits on Lake Témiscamingue to the Braeside mill, ended in 1990. The last log-drive in all of the Valley, the drive that brought pulpwood down the Gatineau River from as far as Lac-des-Outaouais to the Canadian Forest Products mill in the City of Gatineau, came to an end a year later. The construction of hydroelectricity generation dams along these rivers had slowed the movement of the logs, and it was taking them two to three years to reach their destination. At the same time, better highways were making trucking a more efficient means of delivery.[4]

It seems amazing that after two centuries of cutting (and forest fires), there was still enough timber left in the Valley for lumber and pulp-and-paper companies to continue operating. It shows how rich in timber the Ottawa Valley had been. For lumber companies, there was still wood to be cut — scattered stands of red and white pine that had been overlooked, as well as abundant spruce and some cedar. Then there were the hardwoods that had escaped logging in the past because of the difficulty of floating them on rivers; trucks now made it possible to get these valuable species to the sawmill. Pulp mills, on the other hand, were not picky; in addition to spruce, they would also take hemlock, larch, balsam, and even jack pine. In a few places, old timber limits that had been cut-over long ago had sprouted new stands of timber that were now mature enough to cut. These patches of second growth, however, had come about through natural regeneration; they were not the results of reforestation by man. The timber barons and lumber kings cannot be accused of clear-cutting to the destructive levels seen in more recent times in Canada, for they did not have the technology to do so. But there is no doubt that over the decades, they had removed tens of millions of trees from Crown lands and planted none in return. Provincial governments were not much better; they were slow to restock the Crown timberlands for which they had custodial responsibility. The provinces did not begin serious reforestation work until the 1960s, so no restocked Crown timberland is ready yet for harvesting.[5]

There are still some tracts of "old-growth" (virgin) forest remaining in the Valley today. The most extensive lie along the upper Ottawa River beyond Lac Simard, in areas too remote to be cut for commercial use. There are also a few impressive timberlands closer to the more inhabited areas of the Valley, but they are small and scattered (and often not entirely untouched by the saw); examples can be found in Gatineau, Algonquin, Mont-Tremblant, and La Vérendrye parks. A more accessible example is the "Gillies Grove" at Arnprior, a privately preserved woodland with a long history. As early as the 1870s, the lumber king Daniel McLachlin set aside a tract of pines close to his home to protect it from the logger's saw. In 1878 a journalist raved about the "magnificent McLachlin estate and a grove, which, for general beauty and lovely bits of sylvan scenery, I have never seen surpassed — all happily thrown open to the public, and I am glad to say, highly appreciated."[6] The property was later bought by the lumber king David Gillies, who was also committed to preserving its integrity. The grove itself consists of 57 acres of mixed forest, and includes magnificent specimens of mature white pines. Some of the pines are more than 170 years old, and one (more than 47 metres in height) is believed to be the tallest in

Ontario. In the 1990s a local conservancy group raised money to buy the grove and ensure that it would remain untouched by development but open to the public.[7]

In its heyday the forest industry had an immense impact on the Ottawa Valley, but today physical evidence of its past is difficult to find. The industry's infrastructure, after all, was highly perishable. Shanties, timber slides, sawmills, and the like were, no surprise, built with the wood at hand and have largely disappeared over the years through fire and decay. Still, a few Booth and Eddy buildings at Chaudière Falls, constructed of more durable masonry, have been retained and adapted to modern uses. Smaller remainders of the industry — tools, pointer boats, mill machinery, and such — can be found in local museums. The most lasting impact of the forest industry may lie in Valley place names, in which so many timber barons and lumber kings have been immortalized. Their names can be seen in the towns of Eganville, Mackey, Edwards, Bryson, and Davidson. There are Eddy and Edwards townships in Témiscamingue County and Bryson and Gillies townships in the Pontiac. Ottawa has streets named Bronson, Booth, Gilmour, Hurdman, Maclaren, and Skead; Hull has its Eddy, McConnell, and Wright streets. In these names, the forest heritage of the Valley is heard every day, though not everyone may be aware of it.

NOTES

Chapter 1

1 Guy Gaudreau, *Les récoltes des forêts publiques au Québec et en Ontario*, 1840-1890 (Montreal, 1999), pp. 23, 64.

2 Charlotte Whitton, *A Hundred Years A-Fellin'* (Ottawa, 1974), p. 62.

3 Johanne Trew, "Ottawa Valley Fiddling: Issues of Identity and Style," *British Journal of Canadian Studies*, II: 2 (1996), p. 339.

4 Joan Finnigan, *Giants of Canada's Ottawa Valley* (Burnstown, Ont., n.d.), p. 8.

5 Michael Cross discusses Ottawa Valley violence extensively in his doctoral thesis "The Dark Druidical Groves: The Lumber Community and the Commercial Frontier in British North America to 1854"(University of Toronto, 1968); see also his "Violence and Authority: The Case of Bytown," in D.J. Bercuson and L.A. Knafla (eds.), *Law and Society in Canada in Historical Perspective* (Calgary, 1979). Richard M. Reid, *The Upper Ottawa Valley to 1855* (Ottawa. 1990), pp. xxxii-xl. For instances of drinking and fighting among Ottawa Valley shantymen, see Joshua Fraser, *Shanty, Forest and River Life in the Backwoods of Canada* (Montreal, 1883), pp. 330ff.

6 Gina Gilchrist, *The Nature and Cultural Significance of Step-Dancing in the Ottawa Valley* (unpublished paper, Ottawa Public Library, 1989). Trew, pp. 339-44. Raymond Beauchamp et al., *La danse traditionnelle dans la vallée de la Gatineau* (Drummondville, Québec, 2000).

7 J.K. Chambers, "The Ottawa Valley Twang," in J.K. Chambers (ed.), *Canadian English: Origins and Structures* (Toronto, 1975). Ian Pringle and Enoch Padolsky, "The Irish Heritage of the Ottawa Valley," *English Studies in Canada*, 7 (1981), pp. 338-52. Ian Pringle and Enoch Padolsky, "The Linguistic Survey of the Ottawa Valley," *American Speech*, 58-4 (1983), pp. 325-44.

8 Pierre-Louis Lapointe, "Les fleuves unissent et les montagnes divisent: le bassin de l'Outaouais, une réalité géohistorique et culturelle méconnue," in Pierre-Louis Lapointe, *L'Outaouais: actes du colloque sur l'identité régionale de l'Outaouais* (Hull, 1981). Gaston Carrière, "L'Église catholique romaine et l'évolution de l'Outaouais: importance de sa contribution," in Pierre-Louis Lapointe, *supra*.

Chapter 2

1 Richard Tatley, *Industries and Industrialists of Merrickville*, 1792-1979 (Ottawa: Parks Canada, MRS #423, 1979), pp. 26-31. Glenn Lockwood, *Montague: A Social History of an Irish Ontario Community* (Smiths Falls, 1980), pp. 19-50. Ruth Burritt, *Burritt's Rapids*, 1793-1900 (Thornbury, 1993), pp. 9-11.

2 G. F. McGuigan, "Administration of Land Policy and the Growth of Corporate Economic Organization in Lower Canada," in W.T. Easterbrook and M. H. Watkins (eds.), *Approaches to Canadian Economic History* (Toronto, 1967), p. 101.

3 Andrew Picken, *The Canadas* (London, 1832), appendix, pp. xii-xvii.

4 Thomas Malone, quoted in *The Canada Lumberman* (hereafter cited as *CL*), 1 July 1923, p. 39. See also John J. Bigsby, *The Shoe and the Canoe*, vol. 1, (London 1850), p. 153.

5 H.P. Biggar (ed.), *The Works of Samuel de Champlain*, vol. III (Toronto, 1929), pp. 37-38.

6 Arthur Buies, *L'Outaouais Supérieur* (Québec, 1889), p. 61.

7   Picken, pp. xxviii.

8 A.R.M. Lower, *Great Britain's Woodyard: British North America and the Timber Trade*, 1763-1867 (Montreal-Kingston, 1973), p. 22-23.

9 Library and Archives Canada (hereafter cited as LAC), Wright Family Papers, MG 24, D8, vol. 114, *Orderly Day Book*, 1806. Late in life, Wright claimed it took him 35 days to get through the rapids. Picken, p. xxviii.

10 LAC, Wright Papers, *Orderly Day Book*, 1806. Picken, pp. xxviii-xxx.

11 LAC, Wright Papers, vol. 15, "R. Wright to his brother," 30 Nov. 1826, pp. 5523-24.

12 Fernand Ouellet and Benoît Thériault, "Philemon Wright," *Dictionary of Canadian Biography* (hereafter *DCB*), vol. VII, pp. 926-28. Bruce Elliott, " 'The Famous Township of Hull': Image and Aspiration of a Pioneer Quebec Community," *Histoire Sociale*, Nov. 1979, pp. 339-67.

13 D'Arcy Boulton, *Sketch of His Majesty's Province of Upper Canada* (London,

1805), pp. 27-28. H.N. Muller, "Floating a Lumber Raft to Quebec City, 1805: The Journal of Guy Catlin of Burlington," *Vermont History*, Spring 1971, pp. 116-24.

14 Lower, *Great Britain's Woodyard*, pp. 77-95.

15 Cole Harris, "Of Poverty and Helplessness in Petite-Nation," *Canadian Historical Review*, March 1971, pp. 23-50. Richard Chabot, "Joseph Papineau," *DCB*, vol. VII, pp. 673-77. Claude Baribeau, "Denis-B. Papineau," *DCB*, vol. VIII, pp. 678-80. Fernand Ouellet, "Louis-Joseph Papineau," *DCB*, vol. X, pp. 564-78. *Rapport de l'Archiviste de la Province de Québec* (1951-1953), pp. 171-73.

16 R.P. Gillis, "David Pattee," *DCB*, vol. VIII, pp. 688-89. Lucien Brault, *Histoire des Contés Unis de Prescott et de Russell* (L'Orignal, Ontario, 1965).

17 Picken, p. 126. Reid, *The Upper Ottawa Valley*, p. LV. Elaine Mitchell, *Fort Temiskaming and the Fur Trade* (Toronto, 1977), pp. 162-72. Richard Reid, "John Egan," *DCB*, vol. VIII, pp. 268-70.

18 Lorne Hammond, *Capital, Labour and Lumber in A.R.M. Lower's Woodyard: James Maclaren and the Changing Forest Economy, 1850-1906*," (Ph.D. thesis, University of Ottawa, 1994), pp. 46-51. C.C.J. Bond, "The Hudson's Bay Company in the Ottawa Valley,"*The Beaver*, Spring 1966.

19 Canada, Census, 1911, vol. II, *Religions, Origins of the People, Birthplaces*. The census districts examined were Pontiac, Wright, Labelle, and the western townships of Argenteuil (Rouge River Valley) in Quebec; Lanark North and South, Renfrew North and South, Russell, Prescott, Carleton, Ottawa City, and the eastern areas of Nipissing.

Chapter 3

1 R. J. Surtees, *Indian Land Surrenders in Ontario, 1763-1867* (Ottawa, 1984), pp. 34, 139. Lockwood, pp. 26-28.

2 Peter Cumming, Neil Mickenberg, *Native Rights in Canada* (Toronto, 1972), pp. 65-67. Larry Villeneuve and Daniel Francis, *The Historical Background of Indian Reserves and Settlements in the Province of Quebec* (Ottawa, 1984), pp. 40-41.

3 Surtees, *Indian Land Surrenders*, pp. 19-25, 28-34, 73-74, 94-100. Robert Surtees, *The Williams Treaties* (Ottawa, 1986). As for the lightly populated reaches of the Ottawa Valley north of the Mattawa, Indians there gave up their lands in return for cash and annuities in a treaty negotiated in 1850.

4 Sandra J. Gillis, *The Timber Trade in the Ottawa Valley, 1806-54* (Ottawa: Historic Sites and Monuments Board of Canada, 1985), pp. 1-10, 210-15. Reid, *The Upper Ottawa Valley*, pp. L-LI, 81-82.

5 Sandra Gillis, *The Timber Trade*, pp. 210-13. Robert P. Gillis, "George Hamilton," *DCB*, vol. VII, pp. 379-83. Gillis, "Pattee," *DCB*, vol. VIII, pp.

688-89. Robert P. Gillis, "Charles Shirreff," *DCB*, vol. VII, pp. 796-97.

6 A. J. Russell, *"Historical Memorandum on the Management of the Crown Timber Forests"* (1867), Archives of Ontario, RG 1, F-1-8, vol. 57, pp. 4-5.

7 LAC, RG 5, A 1, vol. 64, pp. 33,818-19; vol. 66, pp. 34,882-85. LAC RG 7, G 16, C, vol. 13, pp. 170-71. Eva Taylor and James Kennedy, *Ottawa's Britannia* (Ottawa, 1983), p. 9.

8 Wright Family Papers, vol. 237, pp. 27ff.

9 Russell, "Historical Memorandum," p. 6.

10 Reid, *The Upper Ottawa Valley*, pp. 92-93.

11 Richard Lambert and Paul Pross, *Renewing Nature's Wealth: A Centennial History of the Management of Lands, Forests & Wildlife in Ontario, 1763-1967* (Toronto, 1967), pp. 111ff. Sandra J. Gillis, *The Timber Trade*, pp. 215-35.

12 A system of duties and rents had been installed in New Brunswick a few years earlier, however. See Graeme Wynn, *Timber Colony: A Historical Geography of Early Nineteenth Century New Brunswick* (Toronto, 1981).

13 Province of Canada, *Journals of the Legislative Assembly* (hereafter *JLA*), 1849, App. PPPP.

14 Lambert, Pross, pp. 127ff. Anson Gard, *The Hub and the Spokes, or The Capital and Its Environs* (Ottawa, 1904), p. 253.

15 Québec, Documents de la Session (hereafter QDS), vol. 53, (1918-19), No. II, *Rapport du Ministre des Terres et Forêts*, Appendice No. 16. CL, 1 May 1910, pp. 22, 26. John Guthrie, *The Newsprint Paper Industry: An Economic Analysis* (Cambridge, Mass., 1941), pp. 32-33.

16 Reid, "John Egan," p. 268. Reid, *The Upper Ottawa Valley*, pp. 141-46. JLA, 1849, App. PPPP. Russell, "Historical Memorandum," pp. 42-44.

17 QDS, vol. 22, (1889), #114, pp. 7-9. Inflation calculation from Bank of Canada Web site.

18 Lambert and Pross, *Renewing Nature's Wealth*, pp. 118, 261. CL, June 1897, p. 8; CL, July 1897, p. 5.

19 H.V. Nelles, *The Politics of Development: Forests, Mines & Hydro-electric Power in Ontario, 1849-1941* (Toronto, 1974), p. 18. Jean Hamelin and Yves Roby, *Histoire économique du Québec, 1851-1896* (Montréal, 1971), p. 209.

20   TABLE ONE

Proportion of total timber duties and ground rents contributed by the Ottawa Valley to the treasury of the provinces of Canada, Quebec, and Ontario.*		
Province of Canada (*union of Upper & Lower Canada*)	Province of Quebec	Province of Ontario
1858 . . . . 73%	1867-68 . . . . 69%	1868 . . . . 45%
1863 . . . . 69%	1878-79 . . . . 65%	1878 . . . . 46%
	1888-89 . . . . 80%	1889 . . . . 35%
	1898-99 . . . . 56%	1898 . . . . 14%
	1908-09 . . . . 45%	1908 . . . . 13%
	1918-19 . . . . 38%	1918 . . . . 3%

*Computed from statistics in Prov. of Canada, Report of the Commissioner of Crown Lands, 1858, 1863; Prov. of Ontario, Report of the Commissioner of Crown Lands, 1868, 1878, 1889, 1898, 1908, 1918-19; Prov. de Québec, Rapport du Commissaire des Terres et Forêts, 1867-68, 1878-79, 1888-89, 1898-99, 1908-09, 1918-19.

21 Nelles, Politics of Development, p. 65. CL, July 1896.

22 CL, Jan. 1904. J. E. Defebaugh, History of the Lumber Industry of America (Chicago, 1906), vol. I, p. 184.

23 Robert Legget, Ottawa Waterway: Gateway to a Continent (Toronto, 1975). Robert Passfield, Building the Rideau Canal: A Pictorial History (Don Mills, 1982). Judith Tulloch, "The Rideau Canal: Defence, Transport and Recreation," History and Archaeology, No. 50 (Ottawa, 1981). Normand Lafrenière, The Ottawa River Canal System (Ottawa, 1984).

24 Marsha Hay Snyder, "Industrial Development in the Rideau Corridor to 1920," Microfiche Report Series, No. 223 (Parks Canada, 1980), pp. 19-20, 213-214. S. Gillis, The Timber Trade, p. 93.

25 J. L. Gourlay, History of the Ottawa Valley (Ottawa, 1896), p. 137. CL, Nov. 1889, p. 6.

26 Lafrenière, Ottawa River Canal System, pp. 57, 75-78.

27 Revenue from Timber Trade of the Upper Ottawa, Archives of Ontario, RG 1, E 5, vol. 16, p. 4, converted to pounds at the rate of £4.74 per dollar. S. Gillis, The Timber Trade, p. 275. Reid, "John Egan," pp. 196-97.

28 John MacTaggart, Three Years in Canada (London, 1829), pp. 245-47. S. Gillis, The Timber Trade, pp. 276-82.

29 Joseph Bouchette, The British Dominions in North America, vol. I (London 1832), p. 200.

30 Legget, Ottawa Waterway, pp. 165ff.

31 Harold Innis and A. R. M. Lower (eds.), *Select Documents in Canadian Economic History, 1783-1885* (Toronto, 1929), pp. 506-508. Canada, Parliament, *Sessional Papers* (hereafter CSP), 1866-67, No. 8, App. 13, pp. 103-105. CSP, 1916, No. 19a, pp. 9ff. *CL*, 1 June 1909, pp. 18, 34. R.G. Morgan, "The Georgian Bay Ship Canal," *Canadian Geographical Journal*, March 1969.

32 Reid, "John Egan." Legget, *Ottawa Waterway*, p. 174.

33 S. Gillis, *The Timber Trade*, pp. 266-72.

34 MacTaggart, *Three Years in Canada*, p. 95. Bruce S. Elliott, The City Beyond: A History of Nepean, *Birthplace of Canada's Capital, 1792-1990*, (Nepean, 1991), p. 83.

35 *Memorials, Documents and Affidavits Submitted to the Executive Council by Ruggles Wright Esq. with Reference to his Slides at the Chats and Chaudiere* (Montreal, 1849). Thomas C. Keefer, *Montreal and the Ottawa*, (Montreal, 1854), p. 39.

36 Joseph Tassé, *Philemon Wright ou Colonisation et commerce de bois* (Montreal, 1874), p. 63.

37 *JLA*, 1849, App. NNNN.

38 CSP, 1883, No. 10A, App. 22, p. 663. Canada, Report of the Commissioner of Public Works (hereafter, RCPW), 1866-67, pp. 102-105. S. Gillis, *The Timber Trade*, p. 292.

39 Patrick M. O. Evans, *The Wrights* (Ottawa, 1978), p. 55A.

40 LAC, RG 11, Dept. of Public Works, Series II, No. 8143, Rubidge to T.A. Begley, 6 Sept. 1845. Ibid., No. 930, Report on the Ottawa Works by T.C. Keefer, 23 Oct. 1846. T.C. Keefer, "President's Address," *Transactions of the Canadian Society of Civil Engineers* (1888), pp. 24-27. Canada, RCPW, 1866-67, App. 17, p. 134.

41 Canada, RCPW, 1866-67, App. 17, pp. 134-53; ibid., 1873-74, p. 39.

42 CSP, 1883, No. 10A, App. 22, pp. 668, 697. Ibid., 1860, App. D. Ernest Marceau, "The Carillon Canal, Dam and Slide," *Canadian Society of Civil Engineers Bulletin*, 11 Oct. 1900, pp. 102-16.

43 Canada, RCPW, 1866-67, App. 17, pp. 134-53. Canada, Parlement, *Documents de la Session*, 1916, #19a, pp. 13, 22, 27.

44 Ibid., 1871-72, p. 28; ibid., 1887-88, p. 156.

45 Francis B. Head, *The Emigrant* (London, 1846), p. 108. Joseph Pope, *The Tour of Their Highnesses, The Duke and Duchess of Cornwall and York* (Ottawa, 1903), pp. 59-60. Lady Dufferin, *My Canadian Journal*, G. C. Walker, ed., (Don Mills, 1969), pp. 7, 110. CL, 15 June 1883, p. 188. Sandra Gwyn, *The Private Capital: Ambition and Love in the Age of Macdonald and Laurier*

(Toronto, 1984), pp. 320-21. See also G. T. Borrett in Gerald Craig (ed.), *Early Travellers in the Canadas, 1791-1867* (Toronto, 1955), pp. 283-85.

46 *CSP*, 1883, No.10A, App. 22, p. 663. Omer Lavallée, *Van Horne's Road* (Montreal 1974), p. 179

47 George M. Grant, *Picturesque Canada: The Country as It Was and Is* (Toronto, 1882), pp. 177-78.

48 Canada, RCPW, 1866-67, App. 17, pp. 132-135, 152-57.

49 Canada, RCPW, 1867, App. 17, pp. 156-57; ibid, App. 68, pp. 476-78; ibid., 1871-72, pp. 4, 68; ibid., 1875-76, pp. 48-49; ibid., 1886-87, pp. cxx, 156; ibid., 1887-88, p. 156; ibid., 1893-94, pp. 20, 170-71; ibid., 1897-98, vi, pp. 11, 13.

Chapter 4

1 *CL*, 15 Sept. 1883, p. 279; 15 June 1913, p. 36. Gourlay, *History of the Ottawa Valley*, p. 7. Reid, *The Upper Ottawa Valley*, pp. 149, 153.

2 Herman H. Chapman calculates the wastage at 36.4 percent in his work, *Forest Mensuration* (New York, 1921), p. 33.

3 A.W. Cowan, "*The Canadian White Pine Trade with the United Kingdom, 1867-1914*" (M.A. thesis, Carleton University, 1966), pp. 62ff. CL, 15 June 1913, pp. 36-37.

4 *Comparative Statement of Timber Passed down the Ottawa …1847 to 1857*, Ontario Archives, RG1, E5, vol. 16. Canada, JLA, 1859, App. 17, R. Prov. of Ontario, *Sessional Papers* (hereafter OSP), 1889, no. 26, pp. 14-15. QDS, 1889, no. 26, p. 244.

5 Lambert and Pross, *Renewing Nature's Wealth*, p. 573.

6 Report of 25 Oct. 1880, reprinted in *CL*, 1 Aug. 1916, p. 29.

7 James Little, *The Lumber Trade of the Ottawa Valley* (Ottawa, 1872), p. 16. Kermot Moore, *Kipawa: Portrait of a People* (Cobalt, 1982), pp. 99-101.

8 George S. Thompson, *Up to Date, or the Life of a Lumberman* (Peterborough, 1895), p. 77.

9 *CL*, 1 Sept. 1910, p. 22.

10 Peter Baskerville (ed.), *The Bank of Upper Canada: A Collection of Documents* (Toronto, 1987), pp. 106-107, 110-111. S. Gillis, *The Timber Trade*, pp. 182-99, 359. Lower, *Great Britain's Woodyard*, pp. 140-47, 153-57.

11 Canada, JLA, 1853, App. MMMM, p. 17.

12 Little, , pp. 32-33.

13 Robert Jones, *History of Agriculture in Ontario* (Toronto, 1946), p. 116. Keefer, *Montreal and the Ottawa*, p. 69. Douglas McCalla, *Planting the Province: The Economic History of Upper Canada, 1784-1870* (Toronto, 1993), p. 58.

14 Lafrenière, *Ottawa River Canal System*, pp. 59, 75-77.

15 Cynthia Craigie, *The Influence of the Timber Trade and Philemon Wright on the Social and Economic Development of Hull Township*, (M.A. thesis, Carleton University, 1969), p. 33. E.C. Grant, "In the Lumber Woods," *Canadian Magazine*, April 1894, pp. 549-56. S. Gillis, *The Timber Trade*, pp. 146-47. Canada, *JLA*, 1853, App. MMMM, pp. 1, 7, 12. *CL*, 1 Dec. 1881, p. 6. Pontiac Heritage Group, *Architectural Heritage of the Pontiac* (Quebec, 1981), p. 17. Allan Gilmour was reported operating nine logging farms, totalling 1,500 acres, in 1872: Little, *The Lumber Trade*, p. 42.

16 W. H. Smith, *Canada: Past, Present and Future* (Toronto 1851), II, pp. 3-6, 375. Canada, RCPW, 1866-67, App. 13, p. 115. *CL*, Nov. 1888, p. 5; 15 Dec. 1931, p. 30. George Spragge, "Colonization Roads in Canada West, 1850-1867," *Ontario History* (Winter 1957), pp. 1-17. Brenda Lee-Whiting, "The Opeongo Road; An Early Colonization Scheme," *Canadian Geographical Journal*, March 1967, pp. 76-83.

17 Craigie, *Influence of the Timber Trade*, p. 118.

18 Michael Cross, "Daniel McLachlin," *DCB*, vol. X, pp. 480-481. Canada, JLA, 1853, App. MMMM, pp. 5, 7, 14. John Hughson and Courtney Bond, *Hurling Down the Pine* (Chelsea, 1964), p. 99.

19 *CSP*, 1909, 19a. Ouellet, Thériault, *"Philemon Wright."* Henri Pilon, "Joseph-Ignace Aumond," *DCB*, vol. X, p. 23. Arthur Buies, *L'Outaouais supérieur* (Québec 1889), pp. 128-131. *CL*, 1 June 1882, p. 170; June 1901, p. 6.

20 S. Gillis, *The Timber Trade*, pp. 49-54.

21 Jones, pp. 117-18. William S. Hunter, *Hunter's Ottawa Scenery: In the Vicinity of Ottawa City, Canada* (Ottawa, 1855), p. 13. *CL*, 1 Feb. 1883, p. 41.

22 *CL*, 1 Sept. 1916, p. 58.

23 Donald MacKay, *The Lumberjacks* (Toronto, 1978), p. 80. *CL*, 15 May 1885, p. 176; Dec. 1903, p. 17.

24 Keefer, *Montreal and the Ottawa*, pp. 64-65.

25 Ottawa Citizen, 9 Sept. 1854. Anon., "A Trip to the Timber Makers," *Once a Week* (London, Eng.) 4 Jan. 1862, p. 49 (continued, 22 Feb. 1862); this account, written by an anonymous English writer who, around 1860, spent a season with the shantymen of the Ottawa Valley, is rich in detail.

26 For example, see Head, *The Emigrant*, p. 91.

27 Hughson and Bond, p. 80. Reid, p. 149. Joseph Tassé, *La Vallée de l'Outaouais*

(Montreal, 1873), p. 33. *CL*, 30 Nov. 1880.

28 Gourlay, *History of the Ottawa Valley*, p. 138. Anson Gard, *Pioneers of the Ottawa Valley* (Ottawa, 1908), part IV, p. 28. Grant, *Picturesque Canada*, p. 220. "A Trip to the Timber Makers," p. 51. *CL*, 1 Sept. 1916, pp. 58, 60.

29 Alexander Koroleff et al., *River Drive of Pulpwood: Efficiency of Technique* (Pulp & Paper Inst. of Canada, 1946), pp. 168ff.

30 *CL*, 15 Dec. 1931, p. 31.

31 J. Barnwell Jackson, *The Lumberman's Timber Mark Guide* (Montreal, 1874). Diane Aldred (comp.), *Registered Timber Marks of Eastern Canada from 1870 to 1984* (Ottawa, 1985).

32 A. Koroleff, *River Drive of Pulpwood*, pp. 168ff.

33 A.R.M. Lower, "The Forest in New France," *Canadian Historical Association, Annual Report*, 1928, pp. 80-89.

34 Picken, p. xxiv.

35 Joshua Fraser, 340-43. Thompson, p. 63. Grant, *Picturesque Canada*, pp. 176, 231. Keefer, *Montreal and the Ottawa*, pp. 67-68. *CL*, July 1892, p. 8; Sept. 1893, p. 8; July 1896, p. 13; Sept. 1896, p. 14; 15 July 1908, p. 33.

36 *CL*, Nov. 1886, p. 7; Sept. 1893, p. 8; 14 Feb. 1906.

37 Fraser, p. 340. *CL*, Nov. 1892, p. 10; July 1896, p. 13. Canada, RCPW, 1860, App. D. Lafrenière, App. C.

38 *CL*, Sept. 1889, p. 6.

39 Anon., "All Down the River," *Once a Week*, 22 Feb. 1862, pp. 243-49. Keefer, *President's Address*, p. 25. Fraser, p. 340. *CL*, July 1896, p. 13.

40 "All Down the River," pp. 245-47. Fraser, p. 342. Keefer, *Montreal and the Ottawa*, p. 67. S. Gillis, p. 175. Michael Cross, "Dark Druidical Groves," p. 280. *CL*, 1 June 1882, p. 170.

41 *CL*, 15 Sept. 1881, p. 19; 1 Oct. 1881, p. 1; 1 Nov. 1881, p. 10; 2 July 1883, p. 201; Aug. 1900, p. ii; 9 March 1904, p. iii. CSP, 1911, no. 19, part vi, p. 8.

42 Edward Bush, *Commercial Navigation on the Rideau Canal, 1832-1961* (Ottawa: Parks Canada), MRS #247, p. 243.

43 P-André Sévigny, *Trade and Navigation on the Chambly Canal: A Historical Overview* (Ottawa, 1983), pp. 32ff. *CL*, 15 Jan. 1911, p. 8.

44 S. Gillis, p. 103. *CL*, Aug. 1894, p. 8. Lower, *Great Britain's Woodyard*, pp. 202-203. Graeme Wynn, *Timber Colony: A Historical Geography of Early Nineteenth Century New Brunswick* (Toronto, 1981), p. 67.

45 Archives of Ontario, RG 1, F-1-8, vol. 57, p. 52.

46   TABLE TWO

Ottawa Valley output of squared red and white pine timber cut on Crown land compared to total production in the Province of Canada.*		
Year	Province of Canada output	Ottawa Valley share of total
1844	13,328,266 cubic feet	81%
1845	18,276,831 cubic feet	78%
1846	20,517,447 cubic feet	69%
1856	11,578,554 cubic feet	93%
1857	14,596,367 cubic feet	92%
1858	10,609,510 cubic feet	92%

*Computed from statistics in: A.R.M. Lower, *Great Britain's Woodyard*, p. 208; Prov. of Canada, *Report of the Commissioner of Crown Lands*, 1856, 1857, 1858.

Richard Reid has calculated that in 1846 the Valley produced 63.5 percent of the white pine timber in the Province of Canada, a proportion that increased to 81.0 percent by 1851 (Reid, p. lxv, n. 82). See also S. Gillis, pp. 103-04. It should be noted that this table refers exclusively to timber cut on Crown lands. Square timber was also produced on freehold land owned by farmers who had settled in the Valley, but the volume is difficult to track. See C. Grant Head, "Nineteenth Century Timbering and Sawlogging in the Ottawa Valley: Documentary Sources and Spatial Patterns," in V. Ivanoffski, S. Campbell (eds.), *Exploring Our Heritage: The Ottawa Valley Experience* (Toronto, 1980), pp. 52-57.

47   TABLE THREE

Ottawa Valley output of squared red and white pine timber cut on Crown land compared to total production in Ontario and Quebec.*		
Year	Ontario — Quebec output	Ottawa Valley share of total
1885	2,591,756 cubic feet	57%
1887	1,751,932 cubic feet	58%
1889	2,715,180 cubic feet	48%
1891	1,277,245 cubic feet	51%

*Computed from statistics in Québec, *Documents de la Session*, 1886, no. 4; 1888, no. 4; 1890, no. 4; 1892, no. 4; and Ontario, Sessional Papers, 1886, no. 33; 1888, no. 20; 1890, no. 22; 1892, no. 24.

48 In 1845 New Brunswick produced 8,960,000 cubic feet of squared pine timber; in 1821 it turned out 17,320,000 cubic feet. See statistical tables in Peter McClelland, "The New Brunswick Economy in the Nineteenth Century," (Ph.D. thesis, Harvard University, 1966), Table XXXII, pp. 110-111. These fig-

ures, cited in tons, have been converted on a ratio of 40 cubic feet to the ton. [See R.G. Lewis, *Forest Products of Canada* (Ottawa, 1913), p. 31]. Also, while these figures refer to exports, very little square timber would not have been exported. For comparisons with the Ottawa Valley see Note 44 above.

49 *CL*, 15 July 1908, p. 33; 15 Jan. 1911, p. 7.

50 *CL*, 16 Jan. 1882. *CSP*, 1911, No. 19, part vi, p. 10.

51 *CL*, 1 April 1925, pp. 47-48; 1 Jan. 1930, p. 30; 15 March 1930, p.79

Chapter 5

1 Lower, *Great Britain's Woodyard*, pp. 113-18. S. Gillis, pp, 51-61. McCalla, p. 263. Forbes Hirsch, "William Stewart," *DCB*, vol. VIII, pp. 839-40.

2 Richard Scott, *Recollections of Bytown* (Ottawa, 1908), p. 16.

3 Canada, *Census*, 1870-71, vol. 4 (1851-52), pp. 198, 218. Terry Reynolds, *Stronger than a Hundred Men: A History of the Vertical Water Wheel* (Baltimore, 1983).

4 R. P. Gillis, "George Hamilton," *DCB*, vol. VII, pp. 380-83; "John Hamilton," *DCB*, vol. IX, pp. 379-81. Rev. J. Abbott (ed.), *Phillip Musgrave, or Memoirs of a Church of England Missionary in the North American Colonies* (Londong, 1846), p. 60. Lower, *Great Britain's Woodyard*, pp. 171ff. Canada, *JLA*, 1855, App. MM. One standard deal measured 27.5 board feet [Canada, *House of Commons, Journals*, 1876, App. 3, "Report of the Select Committee on the Causes of the Present Depression," testimony of A. H. Baldwin, p. 8].

5 Hughson and Bond, *Hurling Down the Pine*, pp. 35-39. R. P. Gillis, "Allan Gilmour," *DCB*, vol. XII, pp. 366-68. John H. Taylor, *Ottawa: An Illustrated History* (Toronto, 1986), p. 51. *JLA*, 1853, App. MMMM, p. 15.

6 E. F. Bush, "Thomas McKay," *DCB*, vol. VIII, pp. 551-54. Smith, p. 370. Reid, pp. 163-64.

7 LAC, RG 11, Ser. II, No. 8143, F. P. Rubidge to T. A. Begley, 6 Sept. 1845. Elliott, p. 97.

8 RCPW, 1866-67, p. 103.

9 LAC, RG 1, E 1, book M, vol. 75, pp. 264-65. LAC, RG 11, B-3, vol. 4326, f. 2991-1-A-A, Memoranda from H. H. Killaly, 30 June and 9 July 1852.

10 *Bytown Citizen*, 4 Sept. and 2 Oct. 1852. RCPW, 1852-53, pp. 11, 30.

11 Scott, pp. 20-21. *Ottawa Tribune*, 10 October 1860. *Liste des limites à bois, affermées dans la province de Québec, donnant le nom des acquéreurs primitifs* (Quebec, 1918), p. 15. More recently, an Ottawa historian has suggested

that it may have been John Egan, the timberman and local Member of the Legislative Assembly, who arranged the deal (Taylor, p. 52).

12 *CSP*, 1869, No. 8, App. 13, pp. 79ff.

13 Robert Peter Gillis, "Henry Franklin Bronson," *DCB*, vol. XI, pp. 112-13. Elliott, *The City Beyond*, pp. 98-99, 117. R. Peter Gillis, "The 'American Community' at the Chaudière: The Beginning of the Sawmill Industry in Ottawa-Hull, 1851-1866," in Pierre-Louis Lapointe, pp. 55ff. *The Canadian Biographical Dictionary and Portrait Gallery of Eminent and Self-made Men, Ontario Volume* (Toronto, 1880), pp. 127-29, 492-97.

14 Odette Vincent-Domey, "Ezra Butler Eddy," *DCB*, vol. XIII, pp. 318-20. *CL*, Sept. 1898, pp. 3-4; June 1904, p. 26.

15 Little, pp. 33-45.

16 In 1889, all Chaudière lot-owners agreed to return title of their lands to the Crown and leased their lands thereafter: see Lease, 19 Nov. 1889, in LAC, RG 11, vol. 4326, f. 2991-1-A.

17 1851-52 figures in Canada, *Census, 1870-71*, vol. 4, pp. 198, 218. For 1860-61, *Canada, Census, 1860-61*, vol. 2, pp. 230-31, 260-61.

18 Charles Marshall, *The Canadian Dominion* (London, Eng., 1871), p. 46. A.R.M. Lower, *The North American Assault on the Canadian Forest* (Toronto, 1938), pp. 150-52.

19 Canada, *House of Commons, Journals*, 1876, App. 3, Report of the Select Committee . . . , pp. 5, 11. *CL*, Nov. 1897, pp. 5-6. Gillis, "Bronson," *DCB*, XI, p. 113.

20 S. R. Elliot, *The Bytown and Prescott, 1854-1979* (Ottawa, 1979). C. C. J. Bond, "Tracks into Ottawa: The Construction of Railways into Canada's Capital," *Ontario History*, Sept. 1865, pp. 123-34. Taylor, pp. 48-49.

21 Robert W. S. Mackay (comp.), *The Canadian Directory* (Montreal, 1851), pp. 43ff. Reid, "John Egan." Bush, "Thomas McKay."

22 Scott, pp. 6-9. Taylor, pp. 48-49. Reid, p. lxxxvi.

23 David B. Knight (ed.), *Choosing Canada's Capital: Jealousy and Friction in the Nineteenth Century* (Toronto, 1977), pp. 158, 168.

24 R. P. Gillis, "William Goodhue Perley," *DCB*, vol. XI, pp. 681-83.

25 Reid, pp. lxxxii, 210.

26 Whitton, pp. 58ff. *CL*, 15 Aug. 1881, p. 6. *The North Shore Railway: The St. Lawrence Railway: The Canada Central Railway, A Sketch* (Quebec, 1870). Wayne Tassé, *Pacific Extension: The Building of the Canada Central Railway* (Smiths Falls, 1984). Wayne Tassé, *Broad Gauge in the Ottawa Valley: The Building of the Brockville & Ottawa Railway* (Smiths Falls, 1993).

27 Michael Bliss, *Northern Enterprise: Five Centuries of Canadian Business* (Toronto, 1987), p. 322; Lower, *Assault*, p. 167.

28 Gillis, "Perley." Canada, *Statutes*, (1879), 42 Vict., cap. 57.

29 Allan Bell, *A Way to the West* (Mallorytown, 1976), pp. 22, 177.

30 Canada, *Statutes*, (1891), 54-55 Vict., cap. 93.

31 G. R. Stevens, *Canadian National Railways*, vol. I (Toronto, 1960), pp. 365-66. Niall Mackay, *Over the Hills to Georgian Bay* (Erin Mills, 1984). Bell, pp. 50ff. R. P. Gillis, "E.H. Bronson and Corporate Capitalism: A Study in Canadian Business Thought and Action, 1880-1910," M.A. thesis, Queen's University, 1975, pp. 62-64. *CL*, Sept. 1898, pp. 3-4. The OA&SPR also did considerable business carrying western wheat to eastern markets; for this, Booth built grain elevators at Depot Harbour.

32 *CL*, 19 Feb. 1902, 20 Jan. 1904, Oct. 1904; May 1905; 15 Feb. 1909. Bell, pp. 143, 163.

33 *CL*, Dec. 1895, Feb. 1896, Sept. 1898. Brian Westhouse, *Whitney: St. Anthony's Mill Town on Booth's Railway* (Whitney, 1995).

34 Nelles, pp. 120-22. Jean-Guy Perras, *La Saga de Thurso* (Saint-André-Avellin, 1985), pp. 71ff. John Duffield, *Artifacts and Remnants of 200 Years of Lumbering in the Ottawa Valley*, vol. II (Ottawa, 1996), p. 11.

35 *Liste des limites à bois . . .*, p. 21.

36 Reid, p. 248.

37 *CL*, Nov. 1886; Sept. 1893; 15 Sept. 1910. George Perry, *The Staple Trade of Canada* (Ottawa, 1862), p. 27.

38 *CL*, 1 Sept. 1910, p. 24; 15 Sept. 1910, pp. 22-24; 1 Sept. 1916, p. 77. Grant, pp. 220-222.

39 *CL*, Dec. 1889; 26 Nov. 1902; May 1905. Hughson and Bond, p. 77. C. Ross Silversides and Richard A. Rajala, *Broadaxe to Flying Shear: The Mechanization of Forest Harvesting East of the Rockies* (Ottawa, 1997), p. 135.

40 Aubrey White, *A History of Crown Timber Regulations from the Date of the French Occupation to the Year 1899* (Toronto, 1899), p. 262. Canada, *Statutes*, 16 Vict., cap. cxci. RCPW, 1867, App. 17, pp. 145, 153.

41 Hammond, "Capital, Labour and Lumber," pp. 55-77.

42 E. L. Jamieson, *Caldwells of Lanark*, (n.p., 1973), p. 5. B. H. Morrison, "John Godfrey Spragge," *DCB*, vol. XI, p. 844. Jamie Benidickson, "Private Rights and Public Purposes in the Lakes, Rivers and Streams of Ontario, 1870-1930," in David H. Flaherty (ed.), *Essays in the History of Canadian Law*, vol. II (Toronto, 1983), pp. 372-73. A. Margaret Evans, *Sir Oliver Mowat* (Toronto, 1992), pp. 157, 171.

43 CL, 15 Nov. 1910, p. 36.

44 "Rapport d'une exploration de la Gatineau . . . ," QDS, 1911, vol. II, no. 5, App. 59.

45 CL, Oct. 1900, pp. 5-6. Hughson, pp. 105-107.

46 Moore, pp. 106-10.

47 Brenda Lee-Whiting, "The Pointer Boat," Canadian Geographic Journal, Feb. 1970, pp. 47-51. Lana Shaw, "The Cockburn Pointer Boat," Historical Society of Ottawa, pamphlet no. 47, Jan. 1994. The Pointer Boat (Ont., Dept. of Lands and Forests, 1963). Thompson, p. 32. CL, 1 Sept. 1912.

48 CL, Nov. 1886; 15 April 1911. Ottawa Citizen, 12 March 1990. The Upper Ottawa Improvement Company: Charter, General Acts, Private Acts and By-Laws (Ottawa 1915). In 1919 the government decided to lease all its slides and other Ottawa River improvements to ICO (LAC, RG 2, Order-in-Council, #1791, 26 Aug. 1919).

49 Canada, Dept. of Public Works, Annual Report, 1873-74, App. 11, p. 53. George H. Cole, Lumbering in the Ottawa Valley . . . Logging and Milling Operations of McLachlin Bros. Ltd. at Arnprior, Ont. (study prepared for the New York State College of Forestry, Syracuse, N.Y., 1924), pp. 53-56. CL, 15 May 1882; Aug. 1887; May 1888; June 1888; June 1893. Ottawa Citizen, 24 May 1893.

50 CL, 16 May 1881; Nov. 1886; Nov. 1896; 15 April 1911.

51 A photo of the pile can be seen in CL, Feb. 1898, p. 9.

52 CL, Dec. 1888, p. 6; 1 Feb. 1920, p. 43. Lower, Great Britain's Woodyard, pp. 132, 171-80. R. P. Gillis, "George Hamilton," DCB, vol. VII, pp. 380-83. CSP, 1917, No. 10c, pp. 191-93. The "Timber Trades Journal" List of Shipping Marks on Timber (New York, 1923), p. 85.

53 C. J. Telford, Small Sawmill Operator's Manual (Washington, 1952), pp. 114-18. CL, Nov. 1886, March 1896, 18 April 1900. The Wood Industries of Canada (London, England, 1897), p. 44.

54 Russell Sturgis (ed.), A Dictionary of Architecture and Building (London and New York, 1902), I, pp. 314, 752; II, pp. 811-812; III, p. 156. Brooke Hindle, Material Culture of the Wooden Age (New York, 1981), pp. 23, 88.

55 Little, pp. 33ff. CL, 15 June 1881, p. 8.

56 Reid, p. 163. W.H. Smith, pp. 370, 378.

57 Little, pp. 33ff. Ottawa Citizen, 19 April 1875. Marshall, Canadian Dominion, pp. 42-43. Edward Knight (ed.), Knight's American Mechanical Dictionary, vol. 3 (Boston 1876), pp. 2041-42.

58 Felicity Leung, Direct Drive Waterpower in Canada: 1607-1910 (Presentation

to the Historic Sites and Monuments Board of Canada, 1986), pp. 94-103. Gerald and Elizabeth Bloomfield, *Water Wheels and Steam Engines: Powered Establishments of Ontario* (Guelph, 1989), p. 40. Canada, *Journals of the Senate*, 1888, App. 2, p. 56. Lower, *Assault*, p. 48.

59 Hughson and Bond, pp. 39-40, 44-50. *CL*, Feb. 1896, p. 8; Nov. 1896, pp. 12-16. Elliott, *Nepean*, pp. 119-20.

60 One such mill was that at Balaclava, Ont., near Renfrew. See Brenda Lee-Whiting, "Saga of a Nineteenth Century Sawmill," *Canadian Geographical Journal*, Feb. 1967.

61 Sing C. Chew, *Logs for Capital: The Timber Industry and Capitalist Enterprise in the Nineteenth Century* (Westport, Conn., 1992), p. 76. William Fox et al., *The Mill* (Toronto, 1976), p. 178. Edward Knight, p. 2041. *CL*, Nov. 1896, pp. 12-16; April, 1890, p. 6; Aug. 1900, p. 27; Dec. 1904, p.18.

62 Edward Knight, p. 2041. *CL*, 1 June 1883; Dec. 1895.

63 *CL*, 1 June 1883, p. 162; May 1902, p. 11; Oct. 1907, p. 13.

64 Rodney C. Loehr, "Saving the Kerf: The Introduction of the Band Saw Mill," *Agricultural History* 23 (1949), pp. 168-72. *CL*, 15 Jan. 1883; June 1888; Oct. 1888; May 1891; Jan. 1897. Cole, pp. 93-94, 100.

65 *CL*, 1 July 1881, p. 5; 15 July 1881, p. 10; Oct. 1895, p. 10. Grant, p. 174. The first Canadian use of electricity in an industrial setting seems to have taken place in Montreal in 1880, but the power may not have come from hydro sources; see Loris Russell, *A Heritage of Light: Lamps and Lighting in the Early Canadian Home* (Toronto, 2003), p. 311.

66 Leung, pp. 108 -12, 125. *CL*, 1 Nov. 1908, pp. 18-19; 15 Nov. 1910, p. 23.

67 *CL*, Feb. 1895; Feb. 1898.

68 *CL*, Nov. 1895, p. 11. See also *CL*, Aug. 1894, p. 9; Sept. 1898, p. 3; and *The Wood Industries of Canada* (London, Eng., 1897), pp. 33, 35.

69 *CL*, Feb. 1907, p. 74.

70 *CL*, Sept. 1888. Cole, pp. 121-24.

71 "Legislation in Canada for the Protection of Persons Employed in Factories," *The Labour Gazette*, Nov. 1900, pp. 104-12. Eric Tucker, "Making the Workplace 'Safe' in Capitalism: The Enforcement of Factory Legislation in Nineteenth Century Ontario," *Labour*, Spring 1988, pp. 45-85. Lorna Hurl, "Restricting Child Factory Labour in Late Nineteenth Century Ontario," *Labour*, Spring 1988, pp. 87-121. *Report of the Royal Commission on the Relations of Labor and Capital in Canada* (Ottawa 1889), vol. 4, pp. 1105, 1134-36, 1149-52, 1178-79; vol. 5, p. 1360. *Pulp and Paper Magazine Canada* (hereafter *PPMC*), 1 Dec. 1913.

72 *CL*, Sept. 1893. Other cases of death by saws were periodically reported; see,

for example, *CL*, 15 Oct. 1884; Michael Newton (ed.), *The Bytown Packet /
The Ottawa Citizen, 1846-1879, Birth, Marriage and Death Notices* (Ottawa,
1990), vol. 1, #368.

73 Little, pp. 36, 39, 42, 47. *CL*, Nov. 1892; Nov. 96. Whitton, p. 145.

74 Cole, pp. 150-55. *CL*, Aug. 1887.

75 R.W. Phipps, "Across the Watershed of Eastern Ontario," *Forest History*, Oct.
1965, pp. 2-8. See also, Ishbel Gordon, Lady Aberdeen, *Through Canada with
a Kodak* (Edinburgh, 1893), pp. 84-85.

76 J. E. Defebaugh, *History of the Lumber Industry in America*, vol. II (Chicago
1906), pp. 125-32. *CL*, Jan. 1900, p. 6; Dec. 1901, p. 10; 1 Sept. 1911, p. 71;1
Feb. 1920, p. 43; 15 Sept. 1924, pp. 116-17.

77 *CL*, March 1889, p. 19.

78 *CL*, Feb. 1887, p. 4; Feb. 1894, p. 8; Sept. 1898, p. 3; Nov. 1888, p. 9. Gillis,
"E.H. Bronson and Corporate Capitalism," p. 26. Defebaugh, vol. II, pp.
172-73.

79 John Rankin, *A History Of Our Firm* (Liverpool, 1921). Canada, *Journals of
the House of Commons*, 1876, App. 3, pp. 2, 4, 8, 171. *CL*, Jan. 1887, p. 10;
March 1888, p. 8; Feb. 1897, p. 7.

80 Little, p. 34. *CL*, 15 July 1881, p. 10; 1 May 1882, p. 138. Chew, p. 84.

81 Hughson, pp. 77, 110-13. Gard, *Hub and Spokes*, p. 329. *CL*, 15 July 1881, p.
10. There is evidence that some barges could carry up to 750,000 board feet
of lumber: *CL*, June 1893, p. 8.

82 Bell, p. 162. *CSP*, 1895, No. 8A, Table 2. Lafrenière, App. C. *CL*, 1 April
1884; July 1887; May 1888; 30 Oct. 1901; Feb. 1903; 15 July 1911. *Ottawa
Journal*, 12 March 1917, p. 9.

83   TABLE FOUR

Lumber production of Ottawa Valley large-scale sawmills (in board feet), including deals, dimension timber, and boards and planks.*			
Year	Board feet	Year	Board feet
1860	92,802,000	1901	586,000,000
1874	438,750,000	1907	532,000,000
1882	800,000,000	1914	451,000,000
1889	795,000,000	1919	298,000,000
1895	627,000,000	1925	279,000,000

*1860 output from Prov. of Canada, Census, 1860-61, vol. 2 (Quebec 1964), pp.
230-31, 260-61: eight districts and parts of two others. 1874 output from J.E.
Defebaugh, History of the Lumber Industry of America (Chicago, 1906), vol. I,
p. 270. Remainder: CL, 15 Dec. 1882; Jan. 1890; Feb. 1896; Feb. 1903; 15 Feb.

1909; 15 March 1922; 15 March 1926 (sometimes corrected for inappropriate inclusions).

This table does not include lumber sawn in small mills that served only local markets, but even in the aggregate, their output would not be significant. Indeed, the 1901 census counted 181 sawmills in the Ottawa Valley, but only 18 produced three million or more board feet that year. [Canada, Census, 1901, vol. III, pp. 178-247].

84 *CSP*, 1895, No. 8A, pp. 69-72. Bruce Hodgins et al., "The Ontario and Quebec Experiments in Forest Reserves, 1883-1930," *Journal of Forest History*, Jan. 1982, p. 23. Fred McClement, *The Flaming Forests* (Toronto, 1969), pp. 87-101. *CL*, 8 Aug. 1906. Nelles, pp. 120, 160.

85 *CL*, 15 Aug. 1885, p. 275. Cowan, p. 15. R. P. Gillis, "E.H. Bronson and Corporate Capitalism," p. 30.

86 *CL*, 29 July 1896, p. ii; Feb. 1890, p. 6.

87 *CL*, Nov. 1886, p. 7; Nov. 1893, p. 3. Canada, Parl., *Documents de la Session*, 1916, No. 19A, p. 8. *QDS*, 1907, no. 42, pp. 11, 29. *CSP*, 1911, No. 19A, pp. 29, 46.

88 Lower, *Assault*, pp. 114, 139.

89 George Carruthers, *Paper-Making* (Toronto, 1847), pp. 394-401. R. P. Gillis, "E.H. Bronson and Corporate Capitalism," pp. 111-13. *CL*, May 1889; April 1892; Nov. 1892; 7 Dec. 1898. Gillis, "Perley," *DCB*, XI, pp. 681-83. M. C. Urquhart and K. A. H. Buckley (eds.), *Historical Statistics of Canada* (Toronto, 1965), p. 292.

90 G. W. Shorter, *The Ottawa-Hull Fire of 1900* (Ottawa, 1962). *Ottawa Citizen*, 27 April 1900. *CL*, 2 May 1900. Vincent-Domey, p. 320. *Ottawa Journal*, 4 May 1904.

91 *CL*, 16 May 1900; 30 May 1900; 1 Aug. 1900; 8 Aug. 1900; Feb. 1901; 3 April 1901. Urquhart and Buckley, p. 292.

92 Jon Fear, "'The Lumber Piles Must Go': Ottawa Lumber Interests and the Great Fire of 1900," *Urban History Review* (June 1979). *CL*, June 1903, p. 27; 1 July 1909, p. 34. Elliott, p. 223.

93 R. P. Gillis, "E.H. Bronson and Corporate Capitalism," pp. 111ff. Carruthers, pp. 402-06, 611-12, 656-57. *Phillips' Paper Trade Directory of the World, 1914-15* (London, 1915), pp. 334-45. *PPMC*, Jan. 1904, p. 26; July 1904, p. 216. *CL*, 1 Dec. 1913, p. 58.

94 *CL*, 1 Nov. 1908, pp. 18-19; 1 Aug. 1930, pp. 93-94.

95 Marshall, *Canadian Dominion*, p. 43. *CL*, Oct. 1906, p. 18; see also March 1888, p. 7. *PPMC*, July 1904, p. 222. *The consul's figures show that the Valley supplied $3,438,029 worth of the country's total $6,209,023 of pine exports: CL, Nov. 1888, p. 9.*

Chapter 6

1 Paul Rutherford, *The Making of the Canadian Media* (Toronto, 1978), pp. 49ff.

2 *CL*, Feb. 1900, p. 13; April 1901, p. 16; June 1901, p. 10. Nelson Brown, *Logging; Principles and Practices in the United States and Canada* (New York, 1934), pp. 253ff.

3 Koroleff, p. 5 et passim.

4 *Pulp and Paper Magazine of Canada* (hereafter *PPMC*), Feb. 1936, pp. 153-55.

5 *PPMC*, July 1942, pp. 627-31; Jan. 1974.

6 *PPMC*, Aug. 1904, p. 229. *Le nord de l'Outaouais* (Ottawa, 1938), p. 50.

7 Brenda Lee-Whiting, "The Alligator: Unique Canadian Boat," *Canadian Geographical Journal*, Jan. 1968, pp. 30-33. Bruce Pearce, *Historical Highlights of Norfolk County* (Hamilton, 1973), pp. 113-18. *CL*, May 1893, p. 16; July 1895, p. 14; Nov. 1895, p. 10. *QDS*, 1911, vol. 44, II, no. 5, p. 254.

8 Nathan Reich, *The Pulp and Paper Industry in Canada* (Toronto, 1926), pp. 8-11. *Report of the Royal Commission on Pulpwood* (Ottawa, 1924), pp. 105-106.

9 Reich, pp. 11-12. *Royal Commission on Pulpwood*, pp. 106-07.

10 Carruthers, pp. 390-406. Vincent-Domey, "Eddy," *DCB*, vol. XIII, pp.318-20. *CL*, April 1892; 15 Nov. 1912, p. 52. James Alexander, "A Great Canadian Industry," *Canadian Magazine*, Dec. 1897, pp. 177-86. *Canadian Textile Directory* (3rd ed., 1892), pp. 421-29; (4th ed., 1899), pp. 487-97. *PPMC*, Jan. 1912, p. 7; 1 Aug. 1913, p. 517.

11 *PPMC*, Jan. 1904, p. 26; July 1904, p. 216. Carruthers, pp. 517-22, 656-57. *Canadian Textile Directory* (4th ed., 1899), pp. 487-97 (5th ed., 1907-08), pp. 409-24. *Phillips' Paper Trade Directory of the World*, 1914-15 (London, 1915), pp. 334-63. *Fraser's Wood Products Directory*, 1922-23 (Montreal, 1923), pp. 126-29. Herbert Marshall, *Canadian-American Industry: A Study in International Investment* (New York, 1936), pp. 40-43. R. T. Naylor, *The History of Canadian Business, 1867-1914* (Toronto, 1975), vol. II, p. 82.

12 *Canadian Textile Directory* (3rd ed., 1892; 4th ed., 1899; 5th ed., 1907-08). *Phillips' Paper Trade Directory of the World*, 1914-15. *Fraser's Wood Products Directory*, 1922-23. *CL*, June 1901; 13 June 1906; 15 Nov. 1910. *PPMC*, Jan. 1909, p. 27; Dec. 1909, p. 328; Jan. 1910, p. 9. Bush, pp. 200-201.

13 Reich p. 69. *CL*, Sept. 1903, p. 25; 15 March 1908, p. 22; 1 Nov. 1908, p. 23. *PPMC*, April 1909, pp. 135-38; Nov. 1910, p. 261.

14 *Canadian Textile Directory* (5th ed., 1907-08).

15 TABLE FIVE

Capacity output of Ottawa Valley paper mills compared to capacity of all Canadian mills. *			
Year	Ottawa Valley capacity	Total Canadian capacity	Ottawa Valley share
1892	none reported	196 tons per day	0%
1899	75 tons per day	379 tons per day	19%
1908	168 tons per day	9,701 tons per day	17%
1923	230 tons per day	1,899 tons per day	7%

*Computed from Canadian Textile Directory (3rd ed., 1892), pp. 421-29; ibid. (4th ed., 1899), pp. 487-97; ibid. (5th ed., 1908), pp. 409-24; Fraser's Wood Products Directory, 1922-23 (Montreal, 1923), pp. 126-29.

TABLE SIX

Capacity output of Ottawa Valley pulp mills compared to capacity of all Canadian mills. *			
Year	Ottawa Valley capacity	Total Canadian capacity	Ottawa Valley share
1892	23 tons per day	206 tons per day	11%
1899	117 tons per day	1,083 tons per day	10%
1908	355 tons per day	2,401 tons per day	14%
1923	725 tons per day	5,533 tons per day	13%

*Computed from the same sources as cited in Table Five.

Chapter 7

1 Cuthbert Cummings in The Hargrave Correspondence, 1821-1843, edited by G. T. Glazebrook (Toronto: Champlain Series, 1938), p. 33. See also the condemnations of John McGregor in his Historical and Descriptive Sketches of the Maritime Colonies of British America (London, 1828), p. 166; and Hamnet Pinhey in Reid, p. 90.

2 Cross, "Dark Druidical Groves," pp. 264-67. Reid, pp. 40-41.

3 Ian Radforth, "The Shantymen," in Paul Craven (ed.), Labouring Lives: Work and Workers in Nineteenth Century Ontario (Toronto, 1995), p. 221.

4 Vernon Jensen, Lumber and Labor (New York, 1945), pp. 22ff.

5 MacTaggart, p. 244.

6 Michel Oriano, *Les travailleurs de la frontière: étude socio-historique des chansons de bûcherons, de cowboys et de cheminots américains au 19e siècle* (Paris, 1980).

7 Gérard Goyer and Jean Hamelin, "Joseph Montferrand," *DCB*, vol. IX (Toronto, 1976), pp. 561-565. Jennifer O'Connor, "The Legend of Joseph Montferrand and Its Scientific Context in the 1880s," *Canadian Folklore Canadien* 8 (1986). Bernie Bedore, *Tall Tales of Joe Mufferaw* (Arnprior, Ont., 1963).

8 Pope, pp. 59-60. *Montreal Gazette* and *Toronto Globe*, 24 Sept. 1901. Norman Patterson, "Touring a Continent," *Canadian Magazine*, Nov. 1901. Birge Harrison, "The Habitant in Winter," *Scribners* magazine, March 1908, pp. 283-90. Stewart White, *The Riverman* (New York, 1908).

9 See, for example, Arthur Heming, "The River-Drivers of the Ottawa Valley," *Harper's Weekly*, 16 April 1898. Earlier romanticised examples of Ottawa Valley shantymen can be seen in the poetry of James Ernest Campbell, particularly his *Songs of the Pines* (Toronto, 1895).

10 A National Film Board of Canada production, 1979, based on Wade Hemsworth's song of the same name.

11 Very few Ottawa Valley shantymen left first-hand accounts of their experiences in the bush; see Joshua Fraser, *Shanty, Forest and River Life in the Backwoods of Canada* (Montreal, 1883); James Hillis, "Life in the Lumber Camp," *Ontario History*, Sept. 1967, pp. 157-62; Charles Macnamara, "The Camboose Shanty," ibid. (Spring 1959), pp. 73-78; George S. Thompson, *Up to Date, or the Life of a Lumberman* (Peterborough, 1895); Hartley Trussler, "The Cookery Was the Heart of the Camp," in Bill McNeil (ed.), *Voice of the Pioneer*, vol 2 (Toronto, 1984), pp. 240-43.

12 CL, Jan. 1890, p. 9. In 1894, a less authoritative source put the figure at 9,000 men: *CL*, Dec. 1894, p. 10.

13 Reid, p. 90.

14 MacTaggart, pp. 241-42. Edward Allen Talbot, *Five Years' Residence in Canada* (London, 1824), p. 189. Johann Kohl, *Travels in Canada* and *Through the States of New York and Pennsylvania*, vol. 1 (London, 1861), p. 263. Peter Ennals and Deryck Holdsworth, *Homeplace: The Making of the Canadian Dwelling over Three Centuries* (Toronto, 1998), pp. 133-35. Pinhey also uses the verb "shantying" in his letter of 1821.

15 LAC, RG 31, A1, 1861 census, Nipissing Dist. *CL*, Dec. 1892; May 1903, p. 21; 1 Sept. 1916, p. 59. Moore, pp. 96ff. C. Marshall, p. 41. Phipps, p. 4. For two good studies of shanties see: Ian Radforth (note 2 above), pp. 204-75 and Lorne Hammond, "Anatomy of a Lumber Shanty: A Social History of Labour and Production on the Lièvre River, 1876-1890," in Donald Akenson (ed.), *Canadian Papers in Rural History*, vol. IX, (1994), pp. 291-322.

16 Once a Week, 4 Jan. 1862, pp. 48-49. Macnamara. Hillis.

17 Chad Gaffield (ed.), *History of the Outaouais* (Québec, 1997), pp. 163-64. Grant, p. 218. *CL*, May 1903; Aug. 1904; 1 Sept. 1910; 1 Sept. 1916.

18 *CL*, March 1901; 6 Aug. 1902. For earlier examples see S. Gillis, pp. 447-48 and *CL*, Nov. 1886.

19 Fraser, pp. 28-38. Radforth, pp. 261-62.

20 Archives of Ontario, *Gillies Brothers Papers*, F 150-13-1-1-1, Box 14.

21 Radforth, pp. 258-62. See also newspaper notice in Doug Fischer (ed.) *Each Morning Bright: 160 Years of Selected Readings from the Ottawa Citizen*, (Ottawa, 2005), p. 6.

22 *Reid*, pp. lxix, 174-78. Canada. *Report of the Royal Commission on the Relations of Labor and Capital in Canada* (hereafter *Roy. Comm.*), vol. 4 (Ottawa, 1889), pp. 1188-89. Newton, *The Bytown Packet ... Death Notices*, vol. II, #658; vol. III, #431, 680, 2313. Fraser, pp. 130-31. Radforth, pp. 222-23.

23 *Once a Week*, 4 Jan. 1862, pp. 50-51.

24 Thompson, p. 23. See also Trussler and Macnamara.

25 *CL*, March 1890; Dec. 1892. *Renfrew Mercury*, 12 Jan. 1883. Alyne LeBel, "La culture matérielle des travailleurs forestiers," *Asticou*, déc. 1985, pp. 15-27. Elliott, *The City Beyond*, p. 50. In 1888 another Ottawa shantyman claimed he had worked 37 years in the bush and was still active: *Roy. Comm.*, vol. 4, p. 1188.

26 Macnamara. CL, May 1903; 1 Dec. 1908.

27 Keefer, "*Rafting...*," p. 81.

28 Marshall, p. 39. Phipps, pp. 6-7. Kennedy, p. 116. MacTaggart, p. 242. Craigie, p. 98. S. Gillis, pp. 140, 456 (n. 74). Lord Elgin, *The Condition and Prospects of Canada in 1854* (Quebec, 1855), p. 81. Kohl, vol. 1, p. 265. Fraser, pp. 36-37. *CL*, 15 Dec. 1880.

29 Lower, *Woodyard*, p. 200.

30 Hillis, pp. 158-59.

31 Fraser, p. 115.

32 *Once a Week*, 4 Jan. 1862, p. 50. Hillis, p. 158. S. Gillis, pp. 445-47. Roy. Comm., vol. 4, p. 1189. Reid, pp. 174-78. Hammond, "Anatomy of a Lumber Shanty," pp. 309-10.

33 Robert Choquette, *L'Èglise catholique dans l'Ontario français au dix-neuvième siècle* (Ottawa, 1984), pp. 156-59. Grant, p. 225. *CL*, March 1888, p. 8; April, 1895, p. 12. Presbyterian Church of Canada, *Report of the Mission to the Lumbermen in the Valley of the Ottawa*, 1871, 1872.

34 *CL*, May 1904, pp. 15-16.

35 James Morrison, *Camps & Classrooms: A Pictorial History of Frontier College* (Toronto, 1989). C. Marshall, p. 41. Radforth, p. 234. *CL*, May 1904, pp. 15-16.

36 In 1900, 2,500 men were recruited to supplement the river-drive work force; in 1903, supplementaries were estimated to total 70 percent of the force: *CL*, 18 April 1900, Oct. 1900; May 1903. *Roy. Comm.*, vol. 4, pp. 1175, 1189.

37 *CL*, 4 July 1906.

38 Rusty Leach, *The Rusty Leach Collection of Shanty Songs and Recollections of the Upper Ottawa Valley* (Shawville, 1984), p. 114.

39 *CL*, Sept. 1888; 1 Nov. 1908. Fraser pp. 281-82, 308, 330-31.

40 *JLA*, 1847, App. LL. Keefer's figure may include some rafting deaths.

41 "The Cold Black Stream," in Edith Fowke (ed.), *Lumbering Songs from the Northern Woods*, (Austin, Texas, 1970), pp. 146-49. CL, 2 July 1883, p. 201; July 1888, p. 5; July 1896, p. 13.

42 *CL*, 15 July 1885, p. 251.

43 Keefer, "Rafting," p. 81. *Once a Week*, 22 Feb. 1862, pp. 244-45. *Ottawa Daily Citizen Almanac . . . for the Year 1866* (Ottawa, 1865). pp. 6-7. Heming. S. Wyman MacKechnie, *What Men They Were*, (Shawville 1975) p. 87. Aubrey Saunders, *Algonquin Story* (Toronto, 1947), p. 43. Abbé E. Latulippe, *Visite Pastorale de Monseigneur Lorrain, Éveque de Pembroke, Chez les Algonquins du Grand Lac Victoria et du Lac Barrière* (Quebec, 1902), p. 47.

44 Fowke, pp. 95-99, 104-06, 111-13. Newton, *The Bytown Packet*, II, #112.

45 Charlotte Whitton paraphrased this report in her book *A Hundred Years A-Fellin'*, p. 150; she gives 18 April 1890 as the date of the newspaper but unfortunately, no issue of this date is known to exist today. Also, Fraser, pp. 333-35.

46 *JLA*, 1849, App. NNNN. Kohl, pp. 220-21. *CL*, Sept. 1893, p. 8.

47 *CL*, 2 July 1883, p. 193; July 1892, p. 8; Sept. 1893, p. 8; July 1896, p. 13; 15 July 1908, p. 33.

48 *CL*, Aug. 1889, p. 11; July 1896, pp. 13, 15. Grant, p. 231. Newton, *The Bytown Packet*, II, #103, 126, 634; III, #531. See also, "Old Timer" in *CL*, 1 May 1935, p. 43.

49 Cross, "Dark Druidical Groves," p. 238

50 Gertrude van Cortlandt, *Records of the Rise and Progress of the City of Ottawa* (Ottawa, 1858), pp. 13-15. William S. Hunter, *Hunter's Ottawa Scenery* (Ottawa, 1855), p. 19. *Ottawa Citizen*, 26 Aug. 1854.

51 George T. Borrett, *Letters from Canada and the United States* (London, 1865), pp. 44-45.

52 *JLA*, 1847, App. LL.

53 Bigsby, p. 137. Diary of a P. Wright raft journey, 1835, in S. Gillis, pp. 327-71. *Once a Week*, 22 Feb. 1862, pp. 245-49. CL, July 1896, p. 13. Radforth, pp. 233-35.

54 Connor, p. 4.

55 Michael Cross, "The Shiners' War: Social Violence in the Ottawa Valley in the 1830s," *Canadian Historical Review* (March 1973), pp. 1-26. Michael Cross, "Peter Aylen," *DCB*, vol. IX, pp. 13-14. S. Gillis, p. 119. Reid, pp. xxxvii-xxxix, 55ff.

56 Michael Cross says that the Magistrates Appointment Bill of 1846 also helped bring order to the Valley: "Dark Druidical Groves," p. 301. Taylor, pp. 40-45, 216. Edwin Welch (ed.), *Bytown Council Minutes*, 1847-48 (Ottawa, 1978), p. 16. Reid, pp. 149ff.

57 Michael Newton, *Lower Town*, 1854-1900 (Ottawa, 1981), pp. 287-89, 464.

58 *Ottawa Citizen*, 3 Aug. 1876.

59 Radforth, pp. 244-48. Newton, *Lower Town*, pp. 372-73, 822. Hammond, "*Capital, Labour and Lumber,*" pp. 116-17.

60 Newton, *Lower Town*, pp. 816ff. Connor, pp. 229, 251. Radforth, p. 221. Newton, pp. 816ff. CL, Sept. 1889, p. 6. *Report of the Commissioners Appointed to Enquire into the Prison and Reformatory System of Ontario* (Toronto, 1891), pp. 370-74. *Ottawa Journal*, 17 Sept. 1898.

61 For example, CL, Sept. 1889; 1 May 1908.

62 See Leach and Fowke, op. cit.

63 Radforth, pp. 224-25.

64 *Bytown Gazette*, 19 June 1845; CL, July 1888, p. 5.

65 Moore, pp. 112-13. Fraser, p. 312. CL, 1 Feb. 1935.

66 Fowke, pp. 107-10. Radforth pp. 223-26.

67 For a twentieth-century manifestation of these impulses, see Raoul Blanchard, *Le Canada Francais, Province de Quebec*, (Montreal 1960), pp. 133-34

Chapter 8

1 CL, June 1903, p. 20.

2 CL, 15 May 1930, p. 28.

3 CL, Jan. 1903. Reid, "Egan," DCB, vol. VIII, pp. 268-70. Jamie Benidickson,
   "John Rudolphus Booth," DCB, vol. XV (Toronto, 2005). Vincent-Domey,
   "Eddy," DCB, vol. XIII, pp. 318-20.

4 CL, 1 Dec. 1882; 1 June 1883; Sept. 1898. Vincent-Domey, "Eddy," DCB,
   vol. XIII, pp. 318-20.

5 Joseph Schull and J. Douglas Gibson, The Scotiabank Story: A History of the
   Bank of Nova Scotia, 1832-1982 (Toronto, 1982), pp. 123ff. Robert P. Gillis,
   "George Bryson," DCB, vol. XII, pp. 134-35. Richard Reid, "James
   Maclaren," DCB, vol. XII, pp, 664-66. Hammond, "Capital, Labour and
   Lumber," pp. 263-98.

6 See also Nelles, pp. 208-09.

7 Craig Heron, "Factory Workers," in Paul Craven (ed.), Labouring Lives: Work
   and Workers in Nineteenth Century Ontario (Toronto, 1995), pp. 546, 588, n.
   260. Edward McKenna, "Unorganized Labour versus Management: The Strike
   at the Chaudière Lumber Mills, 1891," Histoire Sociale (Nov. 1972), pp. 186-
   211. Greg Kealey and Bryan Palmer, Dreaming of What Might Be: The Knights of
   Labor in Ontario, 1880-1900 (Toronto, 1987), pp. 362-65. CL, Aug. 1888; Oct.
   1891, p. 11; Dec. 1891, p. 17. P. Gillis, "E. H. Bronson and Corporate
   Capitalism," pp. 71-73. Desmond Morton, Working People: An Illustrated History
   of the Canadian Labour Movement (Montreal–Kingston, 1998), pp. 49-50.

8 Pierre-Louis Lapointe, Buckingham, Ville Occupée (Hull, 1983).

9 P. Gillis, pp. 79-80. CL, May 1895, p. 10; June 1895, p. 6; May 1903, p. 33.

10 CL, 15 Aug. 1910, p. 38

11 Michael Bliss, A Living Profit (Toronto, 1974), pp. 68-90.

12 Anson Gard, Hub and Spokes, or The Capital and its Environs (Ottawa, 1904),
   p. 343.

13 CL, Aug. 1888; Dec. 1895. Report of the Royal Commission on the Relations of
   Labor and Capital in Canada, vol. 4 (Ottawa, 1889), p. 1118. Eugene Forsey,
   Trade Unions in Canada, 1812-1902 (Toronto, 1982), p. 338.

14 Fear, p. 55. John Ross Trinnell, J.R. Booth: The Life and Times of an Ottawa
   Lumberking (Ottawa, 1998), p. 90. CL, Oct. 1904, p. 24; May 1905, p. 32; 1
   July 1909, p. 40.

15 CL, 15 Dec. 1924. For another example of political thuggery, see
   MacKechnie, p. 167

16 A. Margaret Evans, *Sir Oliver Mowat*, (Toronto 1992), pp. 279-80.

17 S. Gillis, pp. 308-12. Russell, p. 41. *CL*, 15 Oct. 1881; April 1890.

18 A large-scale sawmill is one deemed to produce at least ten million board feet of lumber a year. In 1882 the five leading firms accounted for 43.4 percent of total Valley production; in 1892, 53.3 percent; in 1902, 54.9 percent; in 1912, 52.3 percent; and in 1922, 52.9 percent. (Computed from figures in *CL*, 15 Dec. 1882; Nov. 1892; Feb. 1903; 1 Feb. 1913; 15 March 1924.) In 1889 J. R. Booth's share of total output was 10.6 percent; in 1897, it was 17.3 percent; in 1906, 16.8 percent; and in 1915, 16.5 percent. (Computed from figures in *CL*, March 1889; Feb. 1899; Feb. 1907; 15 March 1922.)

19 See advertisement for portable and semi-portable sawmills manufactured by Waterous Engine Works of Brantford, Ont., in *CL*, 1 May 1883. *Fourth Census of Canada*, 1901, vol. III, pp. 178-247.

20 Reid, pp. 127-29.

21 *CL*, 15 May 1908; see also 9 March 1904. Bliss, *Living Profit*, p. 39n.

22 Cole, pp. 126-30. *CL*, 28 Feb. 1906. Dean Walker, *Net Worth: The Memories of C.E. Pickering* (Toronto, 1973), pp. 33ff, 109ff.

23 *Ottawa Daily Citizen Almanac for the Year 1866* (Ottawa, 1865), pp. 15-16. Tassé, *L'Outaouais*, pp. 29-30. *Fraser's Directory, 1922-23*, p. 474. *CL*, 1 Aug. 1880; 1 May 1886; May 1891; March 1906. William Fleming, *America's Match King, Ohio Columbus Barber, 1841-1920* (Barberton, Ohio, 1981). Canada, *Census, 1890-91*, vol. III, p. 217. Vincent-Domey, "Eddy," *DCB*, vol. XIII, pp. 318-20.

24 Scott, p. 18. *CSP*, 1899, No. 9, p. 7. *CL*, 7 Dec. 1898; Jan. 1903. Reid, "Maclaren," *DCB*, vol. XII, pp. 664-66. Vincent-Domey, "Eddy," *DCB*, vol. XIII, pp. 318-20.

25 Michael Cross, "The Age of Gentility: The Formation of an Aristocracy in the Ottawa Valley," *Canadian Historical Association Report* (1967), pp. 105-17. William Leggo, *The History of the Administration of the Right Honorable Frederick Temple, Earl of Dufferin* (Montreal, 1878), pp. 206-07. Cynthia Cooper, *Magnificent Entertainments: Fancy Dress Balls of Canada's Governor General, 1876-1898* (Fredericton 1997). Sandra Gwynn, *The Private Capital: Ambition and Love in the Age of Macdonald and Laurier*, pp. 145 *et passim*. See also list of invitees to Lord Dufferin's ball in 1876, *Ottawa Citizen*, 24 Feb. 1876. *CL*, 4 Feb. 1903.

26 *Ottawa Citizen*, 6 Dec. 1875.

27 *Ottawa City and Counties of Carleton and Russell Directory, 1866-7* (Ottawa, 1866). *Ottawa Directory for 1872-73* (Ottawa, 1873).

28 Philip Gabriel, "George Bryson." In *L'Outaouais: Actes du colloque sur l'identité régionale de l'Outaouais* (Hull, 1982), pp. 15-34. *Architectural Heritage of*

the Pontiac (Quebec, 1981), pp. 50ff.

29 Gordon Fulton and Jacqueline Hucker, "Gillies Grove and House," Historic Sites and Monuments Board of Canada, Agenda Paper, 1993-19.

30 *Ottawa Journal*, 26 Feb. 1895

31 Gilmour, *DCB*, vol. XII, pp. 366-68. S. Gillis, pp. 308-12. George M. Rose (ed.), *A Cyclopedia of Canadian Biography* (Toronto, 1886), pp. 627-29. Lady Dufferin, *Journal*, pp. 106, 109. Leggo, p. 125. Gwyn, pp. 210-11. Rebecca Sisler, *Passionate Spirits: A History of the Royal Canadian Academy of Arts, 1880-1980* (Toronto, 1980), p. 32.

32 CL, Nov. 1893, p. 3; Sept. 1898, pp. 3-4. Charles C. Jenkins, "J. R. Booth: On the Job at 95," *Maclean's Magazine*, 15 May 1922. Madge Macbeth, *Over My Shoulder* (Toronto, 1953), p. 23. Philip Dansken Ross, *Retrospects of a Newspaper Person* (Toronto, 1931), p. 78. Benidickson, "Booth," *DCB*, vol. XV.

33 CL, Nov. 1890, p. 15.

34 Michael Bliss, *Northern Enterprise: Five Centuries of Canadian Business*, (Toronto, 1987), p. 134.

Chapter 9

1 Raoul Blanchard, *Le Canada Français, Province de Québec* (Montréal, 1960), pp. 133-34. A. R. M. Lower, *Settlement and the Forest Frontier in Eastern Canada* (Toronto, 1936), pp. 30ff.

2 Chad Gaffield, "Boom or Bust: The Demography and Economy of the Lower Ottawa Valley in the Nineteenth Century," *Canadian Historical Association Review*, 1982, p. 194. Elliott, *City Beyond*, pp. 44-50.

3 Lower, *Settlement*, pp. 45-47. See also, Picken, pp. 130-31. Another lumber historian has concluded that shanty work in the Lièvre River Valley (east of Hull), rather than conflicting with farming, could be complementary to it: Hammond, "Capital, Labour and Logging," p. 143.

4 Jones, pp. 116ff.

5 Chad Gaffield, *Language, Schooling and Cultural Conflict: The Origins of the French Language Controversy in Ontario* (Kingston, 1987), p. 90. Elliott, *City Beyond*, pp. 150-59.

6 Kenneth Buckley, "Role of Staple Industries in Canada's Economic Development," *Journal of Economic History*, Dec. 1958, pp. 439-50. Melville Watkins, "A Staple Theory of Economic Growth," *Canadian Journal of Economics and Political Science*, May 1963, pp. 141-58.

7 CL, 1 May 1882; 15 Sept. 1884; Dec. 1895; Nov. 1896; Aug. 1897; May

1899; Feb. 1900; 1 Jan. 1909; 15 Oct. 1910; 15 Aug. 1913. *Ottawa Journal*, 6 Sept. 1969. Little, p. 34. Charles Heavrin, "The Felling Axe in America," *The Chronicle of the Early American Industries Association*, Sept. 1982, pp. 43-53. Sandra Gillis, "Horace Merrill," *DCB*, vol. XI, pp. 589-90.

8 *CL*, May 1906, 15 Aug. 1913.

9 Little, pp. 35-36. Canada, *Census, 1890-91*, vol. III, pp. 232, 287.

10 James Little, *The Timber Supply Question of the Dominion of Canada and the United States of America* (Montreal, 1876). Robert P. Gillis, "The Ottawa Lumber Barons and the Conservation Movement, 1880-1914," *Journal of Canadian Studies*, Feb. 1974, pp. 14-31. Robert P. Gillis and Thomas R. Roach, *Lost Initiatives: Canada's Forest Industries, Forest Policy and Forest Conservation* (New York, 1986). Gillis, "Bryson," *DCB*. Lambert and Pross, pp. 158ff, 206ff. White, p. 269ff.

11 Audrey Saunders, *Algonquin Story* (Toronto, 1947). Ottelyn Addison, *Early Days in Algonquin Park* (Toronto, 1974). Lambert and Pross, pp. 169ff. Nelles, pp. 16ff, 193ff.

12 *CSP*, 1861, no. 4, App. E.

13 "Report of the Commission Appointed to Enquire into the Condition of Navigable Streams," 1873, *CSP*, 1873, no. 29. "Mr. [John] Mather's Report on the Disposal of Sawdust and Mill-Offals in the Ottawa River," 1877, *CSP*, 1878, no. 1, App. 3. "Examination and Report on Saw-dust Obstructions, River Ottawa, 11 May 1888," *CSP*, 1890, #18, p. 221. Senate Select Committee Report, 1888, *Journals of the Senate*, 1888, App. 2.

14 Report on Navigable Streams, 1873, p. 6. Mather Report, 1877, pp. 12-13. Senate Report, pp. 55-56. *CL*, June 1888.

15 "Report of Sandford Fleming," 1889, *CSP*, 1890, No. 65, pp. 13-24.

16 Tulloch, p. 30. Report on Navigable Streams, 1873, pp. 112, 15. Senate Report, 1888, pp. 3, 31, 38, 74. Fleming Report, 1889, p. 14.

17 *CL*, June 1888; Sept. 1889. Senate Report, 1888, p. 5. *Ottawa Journal*, 11 Feb. 1889. *Ottawa Citizen*, 12 November 1897.

18 Canada, Statutes, 36 Vict., cap. 65.

19 Mather Report, 1877, pp. 12-13. Senate Report, 1888, pp. 6, 12, 45, 62, 69-70. *Ottawa Journal*, 21 Feb. 1889.

20 Ontario, Statutes, 48 Vict., cap. 25.

21 Canada, Statutes, 57-58 Vict., cap. 51. *CL*, July 1897, p. 11; Nov. 1897, p. 15; Oct. 1901, p. 7; Nov. 1901, p. 13. *LAC*, MG 26, Sir Wilfrid Laurier Papers, pp. 58,048-56, 58,938-39.

22 Measurements supplied by Public Works and Government Services

Canada, 16 June 2005.

23 Kevin O'Brien, *Oscar Wilde in Canada* (Toronto, 1982).

24 *CL*, June 1888.

25 R. Peter Gillis, "Rivers of Sawdust: The Battle over Industrial Pollution in Canada, 1863-1903," *Journal of Canadian Studies*, Spring 1986, pp. 84-103.

26 Lower, *Assault*, p. 210. Lower, *Woodyard*, p. 250.

27 Some profits did leave the Valley for a few firms, such as the Gilmours and the Bronsons, had shareholders living outside Canada; as well, the Bronsons and Maclarens invested in Pacific Coast lumbering ventures in the 1890s.

28 Lower, *Assault*, pp. 114-15. Also, Harold Innis, in Preface to Lower, *Assault*, p. xvii.

29 Ron Brown, *Ontario's Vanished Villages* (Toronto, 1999).

Chapter 10

1 *Ottawa Citizen*, 11 Dec. 1925.

2 Forest-industry workers predominated in Hull, but the numbers were much smaller: 1,252 shantymen and others compared to 386 civil servants. The civil-servant category in both cities included a few provincial employees. *Sixth Census of Canada*, 1921, vol. 4, *Occupations*, pp. 36-53, 460-79.

3 R.G. Lewis, "The Passing of the Big Sawmill," *Canadian Forest and Outdoors* (Jan. 1924), pp. 848-49. "Canadian Companies Make Business History: Booth Lumber Limited," *Canadian Business* (Dec. 1958), pp. 20-21.

4 *Ottawa Citizen*, 12 March 1990; Shawn McCarthy, "The Last Drive," *Canadian Geographic*, Dec. 1991, pp. 18-31; Michel Beaudry, "Last of the River Men," *Equinox*, March-April 1991, pp. 54-67.

5 Ken Armson et al., "History of Reforestation in Ontario," in *Robert Wagner and Stephen Columbo* (eds.), *Regenerating the Canadian Forest: Principles and Practice for Ontario* (Toronto, 2001), pp. 3-22.

6 "Arnprior and Vicinity," *Canadian Illustrated News*, 16 Nov. 1878, pp. 310-11.

7 *Ottawa Citizen*, 23 Jan. 2000, pp. C9-11; 14 Dec. 2001, p. E3.

PHOTO CREDITS

INDEX

Aboriginal land claims,
31–33
accidents, 67, 70, 73, 84,
131–132, 170, 179,
180–181, 184, 185–186,
187, 193–194
Albert Edward, Prince of
Wales (later Edward VII),
55
Albert Island, 94
alcohol use, 172–173, 178,
179, 187
Alexandra Bridge, 120
Algonquin Park, 232
alligator amphibious craft,
149–150
Amelia Island, 94
American settlers, 14–15,
29
Arnprior, 53, 69, 103, 146,
219
Art Association of Ottawa,
221
ash, 20, 61
auction
Chaudière lots, 94–95
timber limits, 38, 40,
42–43, 62
Aumond, Joseph, 39, 68,
99, 100, 198
axes, 148, 229
Aylen, Peter, 37, 38, 39, 48,
188, 216
Aylmer, 66, 189

bag booms, 115
Balaclava, 237
Baldwin, Alanson H., 96,
98, 115, 121, 122, 135,
198, 199

Baldwin, W.H., 199
balloon framing, 120–121
balsam, 20, 147
band saw, 126–127
Bank of Montreal, 201
Bank of Nova Scotia, 201
Bank of Ottawa, 201, 210
bankruptcies, 215
banks, 200–201
Beckwith, Walter, 189
Bingham, Samuel, 112–113
blacklisting, 169, 204
Black (Noir) River, 53
black spruce *(Picea marina)*,
19, 147
Blasdell, Julius Caesar, 93,
125
Blasdell, Nathaniel, 229
Bliss, Michael, 205
bobsleds, 75
booms, 57–58, 110, 115,
116
Booth, Jackson, 240
Booth, J.R., 39, 61, 85, 96,
98, 103, 104–105, 109,
115, 119, 120, 121, 127,
128, 129–130, 134, 135,
141–142, 143, 147, 148,
150, 152, 154, 198,
200–201, 206, 208, 209,
211, 216, 219, 222–224,
235, 239
Borden, Sir Robert, 208,
239
Braeside, 103
British Columbia forest
industries, 120, 144
Brockville and Ottawa
Railway, 102
Bronson, Erskine H., 96,

104, 141, 143, 147, 152,
199, 208, 231, 232
Bronson, Henry F., 95–96,
97, 98, 115, 134, 198,
199, 210
Bronsons and Weston
Lumber Co., 96, 121,
128, 135, 139, 193
broomage, 108
Bryson, George, 231, 232
Bryson family, 199
Buchanan, George, 51, 55,
218
Buchanan, George, Jr., 218
bucksaw, 148
bulk-heads, 54
Bunyan, Paul, 161
Burritt, Stephen, 14
Burritts Rapids, 14
bush work
axmanship, 73
camp site, 70–71
cutting gangs, 108
delivery of supplies,
69–70
early season, 62–70
equipment, 64, 72, 75
felling, 71–72
hauling, 74–75, 108–110
hewing, 59–61, 72–73
pay scale, 168
productivity, 73
pulpwood, 147–149
road-making, 109
skidding, 71, 74, 108
stamping, 76–77
By, John, 23, 44, 94
Bytown, 66, 93, 95, 100,
189–192
See also Ottawa

Bytown and Prescott Railway (B&PR), 99–102

cadge roads. *See* tote roads
Caldwell, Boyd, 103, 111
Calumet Falls, 53
Calumet Rapids, 14, 47
camboose shanty, 164–165, 167
Canada Atlantic Railway (CAR), 103–106
Canada Central Railway (CCR), 69, 102–103, 106
Canada Lumber Company, 139
Canada Paper Co., 152
Canadian International Paper Company (CIP), 152–153
Canadian Match Company, 214
Canadian Pacific Railway, 47, 106, 141
Canadian Reading Camp Association, 175
canals, 43–47
cant-hooks, 75
Carillon Canal, 44, 53
Carillon rapids, 14, 44
Carleton County, 32
Carleton Place, 102, 111, 139
cedar, 20
Central Vermont Railroad, 221
chain saw, 148
Champlaine, Samuel de, 17–18
Chats Falls, 14, 26, 47, 51, 53
Chaudière Dam, 47
Chaudière Falls, 14, 26, 46, 51, 53, 66, 93–97, 101
Chaudière Island, 94
Chelsea Falls, 67, 93
chemical pulp, 150
Chenaux Rapids, 14
child labour, 131
Chute-à-Blondeau, 14, 44
circular saw, 123, 127
Clemow, Francis, 235
Cockburn, John, 113, 114, 229

Connor, Ralph, 161, 187
Connors, Stompin' Tom, 162
Conroy, Robert, 39
Consolidated Paper Company, 240
contracts, employment, 169
cooks, 168
Corbett, Crawford, 171
Coulonge River, 53, 66
cribs, 21, 78, 80–83, 86–87
cross-cut saw, 148
cruising, timber, 62–63
Culbute Canal, 47, 68
Culbute Rapids, 14
Currier, J.M., 98, 102, 198, 210, 215, 217

Dalhousie, George, 45
dams, 46–47, 54, 77–78
dancing, 9
Davidson, James, 230
Dawson, W.W., 41
deadheads, 234
deals, 92–93, 119, 120
de Joachims, 53
de Pencier, Theodore, 31
Deschênes Rapids, 14, 46, 66
desertion, 168–170, 178, 193
Des-Joachims Rapids, 14
Deux-Rivières Rapids, 14
Diamond Match Company, 214
dimension timber, 119, 120
diseases, contagious, 171
double-bit axe, 148
double-butter, 123
double-edger, 123
drams, 86
drivers (*draveurs*). *See* river men
dues, timber. *See* duties, timber
Dufferin, Lord, Governor General, 55, 221
Du Moine River, 53
Dunsmuir, Robert, 202
Dustbane, 213
duties, timber, 37–38, 40–42

E.B. Eddy Co., 152, 214
Eddy, E.B., 41, 96, 107, 115, 120, 121, 126–127, 128, 140, 143, 147, 151–152, 154, 198, 199, 200, 213–215, 230
Edwards, W.C., 107, 111, 117, 120, 125, 128, 131, 134, 138, 206, 209, 217, 231
Egan, John, 27, 38, 40, 47, 64, 65, 68, 99, 100, 169, 199, 200, 209, 215
Eganville, 66
elm, 20, 61
Erie Canal, 136

farming, 20, 24, 30, 65–66, 226–227
felling, 71–72, 168
fights, 8–9, 182, 187–188
Finnigan, Joan, 9
fires, 126–127, 137, 138, 141–143
fir timber, 120
Fiset, Louis, 169
Fisheries Act, 235
Fitzpatrick, Alfred, 174–175
Fleck, Helen Gertrude, 198
Fleming, Sanford, 233
forest industries
  and agriculture, 226–227
  American market, 86, 97–99, 146
  bankruptcies, 215
  competition in, 209–211
  cooperation, 210–211
  and depleted forests, 231–232
  diversification, 213–215
  early beginnings, 20–28
  economic contribution, 237–238
  government intervention, 47–58
  lobbying groups, 211
  and manufacturing, 228–231
  mill closures, 237
  pollution, 232–236
  pulp and paper industry, 145–155, 230–231, 241
  seasonal employment, 30,

74, 77, 148, 163, 226–227
second growth, 242
vertical integration, 212
See also timber trade
Fort Coulonge, 28, 69, 218
Fort Tamiskaming, 28
Fortune, William, 31
Fort William, 28
francophone communities, 29
Francophone raftsmen, 80, 183
Fraser, Alexander, 198
Fraser family, 75
free trade. *See* reciprocity
Frontier College, 175
fur trade, 16, 21, 28, 80, 194

gang-saw, 123
Gatineau River, 65, 67, 93, 107
Gatineau River Drive Co., 111, 112
ghost towns, 237
Gillies, David, 206, 219, 239, 242
Gillies, John S., 239
Gillies Brothers, 125, 132, 135, 169, 240
Gillies brothers, 103, 199
Gillies Grove, 242–243
Gilmour, Allan, 63, 91, 93, 119, 121, 132, 135, 198, 199, 205, 212, 217, 219–222
Gilmour, John, 220
Gilmour & Company, 125, 131, 138, 220
Gilmour-Hughson, 111, 119
glance booms, 110
glance-walls, 54
Glengarry County, 29
Glover Steam Logger, 109
Gordon, Charles W. *See* Connor, Ralph
Gore, Francis, 34
Gourlay, J.L., 60
Government intervention
public works, 47–58
railways, 103–104, 105
Gracefield, 65, 67

Grand Trunk Railway (GTR), 100, 105
Grant, George M., 56, 75
Grenville Canal, 44
Grier, J.B., 45
ground pulp, 150
ground rent. *See* stumpage
Gwyn, Sandra, 216

Hamilton, George, 34–35, 37–38, 48, 92, 199
Hamilton, George, Jr., 92
Hamilton, John, 92, 115, 139, 199
Hamilton family, 92, 97, 117, 119, 121, 134, 212, 217
handspike, 75
Hardy, Arthur, 208
Harris, John J., 95, 97
Hawkesbury, 26, 92, 97, 205
Hawkesbury Lumber Company, 139
Head, Sir Francis Bond, 55
hemlock, 20, 139
Herron's Mills, 237
hewing, 59–61, 72–73, 168
horses, 66, 75, 132
Hudson's Bay Company, 28, 194
Hull, 15, 93, 106, 137, 141
See also Wrightstown
Hull Lumber Company, 141, 142, 143
Hunter, W.S., 52
Hurdman, Robert, 91, 96–97, 141, 198, 199, 209, 216
Hurdman family, 75
hydroelectricity, 154, 199

immigration, 28–29
Indians, in forest industries, 22, 62, 183–184
investment capital, 63–64, 89, 90, 91, 147, 200–201
Irish immigrants, 29, 188–189

jackladder, 123
jack pine, 20, 147

James Maclaren Company, 106, 152
James Macleren & Company, 204
joints, 86
joint-stock companies, 110–113, 115–118

Kanasetake, 22
Kazabazua, 67
Keefer, T.C., 179
Kemp, John, 234
King, Mackenzie, 239
Kingston, 85–86
Kipawa, 47, 106, 139
Klock, Robert, 209
Knights of Labor, 203

Labelle, 66
labour relations, 168–170, 203–205
Lac-des-Deux-Montagnes, 22
Lac-des-Quinzè, 42, 47, 106
Lac Expanse, 42, 106, 140
Lac Kipawa, 105
Lac-St-Pierre, 22–23
Lac Simard. *See* Lac Expanse
Lake Capamitchigama, 13
Lake Kipawa, 68
Lake Tamiskaming, 14, 26, 47, 65, 66, 68, 82, 106
land grants, 15
La Petite-Nation seigneury, 26–27
laths, 119, 122, 213
Latour, Olivier, 69
Laurier, Sir Wilfrid, 55, 161, 235
Leamy, Andrew, 189, 222
LeBreton, John, 35–36
Lemoine, J. St. Denis, 234
liner, 72, 168
Little, James, 64
live rollers, 123
log-drive, 110–118, 241
See also river-drive
logging, 107–118
logging farms, 65–66
log-jams, 79, 112–113, 179–180
log-rolling, 177
Long Sault rapids, 14, 15, 21, 44

Lord Elgin Hotel, 213
Lord's Day Act, 176
Lorne, Marquis of,
  Governor General, 55,
  221
Loughrin, P.J., 207
Louise, Princess, 55
Low, 67
Lower, Arthur, 227, 236
lugsails, 84
lumber kings. *See* Ottawa
  Valley forest elites
lumber trade
  "American community,"
  95–96
  American market, 93,
  97–99, 134
  boards, planks, and scantling, 119, 120–121
  careless logging practices,
  138
  Chaudière lumber kings,
  95–97
  competition, 143–144
  cooperation, 110–113,
  115–118
  deals, 119, 120
  declining forest stocks,
  138–140
  delivery methods,
  135–136
  demand for wood, 118
  dimension timber, 119,
  120
  economic conditions and,
  98, 137–138
  grading standards,
  133–134
  great Ottawa-Hull fire
  and, 141–143
  international markets,
  134–135
  investment capital, 91
  mechanization, 109–110,
  121–124
  mill closures, 240
  railways and, 99–107,
  135, 137
  rise of, 90–93
  selling mechanism,
  134–135
  water power, 17, 93–97
Lumsden, Alex, 69, 114

Lusitania, 61

Macdonald, Sir John A.,
  103, 208
Mackenzie, Alexander, 221
Mackey, William, 39,
  199–200, 215
Maclaren, Albert, 199, 204,
  211
Maclaren, James, 215
Maclaren family, 201, 217
MacTaggart, John, 159
Madawaska River, 26, 53,
  65, 107
Madawaska River
  Improvement Co., 111,
  210
Maitland, Sir Peregrine, 36
Maniwaki, 106
Maniwaki reserve, 32
manufacturing, 228–231
maple, 20
Marlborough township, 14
Marquell, William, 132
Mason, William, 125, 142,
  215
mass-circulation journalism,
  145–146
Master and Servant law, 169
Matheson, Alexander, 36
Mattawa, 28, 47, 66, 69
Mauretania, 61
May, Princess (later Queen
  Mary), 55
McConnell family, 27, 28
McDonell, Alexander, 35,
  37, 38, 39, 65
McKay, Thomas, 93, 101
McKinnon, John, 93, 101
McLachlin, Claude, 104
McLachlin, Daniel, 61, 94,
  100, 103
McLachlin, Daniel, II, 239
McLachlin, David, 242
McLachlin family, 125, 134,
  135, 139, 150, 199, 205,
  216, 232
McLaren, Peter, 103, 111,
  120, 139
Mclaren family, 143, 147
McLaren v Caldwell, 111–112
McNab, Laird, 24
Mears, Thomas, 26, 34, 35

mechanical pulp, 150
Meighen, Arthur, 239
merchants, 200
Merrick, William, 14, 23,
  33, 91
Merrickville, 14
Minto, Earl of, Governor
  General, 55
missionaries, 174–175
Montague township, 14, 31
Montferrand, Joe, 7, 51, 160
Mountain Chute, 53
Mowat, Oliver, 208
Mufferaw, Joe, 160–161
  See also Montferrand, Joe
Murphy, Denis, 137
music, fiddling, 9

Napoleon I, 20
National Gallery of
  Canada, 221
National Policy, 208
newsprint, 145, 151
99th Regiment, 29
North Nation Mills, 237
North West Company, 21,
  194
notcher, 108

oak, 20, 44, 61
Ogdensburg and Lake
  Champlain Railroad, 100
Ontario Lumberman's
  Association, 211
Opeongo Road, 66
Ottawa, 100–101, 114, 137,
  141
  great fire, 141–143
  newspapers, 146
  public security, 189–192
  roads, 66–68
Ottawa, Arnprior & Parry
  Sound Railway
  (OA&PSR), 104–105, 232
Ottawa Association of
  Lumber Manufacturers,
  211
Ottawa Electric Company,
  143
Ottawa River, 13–14, 17,
  46–47, 53, 232–236
Ottawa River canals, 43–45,
  93, 136

Ottawa Saw Works
 Company, 229
Ottawa Transportation
 Company, 137
Ottawa Valley
 diversity, 29–30
 forestry economy, 7–8
 old-growth forests, 242
 region, 11
 settlement, 14–16, 28–30
 society, 8–10
 timbering era, 87–88
 timberlands, 16–20
Ottawa Valley forest elites,
 197–224
 background, 198
 and competition, 209–211
 entry into business,
  199–202
 homes, 217–219
 intermarriage, 210
 labour relations, 203–205
 paternalism, 205–206
 and politics, 198,
  206–209
 public image, 200–212,
  224
 social standing, 216
oxen, 66, 74–75

paper manufacturing,
 151–152
Papineau, Joseph, 25–26
Papineau, Louis-Joseph,
 26
Paquette Rapids, 14
Pattee, David, 26, 34, 35
Pattee, Gordon B., 96, 132,
 141, 198
peavy, 75
Pembroke, 47, 66, 69, 103,
 114, 146
Pembroke Lumber Co.,
 120, 135
Perley, George, 206, 239
Perley, W.G., 96, 97, 98,
 103, 104, 105, 115, 119,
 132, 141, 198, 199, 210,
 217
Perley & Pattee Co., 109,
 121, 122–123, 126
Perth, 66, 189
Petawawa River, 65

Phinhey, Hamnet, 163
Pickering, Chester, 213
piers, construction of, 54
pilot, 80–82, 183, 184, 185
pine, 18–19, 45, 61, 87, 91
pine deals, 92–93
Pink, Thomas, 229
planks, 119, 120
Plantagenet, 53
poaching, timber, 33–37,
 62
pointer boat, 113–114
pollution, 232–236
Pontiac County, 47
Portage-du-Fort Rapids, 14
Powell, John, 35
pulp and paper mills,
 151–155
pulpwood
 sources of, 148–149
 species, 147

Quebec, Montreal, Ottawa
 & Occident Railway, 85
Quebec Limitholders
 Association, 211
Quinze rapids, 82

Radforth, Ian, 169, 193
rafting, timber, 20–23,
 80–87, 182–188
raftsmen, 183-184
raft-towing, 85
railways, 85, 99–107, 109,
 135, 137, 140
rangers, 41–42
reciprocity, 25, 97–98
red pine (Pinus resinosa),
 19, 61, 87
Remic Rapids, 14, 46
Renfrew County, 47
Richmond Road, 66
Rideau Canal, 23, 43–44,
 45, 93, 136
Rideau Hall, 93
Rideau Purchase, 32
Riordon, Charles, 152
river-drive, 77–78,
 149–150, 175–182
 See also rafting, timber
river men, 78–79
Rivers and Streams Act, 111
Rivière-des-Prairies, 22

Rivière-du-Moine Boom
 and Slide Co., 111
robber baron, 200
Rocher Capitaine Rapids,
 14, 53
Royal Canadian Academy
 of Arts, 221
Royal Navy, 33
Rubidge, F.P., 52
Russell, A.J., 87

Saguenay River, slides and
 booms, 57–58
St. Anthony's Lumber Co.,
 105, 109, 125, 127, 135,
 205, 209, 232
St-Maurice River, slides and
 booms, 57–58
sawdust explosions, 234
sawmills, 91–92, 94–77
 electric lighting, 128–129
 fires, 126–127
 hydro power, 129
 mechanization, 121–124
 pay scale, 130
 saws, 123, 127–128
 steam-driven mills,
  124–126
 turbines, 126
 water-driven mills,
  124–126
 working conditions,
  130–132
 See also lumber trade
saws, 123, 127–128, 148,
 229
scantling, 119, 120
scorers, 72, 168
Scott, Richard, 95, 100, 215
Scottish immigration, 29
seasoning, 132–133
Shanly, Walter, 100
shanty, 163, 164–168
shanty foreman, 71, 75,
 168, 174
shantymen
 bad reputation, 157–159,
  190–192
 camp life, 173–174
 drinking, 187–188,
  191–192
 entertainment, 173
 food, 171–173

labour force, 163–164
living conditions,
164–168, 170–171
object of pity, 159–160
pride of vocation,
192–195
public image, 157–162
and river drive, 175–182
romanticized view of,
160–162
word origin, 162–163
Shiners, 158, 188–191
shingles, 119, 122, 213
shipbuilding, 18–19,
20–21, 34
Simpson, George, 28
Singer Sewing Machine Co.,
106
single-stick slide, 50, 53
Skead, James, 52, 98, 102,
125, 200, 210, 215
skid roads, 76
slabber gate-saw, 123
sleds, 75, 108–109
sorting booms, 116
Sparks, Nicholas, 100
speech patterns, Ottawa
Valley dialect, 10
spring river-drive, 77–78
spruce, 19, 61, 139, 147, 149
spruce deals, 120
square timber, 59–60,
72–73
steamboats, 68–69, 85
steam power, 17, 109, 153
step-dancing, 9
Stewart, William, 90
stock gang-saw, 123
strikes, 203–204
stumpage, 38, 40
sulphite pulp mills, 153
swampers, 109

tariff policies, 25, 208
teamsters, 69–70, 164, 168
Temagami region, 106
Temiskaming and Northern
Ontario Railway, 106
The Mill Restaurant, 94
Thompson, Philip, 94
Thomson, Tom, 114
Thurso & Nation River
Railway (T&NRR), 106

Timber Act of 1849, 39–40,
41, 51
timber barons. See Ottawa
Valley forest elites
timber berths. See timber
limits
timber cruiser, 62–63
timber framing, 120
timber limits, 38–39, 40,
42–43, 62, 139
Timber Marketing Act, 77
timber slides, 47–58,
83–84, 185
timber trade
American market, 86
annual cycle, 61–87
boom-and-bust nature of,
37
British market, 59, 61
debt, 63–62
demand for timber,
33–34
expenses, 63–65
investment capital, 63–64
supplies and equipment,
64–66, 69–70
tote roads, 67
transportation
horse-drawn rail service,
68
railways, 99–107, 135,
137
roads, 66–68
shipping, 68–69,
135–136
sleighs, 70
wagons, 69–70
Trent River, slides and
booms, 57–58
truck pay, 205
Twain, Mark, 55

Union, 68
unskilled labourers, 168
Upper Ottawa Drive
Association, 115
Upper Ottawa
Improvement Company
(ICO), 115–118, 183, 210
Usborne Depot, 66

van, 174
Victoria Farm, 65

Victoria Foundry, 229
Victoria Island, 94
violence, 8–9, 35, 36, 48,
182, 187–192
voyageurs, 80

Wakefield, 67
Wales, Prince of. See Albert
Edward, Prince of Wales
(later Edward VII)
Walters family, 229
waney timber, 61, 88
War of 1812, 43
water power, 17, 93–97,
153
Weston, Abijah, 96
White, Andrew, 103
White, Peter, 76, 103, 208
White, Thomas, 231
White Brothers, 125
white pine (Pinus strobus),
18–19, 45, 61, 87
white spruce (Picea glauca),
19, 91, 147
Whitney, 106, 205
Whitney, Edward C., 205
Whitton, Charlotte, 8
Wilde, Oscar, 236
William Mason & Son, 141
Williams Treaties, 33
Winchester Township, 26
Wolford township, 14, 31
Woods, James W., 229
Wright, Alonzo, 77, 222
Wright, Batson & Currier,
121, 124, 125, 151
Wright, Philemon, 15–16,
20–25, 33, 43, 45, 66,
68, 126, 206, 227
Wright, Philemon, Jr., 67
Wright, Ruggles, 24, 36, 37,
38, 39, 40, 48–50, 51,
68, 199, 214
Wright, Tiberius, 21
Wright family, 65, 94, 216
Wrightstown, 16, 66
See also Hull

York, Duke of (later George
V), 55, 161
Young, Levi, 96, 115, 121,
129, 198